Breakdown in Pakistan

# Breakdown in Pakistan

*How Aid Is Eroding Institutions for Collective Action*

Masooda Bano

STANFORD ECONOMICS AND FINANCE
An Imprint of Stanford University Press
Stanford, California

Stanford University Press
Stanford, California

Special discounts for bulk quantities of Economics and Finance are available to corporations, professional associations, and other organizations. For details and discount information, contact the special sales department of Stanford University Press. Tel: (650) 736-1782, Fax: (650) 736-1784

Printed in the United States of America on acid-free, archival-quality paper

Library of Congress Cataloging-in-Publication Data

Bano, Masooda, 1973- author.
  Breakdown in Pakistan : how aid is eroding institutions for collective action / Masooda Bano.
    pages cm
  Includes bibliographical references and index.
  ISBN 978-0-8047-8132-9 (alk. paper)
  1. Economic assistance--Social aspects--Pakistan. 2. Non-governmental organizations--Pakistan.
3. Associations, institutions, etc.--Pakistan. 4. Civil society--Pakistan. 5. Cooperation--Pakistan.
I. Title.
  HC440.5.B365 2012
  361.7095491--dc23                                                        2011051605

Typeset by Bruce Lundquist in 10/14 Minion

*To Hasan,*
*for showing the courage that kept us all going*

# Contents

# List of Illustrations

# Preface

TODAY, 30 PERCENT OF DEVELOPMENT AID is channeled through nongovernmental organizations (NGOs) or community-based collective action initiatives. A growing number of studies show, however, that aid is eroding rather than strengthening cooperation within these groups. Despite increasing evidence, systematic analysis of why aid could have this negative impact is rare. Collective action, whether at the state or the community level, is a result of decisions made at the individual level. Why would individuals who otherwise would choose to cooperate stop doing so when aid is provided? This is a serious dilemma. By providing a micro-level analysis of how aid impacts leaders' and joiners' incentive to cooperate, this book answers this question and presents an explanation of why aid erodes apparently altruistic and other-regarding behavior.

This research inquiry is a product of prolonged engagement with a number of case studies in which I have mapped leaders' and joiners' decision-making processes using survey data, and before and after comparisons. My preference to focus on micro-level decision-making processes was a direct response to the gap I found in existing studies on aid and NGOs. My focus on Pakistan, a country that currently receives one of the largest amounts of aid that the United States and the United Kingdom provide, makes this study timely for policy purposes.

Because this book is designed to show how aid erodes cooperative behavior, it focuses on analyzing the problems within the incentive structures currently offered by aid agencies. However, despite the obvious problems with the existing aid system, the conclusion I personally draw from this research is not that we need to do away with aid, but rather that we need to make a conscious effort to get the incentives right. In the book's conclusion I present an example of how the findings from this research can be operationalized by drawing on an intervention I personally designed for a Quranic school integration program under the Department for International Development's education sector support program in Nigeria. Nadia Naviwala, a former student of the Kennedy School of Government at Harvard University, has used the findings from this research to develop a number of proposals to channel aid to NGOs in Pakistan more effectively. For those who are interested in operationalizing the findings from this book, her paper *Harnessing Local Capacity: U.S. Assistance and NGOs in Pakistan*, available at the Web site of Carr Centre for Human Rights Policy, is a good starting point. Thus, although this book shows how aid is actually crowding out altruistic behavior because development agencies have started with wrong assumptions about the incentive structures that shape collective action decisions, it is very much about improving aid, not abandoning it. I feel the need to emphasize this point because although many individuals in developing societies do genuinely engage in community-based collective action and do solve many of their problems effectively, the challenges of development that one sees in many of these societies are too serious to allow the decision makers in more developed economies to withdraw. Pressure thus needs to be built for better utilization of aid, not for stopping it all together.

Here I would also like to acknowledge the many organizations and individuals who have provided financial, intellectual, and moral support for this project. I am grateful to the Economic and Social Research Council, the Oxford Department of International Development, the Aga Khan Foundation, and the Oxford Centre for Islamic Studies for providing financial support for this research. I have also greatly enjoyed my association with St Antony's College and Wolfson College at Oxford. In addition I am grateful to Elsevier for giving permission to reproduce in Chapter 5 material from my article "Dangerous Correlations: Aid's Impact on NGOs' Performance and Ability to Mobilize Members in Pakistan," published in *World Development* in 2008.

Intellectually, I am indebted to Sabina Alkire, Virginia Appell, Jawad Haroon, Kate Meagher, and Gavin Williams for reading parts or the whole of this manuscript and providing enormously useful comments. Jawad Haroon in particular mulled over each and every line of this work with unimaginable care, critically engaged with the arguments, and most important, having worked in the development sector in Pakistan, constantly reaffirmed the need to adopt the analytical approach that I have developed. I am also extremely grateful to the two reviewers of the manuscript whose comments greatly helped refine the arguments. In particular I am indebted to Margo Beth Fleming, my editor at Stanford University Press, for her great enthusiasm and confidence in this project.

Many friends have also provided wonderful support during this period. Adeel, Devi, Emma, James, Leah, Maysam, Proochista, and Tehnyat have been great companions. Emma has to be thanked in addition for being my ultimate editing adviser, and Leah for feedback on parts of the draft. Arif, Babar, Harris, Mazhar, Saman, and Talat have also supported me by their intellectual engagement with the subject of inquiry as well as by being very caring friends. However, none of this would have been possible without the support of my family. Bahi, Sadia Appa, Appi, and Mona and their partners and children provide that essential comfort zone to which I need to retreat after periods of intense activity, as do Ammi, Amna, and Noreen Khala, who always help put things in perspective. This strong support base has been central to sustaining the intellectual commitment required of a project of this nature.

Last but not least, of all my projects, this book owes a special thanks to Adrian Wood, and he knows why.

*Masooda Bano*
*Oxford, May 30, 2011*

Breakdown in Pakistan

# 1 Revisiting the Collective Action Dilemma

*The fundamental theoretical problem underlying the question of cooperation is the manner by which individuals attain knowledge of each others preferences and likely behavior. Moreover, the problem is one of common knowledge, since each individual, i, is required not only to have information about others preferences, but also to know that the others have knowledge about i's own preferences and strategies.*

**Norman Schofield, "Anarchy, Altruism and Cooperation: A Review," 1985, 218**

*Further, communities of individuals have relied on institutions resembling neither the state nor the market to govern some resource systems with reasonable degrees of success over long periods of time.*

**Elinor Ostrom, *Governing the Commons*, 1990, 1**

THE RURAL AREAS OF SINDH, the southern province of Pakistan, harbor a rich tradition of voluntarism. These rural communities have traditionally supported a large number of voluntary organizations through which community members have pooled resources, at times for charity and at other times to address a collective need. These organizations are known to be much more effective than the state in responding to emergencies; they are particularly good at mobilizing local donations and volunteers. In the 1980s, Oxfam Pakistan initiated a civil society-strengthening program to provide small grants to some of these organizations. The program was premised on the assumption that placing additional financial resources at the disposal of these groups would, in combination with some capacity-building, enable them to expand their work and improve their efficiency. The outcomes were, however, unexpected. Within a year, the groups supported by Oxfam had lost most of their members. Those who were still attached had split into factions, and the hostility that marked these new alliances was starkly visible in the court cases that some members had filed against each other. The welfare work carried out by these groups was a thing of the past.

This story of the negative impact of aid on local community-based collective action structures in rural Sindh is not unique. Many similarities are contained in the story of donor- and NGO-led programs designed to introduce new methods for cultivating quinoa, a traditional crop harvested by smallholder farmers in the highlands of Bolivia. Starting in the 1990s, many donors launched such initiatives under their livelihood-support and income-generation programs, to improve the income of the smallholder farmers. New technologies for cultivation were introduced; for example, farmers were provided with access to modern machines, such as tractors, for use in replacing traditional cultivation practices. Despite increasing the overall yield and the income of these farmers in the short term, the long-term impact of these programs has been markedly detrimental. The support provided by the donors led to a significant decrease in cooperation among the farmers; the resulting individualization and monetarization of agricultural practices restricts the community's ability to play its role of "collective fertility regulator" (Puschiasis 2009), and the unchecked mechanization of agriculture threatens the fragile stability of the ecological and social systems. In recent years there has been growing evidence of soil erosion, which is restricting the yield, and the strong social ties that sustained the cultivation of this crop have been replaced with feuds over land.

In rural Aceh, Indonesia, community members had long participated in many collectively beneficial activities, such as road work and cleaning water drainage systems, under the rubric of *Gotong Royong*, a traditional institution of collective action. Upon the introduction of cash-for-work schemes by international NGOs (INGOs) and multilateral organizations as part of the reconstruction work in tsunami-hit areas, these activities ceased. The cash-for-work schemes had aimed to rehabilitate the local communities by providing short-term employment opportunities that would generate household income and stimulate the rebuilding of the rural and small-scale infrastructure necessary for commerce and the delivery of essential public services (Thorburn 2007). Instead, these schemes led to the erosion of the patterns of voluntary cooperation that the villagers had traditionally manifested in carrying out these activities. By the end of 2005, many practices that had long been sustained as part of *Gotong Royong* had altogether disappeared from Ache (Brusset et al. 2006).

By developing a typology of seven forms of activity undertaken under *Gotong Royong*, ranging from volunteering time to harvesting the fields to taking part in youth cleaning groups, Ewert (2010) shows that the activities that received support under the cash-for-work program were discontinued after the introduction of these schemes, even though the village leaders themselves continually attempted to organize these activities. The possibility that the tsunami itself led to the collapse of the structures that traditionally facilitated this collective action is ruled out in light of the evidence that these activities did not stop immediately; rather, they remained markedly robust for a significant period after the tsunami, disappearing only after the cash-for-work scheme had been in place for a couple of months (Ewert 2010).

All three of the traditional institutions of collective action noted earlier drew on historic patterns and ties of collective action that had evolved and survived in these communities over many centuries, but all three registered dramatic shifts in the members' willingness to contribute to the group when aid was received. Further, these shifts occurred within only a few months or a year. In all three cases, development interventions that introduced cash incentives with the aim of stimulating activities traditionally done voluntarily had the opposite impact. Although in-depth studies analyzing the cases where aid has had a reverse impact are few, the concern that aid is having a negative impact on civil society groups' ability to mobilize members is by now reasonably well established in the development studies literature on NGOs. Thirty percent of development aid is currently being channelled through NGOs, civil society groups, and community-based organizations (CBOs) involved in development work (Riddell 2005). Recent publications on evaluating aid effectiveness, such as Easterly's *The White Man's Burden* and Moyo's *Dead Aid*, by showing the inefficiency of aid channeled through developing countries' governments, indirectly end up supporting calls for channeling increased aid flows through NGOs and civil society groups. However, such calls are worrying when placed alongside growing evidence that civic groups funded by development aid end up having no members. If aid channeled through NGOs and CBOs is to be effectively utilized, the validity of these concerns needs to be tested. If the concerns are borne out, then development theorists must inquire into why aid has this negative impact on individuals' propensities to cooperate to produce a charitable outcome or a collectively beneficial good.

This book fills this gap; however, it first tests whether the concerns are grave enough to be taken seriously. It does this by addressing three core questions: (1) Is the erosion of the individual's propensity to cooperate upon receipt of development aid a widespread phenomenon? (2) Does losing members affect a group's ability to achieve its stated development objective? (3) What are the underlying factors that make individuals engage in collective action, and what are the incentives provided by aid that can break down this cooperation? In *The Logic of Collective Action*, Olson (1971) established why individuals are likely not to cooperate to produce a collective good, and Elinor Ostrom's (1990) seminal work on collective action has shown how communities can overcome this free-rider problem to provide nonstate and nonmarket solutions to many collective-action dilemmas, especially those involving common-pool resources. The lessons learned from debates about these questions have not yet been systematically applied to analyzing why collective action could break down upon receipt of development aid. This book attempts to build on the analytical tools developed by Olson and Ostrom to explain why aid has this unintended impact.

## Collective Action: The Central Puzzle in Development

A collective action situation occurs whenever a desired collective outcome requires the input of several individuals (Gibson et al. 2005); in other words, all productive relationships involve some form of collective action. The problem, however, is that often such collaborative behavior is in short supply: collective action *situations* often become collective action *problems*, in which ensuring cooperation among the relevant actors is a major challenge, despite the fact that collectively they would all be better off if they cooperated (Gibson et al. 2005). The great advancements in the field of new institutional economics in the last three decades have demonstrated how understanding the collective action dilemma rests at the heart of understanding the different development trajectories followed by various countries (North 1990). The growing body of literature in this tradition convincingly demonstrates that the quality of institutions—where institutions are defined as "humanly devised constraints that shape human interaction" (North 1990, 3)—is central to determining how well a society will be able to resolve the challenges to collective action in the sphere of politics, economics, and social organization. Institutions help solve collective action problems by reducing transaction costs—that is, the costs of gathering information and monitoring—and this facilitates exchange (North 1990). Inherent in any collective action decision is the cost of gathering information about the intentions and motivations of other actors (Olson 1971; Ostrom 1990; Schofield 1996). By restricting the choices of individuals, institutions— whether formal (the state, legal systems) or informal (culture, norms, beliefs)— increase the predictability of other individuals' actions and thus make possible outcomes that otherwise would not occur because of the high transaction costs incurred in monitoring others' commitment in the absence of those institutions. As North (1990, 3) puts it, institutions "structure incentives in human exchange, whether political, social, or economic."

The increasing recognition that the development dilemmas faced by many developing countries cannot simply be attributed to lack of resources and that weak institutional arrangements lie at the heart of many such challenges has had direct bearing on donor funding policies. Governance reforms aimed at improving the quality of state institutions in developing countries now form an integral part of the portfolio of most donor agencies. These institutional reforms are given different titles in different donor projects—such as decentralization programs, fiscal reforms, or judicial reforms—but what remains central to these interventions is the desire to replace old-style interventions aimed at ensuring the delivery of the service itself with interventions intended to improve the ability of actors within the recipient country to manage better that activity collectively. Within the education sector, for example, rather than constructing new school buildings, many donors now invest in efforts to improve the governance of existing schools through institutionalizing school management committees and making the central governments devolve school management responsibilities to the district level, thereby helping to resolve the collective action problem that currently exists between state and society and prevents proper governance of schools. Since the late 1990s, all major donors have invested heavily in supporting the introduction of decentralized governance structures in developing countries across Africa, Asia, and Latin America. The logic behind these interventions is to put in place institutional mechanisms that will help make state bureaucracies and elected representatives more accountable to the public and thereby help development reach the poor.

The recognition of the role of institutions in shaping development outcomes has, however, not been restricted to formal institutions of the state. Institutional economists—as well as the donors—have in recent years become equally cognizant of the importance of informal institutions in determining development outcomes, especially in contexts where the formal institutions are weak (North 1990). Informal institutions operate by rules that are not formally endorsed by the state but that are widely adhered to in a given community. Norms, values, and religious beliefs, although often not supported through the legal apparatus of the state, lead individuals to restrict their choices in ways that might not seem entirely rational if seen purely from a wealth-maximizing perspective. Helmke and Levitsky (2004) maintain that *formal* institutions are rules and procedures that are created, communicated, and enforced within officially sanctioned channels; they include political (and judicial) rules, economic rules, and contracts. *Informal* institutions are socially shared rules, usually unwritten, that are created, communicated, and enforced outside officially sanctioned channels (Helmke and Levitsky 2004); these include norms, taboos, and traditions.

Unlike formal institutions, informal institutions are little studied, leading Williamson (2000, 597) to argue that understanding of "the *mechanisms* through which informal institutions arise and are maintained" is still missing. The importance of such institutions in helping the poor meet their immediate development needs is, however, well documented (OECD 2007). An Organisation for Economic Co-operation and Development (OECD) conference on informal institutions and development held in 2006 brought together development academics and experts from leading development agencies who noted not only the widespread prevalence of informal institutions in developing societies, and the opportunities and challenges they present for implementing development programs in these societies, but also the limited understanding of how these institutions work. The limited literature available on informal institutions to date does, however, reflect a trend toward greater recognition that informal institutions are particularly resilient and important in shaping individual and collective decisions in contexts where state institutions are failing (Ostrom 1990; OECD 2007). Thus, in the absence of state-led and commercial banking systems and insurance institutions, impoverished communities have developed their own informal credit societies and insurance networks.

It is worth noting here that not all forms of collective action are conducive to development. When small ethnic clans network closely to ensure control over electoral politics, or when mafia groups in Sicily succeed in winning the strong loyalty of their members, the outcomes of this cooperation are not necessarily conducive to development. The donors, not surprisingly, remain interested in promoting pro-poor forms of collective action, with the hope that, in the long term, enhancing the ability of the poor to engage in collective action will enable them to check the entrenched elites who collude for their own narrow gains. The policy of promoting informal institutions that facilitate collective action has thus mainly translated into supporting CBOs and civil society organizations that produce visible and collectively desirable outcomes for the poor, such as ensuring access to basic facilities in the areas of education, health, basic infrastructure, and so on. At the same time, donors have tried to cultivate a culture of democracy and civic participation in developing countries by supporting

NGOs, civic groups, social movements, and advocacy groups, in the hope that they will build local constituencies that will exert pressure on the existing elites to reshape the formal institutions in favor of the public or the poor. The World Bank Social Development Group, for instance, maintains that strong civil society and community participation is required for making the poor voices be heard and for monitoring the state. Strengthening informal institutions of cooperation is thus seen as a means of ensuring service delivery for the poor in contexts where state bureaucracies are failing, while also contributing to the bigger objective of creating a more proactive civil society in the developing world, with the hope that in the long term such a society will be better able to hold the state accountable.

The dilemma, however, is that these donor efforts—despite their clear intention to support community-based collective action and promote individuals' propensity to galvanize around public interest issues—are in many contexts having the opposite impact. As in the cases introduced at the outset of this chapter, funding provided to civic groups and community-based initiatives that traditionally were successfully self-governing has actually eroded their members' capacity to cooperate. Aid given to improve informal institutional arrangements such as civic culture and cooperation in the broader society has led to the rise of NGOs that have no members. Studies documenting such concerns have proliferated since the mid-1990s; the term *NGO* has actually become distrusted in many societies and rural communities. The studies on aid and NGOs show that the provision of aid to civil society groups since the 1980s has definitely led to a dramatic rise in the emergence of organizations claiming to work for civic causes: NGOs in Nepal increased from 220 in 1990 to 1,210 in 1993 (Rademacher and Tamang 1993); in Bolivia they increased from 100 in 1980 to 530 in the early 1990s (Arellano-Lopez and Petras 1994); in Tunisia there were 5,186 NGOs registered in 1991, an increase from only 1,886 in 1988 (Marzouk 1995). These studies also note, however, that these NGOs have no members.

Many studies argue that donor funding to NGOs in developing countries has created a new elite within the population of such countries, an elite that is better versed in the language of foreign donors than the society it claims to serve (Tvedt 1998; Edward and Hulme 1995; Fowler 2000). Henderson (2002) argues that foreign aid designed to facilitate the growth of civil society in Russia has in reality had the opposite effect. Rather than fostering horizontal networks, small grassroots initiatives, and ultimately civic development, foreign aid has contributed to the emergence of a vertical, institutionalized, and isolated (although well-funded) civic community. She argues that a fairly distinct "civic elite" has developed within the NGO community in Russia and that one of the most visible problems facing many of the funded groups is the "lack of a visible constituency" (142). Sperling (1999) records similar concerns after studying the women's movement in Russia. She argues that of the funded groups, few had volunteers and even fewer had a clear concept of the core group of people they claimed to represent. Sobhan (1997) has described how in Bangladesh an entire class has emerged whose ability to reproduce itself is entirely dependent on its capacity to control the use and distribution of foreign aid. Fukuyama (2001, 2002) records concern that foundations and government aid agencies seeking to promote voluntary associations have often simply managed to create a stratum of local elites who have become skilled at writing grant proposals; the organizations they create tend to have little durability once the funds dry up.

Other researchers note the serious trust-deficiency faced by these organizations. Fowler (2002) notes that in many developing countries, NGOs "are the object of government mistrust and public suspicion." Similarly, Harper (1996) writes that in Vietnam, NGOs are a relatively new type of organization that has been strongly supported by external donors, but their poorly developed links with local communities raise serious questions about legitimacy in that Vietnamese in general view NGOs as profit-making or foreign organizations. Kuratov and Solyanik (1995) make the same observation when they argue that external financial dependency and questionable local accountability are two points that differentiate and detach NGOs from the main body of civil society. This literature indicates that rather than strengthening civil society or building social capital, donor aid has led to the rise of a specific kind of civic group, the NGOs whose members claim to work for a group other than themselves but whose characteristics and modus operandi are very different from those of the groups that traditionally played this role in these societies prior to the arrival of development aid.

Anheier and Salamon (1998), in their work on the nonprofit sector in developing countries, express similar concerns and record that traditional voluntary and nonprofit organizations in developing countries are much older and more complex than the NGOs that are the primary focus of development literature. They argue that within the development literature the concept of a nonprofit sector in the developing world has been obscured due to an exclusive focus on NGOs. Rather than helping to create understanding of the nonprofit sector in such countries, the current literature may instead help to reinforce the "long-standing myth that nonprofit organizations, voluntary associations, charity, and philanthropy are basically 'Western' phenomena that do not naturally exist in the developing world" (4). Their study also, however, does not expand on the empirical or theoretical differences between NGOs and other voluntary groups that do not engage with development aid. All of these critiques indicate that donor aid seems to lead to some unique organizational characteristics within NGOs that were not formerly associated with nonprofit groups in many developing countries. In the language of collective action literature (Ostrom 1990), these organizations, which are being funded to address the second-order collective action dilemma of generating institutional arrangements that will promote cooperation in broader society, are in fact unable to overcome even the first-order collective action dilemma, that is, they are unable to retain their core members.

Greater understanding is needed of the formal and informal institutional arrangements that facilitate community-based collective action and participation in civic groups, and why aid could be crowding out such cooperation. This book provides an answer to these questions by drawing on a set of five empirically rich studies conducted between 2003 and 2009 in Pakistan, where, following the global trend, donors have channeled an increasing amount of development aid through NGOs and civic groups. The next section starts exploring possible solutions to this puzzle by engaging with the theoretical works that form the foundation of the donor policy of channeling aid to civic groups in the developing world.

## Two Proponents: Tocqueville and Putnam

The idea that donors should invest in civic groups in pursuit of vibrant civic culture and community participation is not a recent one; nor is this policy exclusively embedded in theoretical debates on informal institutions. A product of the early 1980s, this policy draws on two works that have greatly influenced international donors in directing aid toward actors who are viewed as strengthening civic culture: Tocqueville's ([1835] 1994) *Democracy in America* and Putnam's (with Leonardi and Nanetti) *Making Democracy Work* (1993). In his much-acclaimed analysis of the working of democracy in America, Tocqueville commended Americans' propensity to form voluntary organizations, which he considered to be a critical ingredient of U.S. democracy. He maintained: "When some view is represented by an association, it must take clearer and more precise shape. It counts its supporters and involves them in its cause; these supporters get to know one another, and numbers increase zeal. An association unites the energies of divergent minds and vigorously directs them towards a clearly indicated goal" (1994, 190). He argued that through these voluntary organizations, "feelings and ideas are renewed, the heart enlarged, and the understanding developed only by the reciprocal action of men one upon another" (515). Putnam (1993, 90) notes that, in the vocabulary of the present-day political scientist, Tocqueville attributes to voluntary organizations the power to inspire "interest articulation" and "interest aggregation." His own work on identifying the reasons for the contrasting democratic and economic performance of northern and southern Italy further strengthens the Tocquevillean understanding of the role of voluntary organizations in development. In *Making Democracy Work*, he argues that dense networks of voluntary associations are the main explanation for northern Italy's greater economic progress compared to the country's progress in the south. Putnam demonstrates that there are strong causal connections between the existence of "civic engagement," reflected in such factors as high levels of voluntary associations (such as sports clubs, music groups, and bird watcher societies), and outcomes that can be labeled "good governance." Participation in civic organizations, he argues, inculcates cooperation skills as well as a sense of shared responsibility for collective endeavors. As a visible sign of the influence of his work, at one point "social capital" was declared the "missing link" in development theory by the World Bank (Harriss 2002).

Drawing on the work of these authors, many donors have argued that for developing countries a strong civil society is important in providing a counterweight to repressive governments while at the same time resolving the seemingly intractable tension between the state and market (Howell and Pearce 2000). Such a society has been assumed "to hold in check the state," "serve as the moral pulse of society," and "further democratic values." It has thus been argued that strengthening civil society should be an important part of international development institutions' interventions in developing countries. Improving the quality of civic culture through supporting the organizations that constitute this informal sphere—namely NGOs, socially oriented social movements, and community-based organizations—has been an important feature of donor aid policies since the 1980s, leading to increased aid flows to NGOs over time (Edward and Hulme 1995; Howell and Pearce 2000). Most of the positive attributes accorded to voluntary organizations as enabling them to strengthen civil society are based on claims regarding their voluntary nature, that they enable like-minded members to articulate a collective interest and mutually work to attain it (Putnam 1993). It is believed that this coming-together of people to cooperate to produce a common good is valuable not just because it helps attain that good, but more importantly because in the process they learn to cooperate and trust one another, or in Putnam's words, to create social capital, which is in turn good for a society's economic and political growth. The question, then, is why should the organizations supported by donors in the hope of promoting civil society and social capital come to lack the very ingredient that is central to Tocqueville's and Putnam's conception of strong civic culture, that is, active members? What explains this dilemma?

When we study these two theoretical works closely to see why a policy emanating from them may in reality have the reverse impact of breaking down cooperation rather than enhancing it, two issues are noteworthy. First, while drawing inspiration from the work of Tocqueville and of Putnam, international donors have formulated a policy of promoting organizations that in fact are not the kind of organizations that were the primary concern of these authors. Tocqueville and Putnam were mainly concerned with membership-based organizations, that is, self-regarding groups whose members come together to produce a good that they use collectively, rather than other-regarding groups, whose members come together to serve a group other than themselves. The latter organizations are mostly referred to as "charities," even though these authors, in some sections of their work, group together both types of organization. International donors instead are engaged with other-regarding groups. This might not appear to be a fundamental issue, but it does at least indicate a lack of understanding of the groups with which international donors engage. A group that promises gains to its participants clearly offers different incentives to individuals to join than one that aims to involve individuals not for their own gain but for the benefit of other people; it cannot logically be assumed that people voluntarily participate in the two forms of groups, one promising a return and the other not, for the same reasons.

Second, although these authors theorize about the links between strong civil society, democracy, and good governance, they do not present a detailed account of the motivations of individuals to cooperate in generating these membership associations and organizations. Tocqueville (1994, 525) assumes that these organizations are an outcome of "self-interest properly understood," that is, self-interest in the context of broader public needs, self-interest that is "enlightened" rather than "myopic," self-interest that is alive to the interests of others. Putnam, on the other hand, analyzes this cooperation through macrosocial phenomena such as norms, values, and networks rather than explaining how those norms of cooperation come about. He highlights the macro factors that facilitate cooperation but provides limited insight into what motivates individuals to cooperate. In policy design, in order to predict the incentives that will make people act in the desired way, it is critical to understand what motivates them to act. Neither Tocqueville nor

Putnam gives us this understanding. This lack of insight makes it difficult to predict why individuals who have come together to form a group behave differently when development aid is made available.

Compared to the civil society literature, the collective action literature provides a better framework for analyzing this puzzle. Olson (1971) established once and for all the importance of studying how individuals who can benefit from a group will not contribute to the cost of running that group because their personal interest will be best served by free-riding, even when such behavior on the part of all individuals will lead to a collectively inefficient outcome. The strong analytical appeal of this paradox has made some argue that it has a "central place in philosophical discussions" (Campbell 1985, 3). While recognizing the role of the free-rider dilemma in undermining collective action, Ostrom (1990) has built on Olson's framework to illuminate how some groups have overcome this challenge. It is therefore important to engage with the collective action literature within institutional economics to find possible explanations for why aid can erode individuals' propensity to cooperate toward the production of a collective good. What explanations does the existing literature on collective action present for this unintended impact of aid on informal institutions of collective action in many developing countries? The next section turns to this literature.

## The Free-Rider Problem: From Olson to Ostrom

The high probability that individuals will not work together to produce a collectively desirable good has been well established by Olson, who, in *The Logic of Collective Action* (1971), shows that the traditional assumption in group theory that individuals with common interests will voluntarily act so as to try to further those interests is misguided (Bentley 1949; Truman 1958):

> The idea that groups tend to act in support of their group interests is supposed to follow logically from this widely accepted premise of rational, self-interested behavior. In other words, if the members of some group have a common interest or objective, and if they would all be better off if that objective were achieved, it has been thought to follow logically that the individuals in that group would, if they were rational and self-interested, act to achieve that objective (Olson 1971, 1).

Olson instead argues that "unless the number of individuals in a group is quite small, or unless there is coercion or some other special device to make individuals act in their common interest, *rational, self-interested individuals will not act to achieve their common or group interests*" (2, emphasis in original). As Ostrom (1990) notes, Olson's argument rests largely on the premise that a person who cannot be excluded from obtaining the benefits of a collective good once the good is produced has little incentive to contribute voluntarily to the provision of that good unless each member's contributions are very noticeable.

The very same logic drives two other influential models shaping debates on collective action: Hardin's (1968) account of the *tragedy of the commons* and the *prisoner's dilemma game.* In the tragedy of the commons, Hardin asks readers to envision a pasture that is open to all and then assess from the perspective of a rational herder the optimal strategies for making the animals graze the pasture. Each herder receives a direct benefit from his own animals and suffers delayed costs from the deterioration of the commons when his and others' cattle overgraze. Each herder is motivated to add more and more animals because he receives the direct benefit from his own animals and bears only a share of the costs resulting from overgrazing. Hardin concludes: "Therein is the tragedy. Each man is locked into a system that compels him to increase his herd without limit—in a world that is limited. Ruin is the destination towards which all men rush, each pursuing his own best interest in a society that believes in the freedom of the commons" (1244).

In the prisoner's dilemma game, the actors face similar incentives not to cooperate. Each player is always personally better off choosing the strategy to defect—that is, not to cooperate, no matter what the other player chooses. Given these assumptions, when both players choose their dominant strategy, they produce a below-optimal equilibrium; this is not a Pareto-optimal outcome in that at least one other outcome is strictly preferred by at least one player that is at least as good for all the other players. This paradox—that individually rational strategies lead to collectively irrational outcomes—has formed the foundation of the analytical debates on collective action in institutional economics. For a long time it has also shaped the policy conclusion that third-party intervention in the form of state-enforced laws or privatization is the key to solving these collective action challenges.

Seen in this context, the evidence of the breakdown of groups when aid is provided should not be surprising, because this framework sets out the inherent challenge faced by any group in sustaining its membership. The issue, however, is that aid is not just often *failing* to generate collective action in newly formed groups, but it is actually eroding cooperation in groups that, prior to provision of aid, worked effectively. The existence of real-life cases in which collective action did prevail without third-party intervention has led to a rich literature highlighting how the collective action dilemmas predicted by Olson can in some contexts be overcome without the involvement of a third party.

In her landmark study *Governing the Commons*, Ostrom (1990) illustrates how societies have developed diverse institutional arrangements for managing natural resources and avoiding ecosystem collapse in many cases, even though some arrangements have failed to prevent resource exhaustion. She identifies eight "design principles" that can help groups overcome their collective action dilemmas (1990, 90): (1) clearly defined boundaries for withdrawing resources, (2) congruence between appropriation and provision rules and local conditions, (3) collective-choice arrangements in which most resource appropriators may participate in the decision-making process, (4) effective monitoring by persons who are also appropriators or accountable to them, (5) graduated sanctions for resource appropriators who violate community rules, (6) mechanisms of conflict resolution that are cheap and easily accessible, (7) recognition by higher-level authorities of the right to be self-determining, and (8) organization of activities into multilayered nested enterprises.

Ostrom notes that "The central question in this study is how a group of principals who are in an interdependent situation can organize and govern themselves to obtain continuing joint benefits when all face temptations to free-ride, shirk, or otherwise act opportunistically" (1990, 29). She maintains that "All efforts to organize collective action, whether by an external ruler, an entrepreneur, or a set of principals who wish to gain collective benefits, must address a common set of problems. These have to do with coping with free-riding, solving commitment problems, arranging for the supply of new institutions, and monitoring individual compliance with sets of rules" (1990, 27).

These design principles, in Ostrom's assessment, help overcome the appropriation and provision problems (1990, 47):

> When appropriators face appropriation problems, they are concerned with the effects that various methods of allocating a fixed, or time-in-dependent, quantity of resource units will have on the net return obtained by the appropriators. Provision problems concern the effects of various ways of assigning responsibility for building, restoring, or maintaining the resource system over time, as well as the well-being of the appropriators. Appropriation problems are concerned with the allocation of the flow; provision problems are concerned with the stock.

In addition, Ostrom places great emphasis on understanding the incremental, sequential, and self-transforming nature of institutional change.

However, she focuses on a specific type of collective action dilemma, that is, one confronted in the management of common-pool resources. Both she and Olson (1971) recognize the importance of the type of good desired in shaping collective action decisions. Both authors note that participation decisions will differ depending on whether the group is inclusive or exclusive. Common-pool resource problems share with public good provision the problems of free-riding, but they also include the problems of overharvesting and of overcrowding. The eight principles identified by Ostrom have been most systematically studied in the context of common-pool resources. They are, however, also useful principles for initiating investigation into any form of collective action dilemma. These eight principles thus have the potential to help explain, partially if not fully, why voluntary organizations in Sindh had traditionally sustained collective action, why the norms of communal cultivation of quinoa survived in the Bolivian highlands for many centuries, and why *Gotong Royong* continued to act as a platform for mobilizing collective works in Aceh for similarly long periods.

Where Ostrom's framework is less useful, however, is in explaining why these institutional arrangements that facilitated collective action could change and break down upon the provision of development aid. She has provided more detailed insights into how institutions can be created to facilitate collective action than she has provided understanding of the reasons for its erosion. In a recent publication (Gibson et al. 2005), she and her coauthors attempt to explain why aid has a negative impact on collective action. Referring to this puzzle as "the Samaritan's Dilemma," they argue that the incentives generated by development aid are important in explaining the breakdown of cooperation. The limitation of their work is that it attempts to address all forms of collective action dilemmas associated with development aid—both those involving state bureaucracies and those involving civil society groups—and thus fails to highlight the specific incentives that could be leading to the withdrawal of members from these groups. Thus, when applied to the dilemma discussed in this book, this joint work tells us that something is amiss with the incentive structure provided to these groups by the donors, but it does not tell us what those incentives are.

A second limitation of the collective action literature in answering the dilemma under study in this book is the same as in the case of civil society and social capital literature. Both Olson and Ostrom largely theorize about incentives to engage in self-regarding rather than other-regarding collective action. Olson establishes the dilemma of collective action by looking at groups engaged in the production of public goods promoted by labor unions, and Ostrom illustrates institutional mechanisms that help overcome this dilemma through the study of common-pool resources. In the *Logic of Collective Action,* Olson in fact notes the need for a separate theory to explain other-regarding action. He argues that his theory can also be applied to charities but cannot be expected to provide a great deal of insight in this regard because his primary focus is on groups that come about for explicit economic gain. He notes that as yet there is no strong theory to explain the rise of charities. More recently, Heyer, Stewart, and Throps (2002), in their edited volume on group behavior, have reaffirmed this gap in the literature. While developing a typology of groups, they highlight the absence of a powerful theory to explain *pro bono groups*, within which category they place charities and NGOs. They argue that "groups performing pro-bono functions also seek to alter distribution of benefits within the society, but they differ from groups performing claim functions in that they are directed mainly towards individuals outside the group, in contrast to claim groups in which functions are pursued by groups on behalf of the group members" (7).

Thus, in its current form, the collective action literature remains focused on self-regarding groups, with the result that its predictive power has not been explored for the very organizations with which the donors are primarily dealing, many of whom fit into the category of other-regarding groups. Most of the NGOs funded by donors actually claim to work for groups other than themselves. This book thus maintains that we first need to develop a consistent account of why individuals come together to form self-regarding as well as other-regarding groups; that is, we need to expand the collective action literature to explain the existence of other-regarding as well as self-regarding groups and see if the rules governing cooperation among the two forms of groups are the same. Only after this can we assess whether similar explanations hold for the crowding out of cooperative behavior upon provision of aid, given that the concerns recorded here have been noted for both types of groups.

## New Propositions

This book proposes that two main adjustments need to be made if we want to develop a theory that holds equal explanatory power with respect to the negative impact of current patterns of aid disbursement on both self-regarding and other-regarding groups. First, I argue that in order to understand why aid can break down collective action within civic groups and community-based initiatives it is important to differentiate between the initiators—those who started the group or are the current leaders—and the joiners—the ordinary members—and to study the dynamic interaction between the strategies of these two actors. This book argues that at the heart of cooperation lies the ability of the initiator to win the trust of the joiners, and that the success of collective action rests in the leader's ability to reduce transaction costs, that is, the costs of negotiating and enforcing contracts (North 1990). Because the joiner has to trust the initiator with his or her money or time, in a context where monitoring is difficult (particularly because the joiner him- or herself is not the beneficiary), material sacrifice on the part of the group initiator becomes an important signal of the initiator's commitment. Other factors that help reduce monitoring costs are clear signs of efficiency established through visibility of work, direct contact, and reputation built over time. This book argues that, as predicted by collective action models that draw broadly on rational choice assumptions, the joiners are always suspicious of the motives of the initiators and thus would cooperate only after they have access to mechanisms for monitoring the initiator's commitment and performance. Material sacrifice on the part of the initiators for the work of the group and visible signs of performance reduce the information-gathering and monitoring costs and thereby facilitate cooperation between initiators and joiners.

In emphasizing the importance of the role of the initiator in generating and sustaining collective action, the analysis developed in this book finds support in *constitutional political economy*, represented by James Buchanan (founder of the Virginia school of political economy) and Vincent Ostrom (of the Bloomington school of institutional analysis). Constitutional political economy emphasizes the role of *public entrepreneurs*, who are viewed as overcoming narrowly selfish behavior and investing in organizing for publicly beneficial collective action in response to incentives such as power, honor, and fame (Kuhnert 2001; Shivakumar 2005), or *self-interest better understood*. However, as seen in the analysis presented in the following chapters, this book presents a much more complex analysis of the inner motivational framework of such a *public entrepreneur* than that recognized in the constitutional political economy literature. Although Elinor Ostrom (1990) also notes the role of "monitors" and social and public entrepreneurs in facilitating collective action, she places limited emphasis on their role; further, she does not systematically analyze the complex motivational framework that shapes their decisions to initiate or sustain collective action. By comparison, Theda Skocpol (2003) places greater emphasis on such an approach by looking at civic activity in the United States as cooperation between "organizers" and "joiners." However, because she is a historical institutionalist, Skocpol's primary concern remains the study of the social and political conditions that have influenced the strategies of the leaders who launch and direct the various kinds of voluntary groups, rather than the strategies of the organizers and joiners themselves.

Second, I argue that understanding why aid reduces the initiator's ability to mobilize or retain members requires that we adjust our understanding of utility; we must recognize not only the difference between material and psychosocial sources of utility, for which there is growing recognition within economics, especially behavioral economics (Bowles 2004), but more importantly, the dynamic interplay between the two. This book illustrates that aid provides wrong incentives because the donors make wrong assumptions about the behavior of individuals who engage in collective action. It argues that involvement in both forms of groups under study is driven by self-interest; however, the notion of self-interest is more complex than is assumed within narrow interpretations of rational choice framework. The book argues that even the apparently self-sacrificing action of initiating an other-regarding group is driven by self-interest, that is, by a search for certain personal reward rather than pure concern for others; the difference is that in the case of altruistic or other-regarding action the search is for psychosocial rather than material rewards. Ironically, however, the donor literature on civil society and collective action—even that produced by the World Bank, an institution that normally is critiqued for being wedded to development models based in crude economic rationality—starts with the assumption that those who engage in other-regarding collective action are driven by altruism and care for the other (World Bank 2000a; 2005). The primary contribution of this research is to show how this misplaced assumption is at the heart of the wrong incentive structures that actually end up eroding collective action.

What we see in this book is that it is not that people don't engage in altruistic or other-regarding action; they do, but they do it because they get something out of it. It is the *makeup* of this *something*—namely psychosocial rewards—that we need to understand if we are to comprehend why aid is actually eroding altruism and other-regarding behavior. In making this case, the book builds on existing literature that argues for a dual notion of self-interest: *ideal* and *material.*

Such a conception of utility is not at odds with economic theory. John Stuart Mill ([1861] 1982) tried to explain altruistic behavior as rational. Margolis (1982) argues that almost no economist would deny the possibility of explaining altruism within rational choice theory; he contends that in recent years, efforts to incorporate altruistic preferences into the conventional framework have become fairly common. Such explanations stem from the basic conception of utility within rational choice, a notion based on Bentham's reasoning that "nature has placed mankind under the governance of two sovereign masters, *pain* and *pleasure*" (1789, 33, emphasis in original). The shift in emphasis in economic theory from wealth to utility, where utility is viewed as a psychological unit of pleasure, has allowed for the explanation of altruistic behavior within the rational choice framework (Becker 1993).

Explaining other-regarding behavior as fitting the self-interest model has, however, also been criticized by those who argue for recognition of non-self-interested motives, such as altruism, in explaining the actions of otherwise rational actors, that is, actors driven to maximize gains for minimum costs (Alkire and Deneulin 2002). The argument is most convincingly spelled out in Sen's (1977) seminal paper "Rational Fools," in which he defines sympathy and commitment as two means by which consideration for others' welfare enters one's set of choices. This view is in line with the traditional view of altruism as action done for the good of others, independent of concerns about the impact that action will have, positive or negative, on one's own well-being (Alkire and Deneulin 2002, 62). The concept of altruistic behavior draws from the notion of *philia*. In Aristotle's political thought, *philia* connotes any sense of affection, of belonging to others or communication with others, whether spontaneous or reflected, due to circumstances or to free choice (Alkire and Deneulin 2002, 62). The empirical findings from the research presented in this book, however, do not support these critiques but instead show that even altruistic action is primarily self-interested. However, as noted by Becker (1993), what constitutes utility is more complex than exclusive pursuit of material gains.

Where this research pushes this debate forward is in its argument that it is not enough to recognize the complexity of the utility calculus; we also need to study the specific rewards associated with the both the ideal and the material utilities; the former offers rewards of a more psychosocial nature, and the latter, of material goods. What is even more important to recognize is that these two types of rewards rarely coexist, because psychosocial rewards are contingent on denial of material rewards for the specific activity being rewarded. As the following chapters demonstrate, it is because of this inverse relation between the two types of rewards that provision of aid to the leaders of self-regarding and other-regarding groups actually leads to breakdown in cooperation. The answer to why aid crowds out cooperation between other-regarding and self-regarding groups rests precisely in understanding this tension between the two types of rewards, and in the realization that ideal rewards come at the cost of material rewards for a given activity. Thus aid packages offering high salaries as incentives to motivate the leaders of NGOs and traditional collective action initiatives to perform better actually end up eroding their commitment. The provision of high material rewards makes it impossible to draw on the psychosocial rewards that were the primary drivers for that action prior to provision of aid. This tension between material and psychosocial rewards erodes commitment, which over time deteriorates performance and the ability to mobilize members.

Finally, this book also notes that the incremental and self-transformative nature of institutional change that Ostrom (1990) identifies as being critical to the supply of new institutions that can overcome free-riding is just as relevant for understanding why aid breaks down collective action. Often the impact of aid is not instant but the result of a gradual process in which change in the activity of one set of actors—normally the initiators—triggers change in the behavior of the other set of actors. Just as Ostrom (1990) predicts that small initial successes build trust that enables bigger contributions later, this book shows that small lapses of performance and accountability on the part of leaders upon receipt of development aid trigger a dynamic that leads over time to the complete breakdown of cooperation. Aid removes the initiator's dependence on joiners, leaving little incentive for leaders to mobilize joiners, who come with their own demands for putting in place visible accountability mechanisms. What such an analysis illustrates is that no one is entirely committed to either material or ideal rewards; rather, most individuals balance the two to maximize their utility, because the two forms of reward have their own distinct appeals. The incentives available in the external context are critical to determining whether the internal utility calculus will tip in favor of pursuing ideal or material pleasures for a specific activity.

## The Methodology

Taking a cue from the limitations of the existing works on NGOs just analyzed, the research project discussed in this book adopts three methodological preferences. First, it aims to study the working of both self-regarding and other-regarding groups, and the impact of aid on both. Second, it focuses on understanding the distinct calculations of the initiators and joiners, and on studying the behavior of both to see why they engage in collective action and how the choices of one affect the choices of the other. Third, rather than starting with the assumptions of rational choice theory, the research was designed to let the fieldwork data determine the motives and decision-making processes of the actors engaging in collective action. Such an approach helps overcome Green and Shapiro's (1994) concern that empirical studies designed to test rational choice theory often adopt a "method-driven rather than problem-driven" approach to research. Rather than formulating bold predictions that are falsifiable by empirical evidence, rational choice theorists tend first to look at the empirical evidence, then design a rational choice model that fits it; they refer to this process as post-hoc theory development (34–35).

The book thus engages in an inquiry into individual action that results in cooperative behavior and the formation of self-regarding and other-regarding groups, without making any prior assumptions about the motives or decision-making processes of the individuals involved. In doing so, it tests many of these fundamental assumptions themselves. Gambetta and Hamill (2005, 15) adopt a similar approach in understanding taxi drivers' decisions about which customers to trust: "A distinctive feature of our research is that we investigate empirically the actual judgement and decision-making processes that taxi drivers, passengers, and mimics use in such situations. In other words, rather than presume full rationality, our study explicates the actual content of the 'street-level epistemologies' of the respective players." In the same way, rather than assuming that individuals have rational, self-interested reasons for joining an altruistic group, this book analyzes the basis of their choices and decisions. Five distinct though interlinked investigations were carried out to understand why aid can crowd out community-based collective action: (1) case-studies of three traditional voluntary organizations (VOs) that drew on rich ethnographies and interviews with more than 350 members of these organizations to develop a theory of why individuals engage in other-regarding collective action; (2) a case study of a self-regarding group in which community members mobilized themselves to protect their right to land when they all had an incentive to free-ride; (3) a countrywide survey of forty prominent civil society organizations in Pakistan (twenty of which drew on development aid and twenty on local donations, hereafter referred to as traditional VOs) to test whether aid impacted the ability of these organizations to mobilize members and their ability to achieve development outcomes; (4) a public-perceptions survey of public trust in civil society organizations that receive development aid; and (5) an in-depth study of the factors that led to erosion of collective action in the organizations supported by Oxfam in Sindh—the case introduced at the outset of this chapter. The results of these studies are systematically analyzed in the chapters of this book.

Chapter 2 starts by inviting the reader to step back and understand the complexity of the civic groups that constitute the civil society landscape in Pakistan. In the process it also assesses whether self-regarding or other-regarding groups owe their origin to inherited beliefs and the value structures of a society, or to opportunities created by the changing socioeconomic and political context. The chapter provides a historical analysis of the origins of and shifts in the prominent forms of self-regarding and other-regarding groups in Pakistan. It traces the evolution of such groups in the Muslim communities of South Asia, in areas that constitute present-day Pakistan, starting from the twelfth century. Noting the existence of four types of groups in the present-day arena of civic associations in Pakistan, the chapter identifies a distinct point of origin for each type. The religiously inspired associational networks, such as the mosques, madrasas, and Sufi *khankahs*, were the first set of organizations to emerge within the Muslim population in South Asia, starting as early as the twelfth century. These were followed by the rise of *anjumans*, welfare-oriented voluntary groups that work for their own religious communities to meet their basic welfare needs; they arose as a response to missionary organizations that entered South Asian civic space with the onset of British rule. During the twentieth century some of these associational networks transformed into political organizations, working for an independent homeland and mobilizing members beyond narrow religious lines. After the partition of the Indian subcontinent into India and Pakistan in 1947, the main period that saw the rise of a new form of voluntary association was the 1980s, when the term *NGO* came into vogue.

Chapter 2 shows that the origin of each of these four groups (the religiously inspired associational networks, the *anjumans*, the political organizations, and the NGOs) was closely tied to the new opportunities and threats created by the changing political and social environment. As at each point new players entered the scene to avail themselves of these opportunities, many of the old players also adapted their strategies to survive in the new context. The madrasas, which in the Mughal Empire provided both religious and secular education to their students, became focused entirely on religious education when they found that competing with the Western-style educational institutions introduced by the British was a failing strategy. The politically oriented groups were either crushed or taken over by the military regimes in postcolonial Pakistan, and some VOs that had emerged in the colonial period acquired a new development language and cultural norms after they started to receive development aid in the 1980s. By tracing this constant reshaping of both the self-regarding and other-regarding groups in response to changing external incentives, the chapter shows how collective action is clearly shaped by a complex interplay of intrinsic and extrinsic incentives. It also notes that in all of these groups, except the NGOs, signs of material sacrifice on the part of their leaders were very important in mobilizing members. The chapter ends by noting how groups that draw on development aid (NGOs) differ in their core features from those that don't.

Chapter 3 looks at the motives and decision-making processes of the initiators (those who start or lead groups) and the joiners (members) of three types of other-regarding groups (religiously oriented, social welfare oriented, and those driven by Marxist philosophy) in Pakistan. It asks why initiators and joiners cooperate to constitute other-regarding groups, and explores the factors that make the joiners join one particular initiator out of the many seeking their cooperation. While Olson and Ostrom both focus on self-regarding groups, this chapter develops a theory of other-regarding groups. Drawing on more than 350 interviews with leaders, staff, and members who contribute their time or money to these groups, the chapter argues that the success of a group depends on the initiator's ability to reduce the transaction costs for the joiners to join the group. It also argues that both initiators and joiners cooperate to create such groups because they appreciate the psychosocial rewards; as is fully recognized in economic theory today, the sense of having done a good deed can increase individual utility (Kuhnert 2001; Bowles 2004). However, what ensures that a group will win members is the initiator's ability to reduce the transaction costs incurred by the joiners in assessing the commitment of the initiators. Because the joiner has to trust the initiator with his money or time, in a context where monitoring is difficult (because the joiner him- or herself is not the beneficiary of the work), material sacrifice on the part of the initiator of these groups becomes an important measure of the initiator's commitment.

Other factors that help reduce monitoring costs are clear signs of efficiency established through visibility of work, direct contact, and reputation built over time. Chapter 3 thus argues that, as predicted by collective action models that draw broadly on rational choice assumptions, joiners are always suspicious of the motives of the initiators and thus will cooperate only after they have access to mechanisms to monitor the initiator's commitment and performance. Material sacrifice on the part of the initiators for the benefit of the work of the group and visible signs of performance reduce information-gathering and monitoring costs and thereby facilitate cooperation between initiators and joiners. Why a group of this nature should break down upon provision of aid is discussed in Chapter 6, but before that, the next chapter tests whether these factors also mobilize members in self-regarding groups, which have been studied more often within the collective action literature.

Chapter 4 undertakes an in-depth analysis of the motives and decision-making processes of the initiators and joiners of a land rights movement led by a low-income tenant farmer community in Pakistan. The chapter shows that many of the eight principles identified by Ostrom as important in overcoming the free-rider problem—clearly defined boundaries, ability to monitor contributions, mechanisms for punishment, and so on—do indeed hold true when applied to this case. The case also fully supports Ostrom's proposition that institutional change is often an incremental and self-transforming process. Despite the high costs incurred by members of this movement—some were even killed during protests—it was able to sustain its membership and check free-riding primarily because of the incremental and self-transforming process of institutional change. As Ostrom predicts, the low initial costs for obtaining the promised benefits and the group's success in meeting its initial targets inspired individual members to make bigger contributions later on—amounts they were not willing to contribute at the outset. However, the case also shows that the presence of leaders who were willing to make material sacrifices in the group's interest was equally important in sustaining this collective action. The chapter thus argues that although most of the factors that Ostrom has found to facilitate collective action in governing common-pool resources apply to sustaining collective action in the production of public goods, the list of important variables prepared by Ostrom needs to include material sacrifice on the part of the leaders of these groups. Given the importance placed on the behavior of the leaders in mobilizing and sustaining collective action in both self-regarding and other-regarding groups, the chapter concludes with the hypothesis that the reason aid breaks down cooperation within civil society groups is that aid changes incentives, which in turn changes the behavior of the leaders of these groups. This hypothesis was tested using two nationwide surveys, reported on in the next chapter.

Chapter 5 presents the findings of a countrywide survey of the forty largest civil society organizations in Pakistan, twenty of which draw on development aid and twenty that do not. Based on a standard questionnaire, the survey studied the group leaders' motivation (by examining salary structures, financial commitments made to the group, and so on), the membership of the groups (by assessing the number of donors and volunteers), and the groups' organizational performance (by evaluating the sustainability of the group's work, its ties with beneficiaries, and so on) in order to test the hypothesis that aid leads to the breakdown of cooperation by changing the behavior of the leaders of these groups and the group's performance. The survey shows that groups whose initiators rely on aid have no joiners, whereas all those that rely on domestic resources have formal and informal donors as well as volunteers. Further, organizations that had joiners better achieved their development outcomes; they were more consistent in working toward stable goals, their activities were more sustainable, they were more accountable to their beneficiaries, and so forth. The chapter therefore argues that aid has a negative impact on collective action, which in turn has a negative impact on an organization's ability to attain its development goals. The chapter complements these rich empirical findings with a public-perceptions survey of NGOs in Pakistan. It shows that in Pakistan the term NGO is clearly associated with development aid and has very negative connotations: NGOs are viewed as elitist, unaccountable, lacking in public trust, and unworthy of public donations.

Whereas the previous chapter compares groups that take aid with those that don't, Chapter 6 takes the reader back to the case introduced at the outset of the book, in which the provision of small grants by Oxfam in Sindh led to a breakdown of cooperation within both other-regarding and self-regarding groups. Tracing the process of this shift, the chapter develops the core theoretical argument of the book and shows that this shift in how self-regarding and other-regarding groups work after they have received aid is inevitable under the current patterns of aid disbursement. The current incentive structure attempts to promote altruistic behavior by providing material incentives to the leaders of these groups. Aid agencies offer high salaries to the initiators of NGOs and community-based groups, assuming that they are committed and professional and thus need to be properly compensated. However, this simple incentive completely upsets the informal rules governing cooperative behavior within these groups. First, it increases the transaction costs for the joiners, because when the leaders of these groups are paid for the work they claim to be doing out of an ideological commitment or because everyone will benefit, the joiners can no longer monitor the leader's commitment. Thus, for the joiners, aid actually introduces a collective action problem that previously did not exist by making it difficult for them to assess the motivation and intentions of the initiator who asks for their contributions.

The checking of financial accounts becomes the only monitoring mechanism for members and this might be practically impossible or, in a context where formal institutions are weak and accounts can be fudged, completely unsuitable. By failing to understand the logic behind the informal mechanisms that communities had put in place to monitor the motivation of other actors, the donors thus introduce a collective action problem. Further, such incentives create an even bigger dilemma for the initiator, because they initiate an internal tension between material and ideal rewards. Connecting with the argument presented in Chapters 3 and 4, that initiators are driven primarily by the search for psychosocial rewards and that such rewards come at the cost of material rewards for a given activity, this chapter shows that the high salaries or incentive structures offered for their work make it impossible for leaders to draw on the ideal rewards that they initially received upon engaging in such activity; the result is that sooner or later they start to look at the group's activity purely in terms of the material rewards it promises, making their behavior vulnerable to free-riding. Thus, by introducing a wrong incentive, donors actually upset a complex balance between the opportunistic and altruistic behavior that shapes any decision and end up eroding altruistic outcomes by the very measures that are meant to promote them.

The book's final chapter looks at the policy implications that this research has for channeling aid to civil society groups and community-based collective action initiatives in the developing world. Whereas all major studies of aid argue that donors should be very careful to get the incentives right, this book attempts to present a specific account of precisely how the incentives embedded in current mechanisms for aid disbursement can corrupt behavior in community-based collective action groups. Chapter 7 presents five clear policy measures to improve the effectiveness of aid channeled through civil society groups and NGOs in the developing world: (1) work with those who are willing to put in time and effort rather than those who want to make a living off the stated cause; (2) invest in building resources for carrying out the group's activities rather than budgeting for salaries; (3) monitor the impact of these organizations by engaging with their members rather than looking at their annual reports; (4) enter the relationship as equals and be willing to understand the local groups' conceptions of desirable ends; and (5) be aware that the nature of interactions among the group's members will change as the project evolves, and that the incentives will need to be adjusted over time.

Theoretically, the chapter situates these empirically driven findings on the complexity of utility calculus and the dynamic interplay between material and psychosocial rewards within the findings of the broader literature on these themes. More generally, it notes how explanations attributed to culture can be misguiding for policy purposes if culture is assumed to be an unquestioned and unchanging set of practices and no attempt is made to understand the logic behind tradition. Most donors dismiss material sacrifice on the part of leaders of successful civil society movements in developing countries as a cultural practice. However, this book shows that there are clear effectiveness-based reasons for the existence of this practice that, once acknowledged, have clear implications for donors' policies of channeling aid to civil society groups. The chapter also presents a concrete example of Quranic schools in the northern Nigerian state of Kano, where donors are trying to use various incentives to make the *malams* (religious leaders) introduce secular subjects into the curricula of these schools. It shows how the donors will have to adjust their policy interventions if they are to take into account the implications of this book's findings. The chapter ends by addressing some methodological issues in studying rational choice-based theories and the optimal balance between using qualitative and quantitative studies.

# 2 Intrinsic or Extrinsic Incentives

The Evolution of Cooperative Groups in Pakistan

*Any society—modern or traditional, authoritarian or democratic, feudal or capitalist—is characterized by networks of interpersonal communication and exchange, both formal and informal.*

**Robert Putnam, Making Democracy Work, 1993, 173**

*The kinds of knowledge, skills, and learning that the members of an organization will acquire will reflect the payoff—the incentives—imbedded in the institutional constraints.*

**Douglass North, Institutions, Institutional Change, and Economic Performance, 1990, 74**

INSTITUTIONS PLACE CONSTRAINTS on individual behavior and thus confine individual choices. However, as is by now well-documented in the new institutional economics literature, institutions themselves also change in response to the actions of individual actors (North 1990; OECD 2007). Since Hobsbawm and Ranger's (1996) critical rethinking of the study of tradition, which questions the notion of tradition as "fixed (normally formalized) practices" (2) and emphasizes the ever-changing nature of apparently traditional practices, even within anthropology and history (disciplines that are more sympathetic to structuralist assumptions), *tradition* is recognized as a problematic categorization. Given that traditions are constantly changing or can evolve very quickly, what is classified as traditional might actually be a recent invention. This chapter traces the origin and processes of change within both self-regarding and other-regarding groups that have emerged in the area constituting present-day Pakistan. It also illustrates how the strategies adopted by the leaders of these organizations have constantly changed in response to changes in socio-economic and political institutions, and how this adaptive mechanism has in turn changed the institutional mechanisms that regulate cooperative behavior. With every major political or economic shift, new organizational players have emerged to capture the changed opportunities in the new environment, and once these players have come into place, they have tried to change in their favor the formal and informal rules governing cooperative behavior. However, certain informal institutional arrangements have remained unchanged—namely the expectation among the members of these groups that their leaders should demonstrate efficiency as well as clear signs that they are making material sacrifices for the advancement of the group's cause. The chapter also illustrates how weak formal institutions have led the public to develop greater reliance on informal institutions for collective action to meet basic survival needs. It does so by analyzing the emergence of religious groups within the Muslim population in India and then maps how other forms of collective action platforms mobilized around more secular or global humanitarian norms have gradually emerged within this community.

## Creating Demand for Informal Institutions

The formal institutions of the state of Pakistan—which was carved out of the Indian subcontinent at the end of British colonial rule in response to demand for a separate homeland for Muslims—have failed to promote the interests of ordinary citizens. Ranked 125 on the United Nations Development Programme's (UNDP's) Human Development Index, Pakistan falls among countries with low human development (UNDP 2010). Just slightly more than half of the population is literate while an equal share has no access to basic health facilities or sanitation. The gross domestic product (GDP) per capita in 2009 was US$2,400 at purchasing power parity (PPP). The estimates for income poverty rest at 66 percent of the population when the poverty line is defined as people living on less than two dollars a day. With a population growth rate of 2.8 percent, the population of 160 million is estimated to rise to 205 million by 2015. The economy is largely agriculture based, with 65 percent of the population still living in rural areas. Income distribution is highly skewed. Due to quotas for women in parliament since 2002, Pakistan ranks slightly better on the UNDP's Gender Empowerment Measure (GEM), at 99.[1]

1. http://hdrstats.undp.org/en/indicators/125.html

The explanation for this poor state of human development, however, cannot be interpreted to indicate a failure of economic institutions. After gaining independence in 1947, Pakistan sustained an impressive annual growth rate of 6 percent for most periods. Overall, Pakistan's real income per capita increased by 231 percent from 1970 to 1993 (Haq 1997). The problem has not been with growth itself but with the inefficient state institutions that have failed to undertake fair distribution. Pakistan's performance on key human development indicators is far below that of other countries with similar income. For example, in 1997, Pakistan's real per capita income (in PPP dollars) was about 75 percent higher than India's. Yet Pakistan lagged behind India in adult literacy and on most other social indicators, and today it has the lowest education indicators across South Asia (Haq 1997). Mahbub ul Haq, founder of the UNDP Human Development Reports and one-time finance minister of the country, identified the following challenges: "highly skewed distribution of income; the absence of any meaningful land reforms; non-existence of income tax on agricultural income; an overwhelming reliance of fiscal policy on indirect rather than direct taxes; the heavy burden of defence and debt servicing on limited budgetary resources; political domination by a rentier class that pre-empts the patronage of the state in its own favour; and very corrupt ruling elite" (Haq 1997, 38).

The key cause of Pakistan's multiple problems, as identified by many authors, has been the failure to establish efficient institutions of state governance (Ali 1983; Noman 1990; Haq 1997; Zaidi 1999a). The country faced a crisis of leadership right from the outset when Muhammad Ali Jinnah, the founder of Pakistan, already very frail by the time of partition, passed away in 1948, a year after the creation of Pakistan. His close confidant Liaquat Ali Khan, the first prime minister of the country, was assassinated in 1951. Their deaths left the civil service and the military, the two institutions that had inherited a strong institutional structure from British colonial rule, in total command (Ali 1983, 43).[2] The problem of weak political leadership was also rooted in the foundation of the Pakistan Muslim League, the party that brought the country onto the world map, a party mainly of the bourgeoisie and big landlords (Gankovsky and Gordon-Polonskaya 1964, 113; Jalal 1990). The members of these two social groups were bound closely together by common interests and personal ties (Gankovsky and Gordon-Polonskaya 1964). Many of the landlords were not only political but also religious leaders in their areas due to their Sufi lineage. This concentration of political power in the hands of a few families, in a context

---

2. For a detailed discussion, see Alavi 1966.

where democratic institutions were weak against the civil and military bureaucracy, introduced perverse incentive structures for the political elites. The politicians became more open to entering into pacts with the civil and military elites, which helped them retain and expand their individual status within the government structure but undermined democratic institutions (Ali 1970, 1983).

A bureaucracy-military alliance led the country until October 1958. In March 1959, President Iskander Ali Mirza formally asked General Ayub Khan, commander-in-chief at that time, to take over political power (Ali 1983); the general obliged with the imposition of martial law. Ali (1983) argues it was fear that the leftist parties would succeed in Pakistan's first-ever general elections that made the civilian bureaucrats invite the army to assume power, and Noman (1990) argues it was due to the fear that power would shift away from the Muhajir-Punjabi elite in West Pakistan to the Bengalis in East Pakistan. Jalal (1990, 6), on the other hand, explains the dominance of the military and the bureaucracy by carefully scrutinizing the different ways in which the "interplay of regional and international factors influenced domestic politics and economy, distorting relations between the centre and the provinces in particular and the dialectic between state construction and political processes in general."

The decade-long control of political power by General Ayub Khan so early in the life of this newly established state gave the military a strong grip on Pakistan's governance structure that continues to this day. The country has spent more than half of its life under military rule. It took Pakistan twenty-three years after gaining its independence to hold its first general election to parliament, in the 1970s, by granting adults the right to vote; it took twenty-six years to produce a constitution that had the support of all the political parties (Noman 1990). This engagement with democracy, which the military allowed only after internal unrest reached threatening levels with the partition of East Pakistan in 1971, was short-lived. In 1979 another military general, Zia ul Haq, toppled the government of the first elected prime minister of the country, Zulfiqar Ali Bhutto. After eleven years of Zia ul Haq's military rule, the country went back to democracy. However, constitutional changes introduced during his regime that gave the president the power to dissolve assemblies resulted in the dissolution of the assemblies every two years. As a consequence, four different governments were formed between 1989 and 1999. In late 1999 the military once again intervened as General Pervez Musharraf, the chief of army staff, toppled the elected government of Nawaz Sharif. Military rule ended again in early 2008, after tension between the judiciary and General Musharraf—whose tenure was unexpectedly strengthened after the events of September 11, 2001, made Pakistan a sought-after ally for the United States—culminated in sustained street protests against the regime. General Musharraf was forced to quit after the Pakistan Peoples Party, whose leader, Benazir Bhutto, had been assassinated two months before, won the February 2008 elections.

Concentration of power in the hands of the military, the bureaucracy, and the landed elite has resulted in the failure of the legislature to undertake basic institutional reforms that could lay the foundation of a more representative and accountable government. Due to alliances among these elites, the interests of a few have been protected, while ordinary citizens have paid the price. Land reforms were never implemented even though development researchers have consistently pointed out that they are critical for income distribution (Haq 1997); in the 1950s, six thousand landlords owned more land than 3.5 million peasant households (Ali 1983, 43). The half-hearted attempts made in the land reform acts of 1959, 1972, and 1977 were neither radical nor effectively implemented (Haq 1997). The landlords with large holdings managed to keep them within an extended joint-family framework. Land ownership remains highly concentrated: more than half of the total farmland is concentrated in farms of fifty acres or more (Haq 1997). At the same time, the state has not invested in social services. On average, only 1 percent of the GDP is spent on health care whereas expenditures on education normally stay below 2 percent of the GDP; together government expenditures in these two critical areas normally amount to just over 7 percent of the government annual budget. By comparison, public expenditure on the military is 4.6 percent of the GDP, and on debt servicing it is 4.8 percent. The state transfers a very low share of its total income to the poor in the form of social security benefits (Haq 1997). Also, instead of directly taxing the rich, the state focuses more on indirect taxation that places a further burden on the poor. The state machinery is extremely corrupt, leading to high rent-seeking, and public trust in the state institutions is very low.

This weak internal legitimacy of the state has resulted in the state seeking external support for its rule. Foreign aid has been critical to strengthening Pakistan's military rulers (Ali 1983). The geostrategic importance of Pakistan at the time of its partition made this newly born nation important to both the United States and the Soviet Union. Jinnah announced a policy of nonalignment, but soon after his death Pakistan joined the U.S. camp. The army and the military agreed to allow establishment of an American military base (Ali 1983). American aid had already established a presence in 1951. "Ghulam Mohammad and Iskandar Mirza, (civil servants) who effectively ran the country as heads of state in the fifties, needed the alliance with the United States to shore up their position at home" (Ali 1983, 51). This dependence on the United States was noted by Zulfiqar Ali Bhutto in the preface to one of his books (1969):

> When in 1958 I entered upon my career in high public office at the compara-
> tively early age of thirty, as Minister for Commerce in the Martial Law Govern-
> ment, the situation Pakistan found itself in was such that every decision of any
> importance, even as regards matters that ought to have been of purely internal
> concern, was affected by some aspect, real or imaginary, of international rela-
> tions, especially of commitment to the United States of America.

External intervention in Pakistan's policy affairs has become even more pronounced since 1988, when General Zia ul Haq decided to enter into structural
adjustment and stabilization programs with the International Monetary Fund
(IMF) and the World Bank. Both the IMF and the World Bank exercise great
influence over Pakistan's economic as well as social policies. September 11
brought an economic boom to Pakistan as, in return for becoming an active
partner in the U.S. "war on terror," the flow of aid multiplied. In 2002, Pakistan
received US$14.3 per capita in development assistance as opposed to US$1.4 for
India, and US$6.3 for Bangladesh. Pakistan has been a receiver of significant
foreign aid from its very beginning. Yet the country also demonstrates well that
international development aid is highly political. The flow of aid to Pakistan
has been highest during the military regimes of Ayub Khan, Zia ul Haq (Zaidi
1999a), and more recently General Musharraf. Ayub supported the anti-Soviet
policy, Zia supported the Afghan jihad funded by the United States, and General Musharraf served U.S. interests by helping to wage the "war on terror." The
dramatic jump in aid flow to Pakistan since it joined the "war on terror" is a
stark reversal of the situation that existed immediately before September 11,
when Pakistan had faced a dramatic decline in aid due to sanctions imposed on
it for executing nuclear tests in 1998.

Nation-building has thus been extremely difficult since Pakistan's inception
and has been marked with consistent failure of the formal state institutions to
lead the nation to collective desirable outcomes. The prevailing formal institutional arrangements are designed to preserve the interests of the elite rather
than the ordinary public. In such a context, a vibrant network of self-regarding
and other-regarding groups has emerged to meet the collective needs of the
community and those of the poor. What institutional arrangements govern
these groups and what motivates the members of these groups to cooperate
when the state institutions are failing? It is argued that in order to understand
the nature and working of these groups in present-day Pakistan, it is useful

to start from the arrival of Islam in the subcontinent and to trace the philanthropic practices that flourished within the Muslim population in this region, parts of which later became Pakistan. Such an approach is justified on the basis of evidence that shows that Islamic beliefs play a critical role in the shaping of collective action in Pakistan (Aga Khan Development Network 2000).

## The Muslim Tradition in the Indian Subcontinent

The Arabs formally entered the subcontinent in the eighth century, during the Umayyad Caliphate of Walid I (705–715) by sending a young Arab general, Muhammad Ibn Qasim, to chastise some pirates off the coast of Sindh (Hussain 1979). The real foundation of the Muslim empire in India, however, was laid during the Sultanate period (1175–1526), and the Islamic Sharia (or code of law) was institutionalized by the end of the fourteenth century (Hussain 1979). Admittedly, it is problematic to talk of Muslim philanthropic practices without taking into consideration the broader Indian society, because the Muslims did not live in isolation from their non-Muslim neighbors. However, as Farhan Nizami (1983, 3–4) argues, "Nevertheless, they [Muslims] did possess a distrust and well-defined identity and here it has seemed legitimate to concentrate on the Muslim religious elite and those facets of Muslim life which were conditioned by their religion."

Also, social histories of India show that religious beliefs, collective action, and philanthropic practices appear to be closely intertwined with the country's religious traditions; for example, Haynes (1992), in his work on the Indian port city of Surat, highlights that the philanthropic practices of the Hindus, Muslims, and Parsis differed according to their religious beliefs. Similarly, Sharma (2001) notes that many colonial observers differentiated between the charitable practices of Muslims and Hindus. Islam places great emphasis on collective action by prescribing that Muslims should give to good causes, and promising high spiritual rewards for these actions—an approach that proves conducive to mobilizing self-regarding as well as other-regarding collective action. The great emphasis within Islam on saying prayers in the mosque rather than at home is justified as a mechanism for generating platforms of social cooperation within the Muslim community and for helping Muslims to synergize their energies in order to meet common needs. At the same time, great emphasis is placed on the sharing of wealth with the poor by engaging in charity and welfare work. It is thus not surprising that with the establishment of Muslim rule, two unique forms of collective action arrangements—the Sufi *khankahs* and the mosque and madrasa complex—evolved within the Muslim community on the Indian subcontinent and gradually became central to the identity of this community.

The madrasa was one of the oldest institutions of learning in the Islamic world; it was the traditional school of learning in which the Islamic sciences were taught. In Muslim India, the madrasas were establishments of higher learning that produced civil servants and judicial officials. They always had an altruistic purpose; both the infrastructure and recurrent costs such as teachers' salaries were recovered not from the beneficiaries of the madrasa—that is, the students—but from state patronage or public donations. From the twelfth century onward the Sufis played a critical role in transmitting Islam to the remote villages and towns of India. They had widespread social appeal, which derived from their liberal approach to humanity, which was based on the concept of *Al-Khalq-u-Ayalullah* (all humans are creations of God). The Sufis were responsible for a large number of conversions to Islam on the Indian subcontinent. Chistiyya and Suhrawardiyya were the two earliest Sufi orders to flourish there. Just as the madrasa system was, the *khankahs*—which consisted of the tomb of a Sufi saint, a mosque, and several rooms for visitors—were always established to serve both self-regarding and other-regarding purposes. While *khankahs* acted as a base for social engagement for those who funded them, their patrons, mobilized by the saints, also served others through the provision of a free *langar* (public kitchen) and free accommodations for the poor and travelers.

Islam provides three clear categories of religious donations for helping others (*zakat, sadaka,* and *khayraat*) and lists clear incentives for indulging in other-regarding collective action. Each type of giving has its own significance, its own guidelines for how to administer it, its own criteria for selecting the recipients, and its own rewards. *Zakat* is obligatory, the other two are optional.

*Zakat* is one of the five pillars of Islam. Denial of one of these pillars is considered tantamount to disbelief. *Zakat* is a compulsory tax on all affluent Muslims. A specified amount is to be deducted from their wealth each year. Occurring thirty-two times in the Quran, the word *zakat* is often joined with the command to offer prayer, the second key pillar of Islam, thus highlighting its importance to believers. Islamic jurisprudence maintains that *zakat* is the right of the poor to the wealth of the rich and has been determined by God. The *Surah-at-Tawba* (verses on forgiveness), one of the passages in the Quran, states that the primary aim of *zakat* is to eliminate poverty and destitution from society. The dispensation of *zakat* is thus one of the basic religious duties of a believing Muslim, who is supposed to dispense it personally if the state does not have a central system for collecting it.

In contrast to *zakat*, *sadaka*, which means "voluntary alms," is nonobligatory. Even though *sadaka* is not obligatory, it is no less emphasized than *zakat*. *Sadaka* and its related verbal forms are used twenty-four times in the Quran and are the subject of many *hadith* (sayings of the Prophet Muhammad). There are explicit guidelines for the giving of *sadaka* that clarify the eligible recipients, the appropriate time and place of the giving, and the nature of the gift itself. Whereas *zakat* is explicitly based on the notion of social justice and the redistribution of wealth in society, and although socially *sadaka* plays the same role, *sadaka* is explained mainly in terms of inner cleansing of the self through self-denial. It is not the monetary value of *sadaka* that is critical but the act of sacrifice. It is preferred that one give to people close by, including one's neighbors and needy relatives, rather than to distant people. This guideline is linked to the emphasis in Islam on social responsibility to one's neighbors and relatives. There is also great emphasis on giving without making it public. The reward of giving voluntary alms in secret is seventy times that of giving such alms publicly.

For the giver of *zakat*, Islamic law fixes the amount due, but the giver of *sadaka* is free to determine both what and how much to give. That is, *sadaka* does not have to be in cash; items such as old clothes in wearable condition can also be given. There is also the concept of *sadaka jariya* ("permanent alms"), which is a gift or deed that will benefit others over time. The giver or doer is promised a reward for the gift or the deed, as long it continues to benefit others.

*Khayraat* is the third main form of giving in Islam. Like *sadaka*, it is highly encouraged but is nonobligatory. *Khayraat* is basically the extension of the notion of social responsibility established through *zakat* and *sadaka*. It entails giving away as much of one's wealth as one can to benefit the public welfare or the poor and the needy. In turn, God promises to reward the giver in this life, by multiplying his wealth to many times the amount he gives, as well as in the hereafter. There are verses in the Quran that ask, "Who is it that will make God a goodly loan so that He will increase it many times" (2:245).

Because of this emphasis in Islam on promoting Muslim brotherhood as well as social justice, the Muslim population in India ended up supporting a large number of self-regarding and other-regarding groups for collective action. People took part in mosque and *khankah* gatherings addressing common problems; those who were affluent enough also funded other-regarding groups to support those who were less well-off. However, of these two platforms for collective action that arose in India with the arrival of Muslims, the madrasas proved over time to be more successful than the Sufi *khankahs* in retaining their other-regarding function. Even during the Mughal Empire, most of the *khankahs* had moved far away from the mission of the saints who had inspired them. These saints had lived very simple lives and had tried to serve humanity, but their descendants who controlled the shrines rarely built on the saints' spiritual power. Instead, over the generations they became more and more involved in worldly affairs. "Unlike their saintly ancestors who lived as ascetics, these *pirs* [professional Sufis] benefited from royal patronage, often receiving landed estates or money to build beautiful mausoleums and shrines in memory of the saints" (Sherani 1991, 225). The majority of the *pirs* inherited neither the knowledge nor the piety of their ancestors, only their tombs, shrines, and devotees (Sherani 1991).

Consequently, although there are still some exceptions, the shrines can no longer be viewed as other-regarding groups. Many have become bases of political and feudal power rather than remaining focused on finding solutions for the concerns of the poor or the ordinary public. The descendants of many of the saints stand alongside the landed elite. *Pirs* in Punjab, for example, supported the National Unionist Party, a coalition of Muslim, Sikh, and Hindu landlords. At the turn of the nineteenth to the twentieth century, the descendants of the great Sufi Baba Farid of Pak-Pattan owned 43,000 acres of land (Ali 1983). Baba Farid himself had lived all his life in a small thatched building constructed of wood and mud, declining all gifts and offers of income from kings as well as devotees (Nizami 1998). One reason the madrasas were better able than the *khankahs* to stick to their original missions over time is that the *khankahs* placed greater emphasis on the hereditary nature of the transfer of authority.

Although these two distinct forms of collective action arrangements both arose on the Indian subcontinent as a result of Muslim influence and in response to a combination of self-regarding and other-regarding concerns, each form evolved in a different way over time.

## Adapting to Extrinsic Incentives

Muslim rule was displaced by gradual strengthening of the British East India Company in the subcontinent, which paved the way for the establishment of direct British rule from 1858 until 1947. It also led to changes in the platforms for collective action within the Muslim population. First, with the demise of the Mughal Empire, the official sources of support to madrasas and Sufi *khankahs* dwindled. The British government changed the policy for *Madad-i-Ma'ash* (revenue-free lands), which had sustained various institutions of Muslim education and learning. The new policy made the leaders of these groups even more dependent on the voluntary financial contributions of their members to sustain these platforms for collective action. Nizami (1983) and Metcalf (1978) document that madrasas, which were unable to shift to public support, eventually closed down. The changes in the administration as well as changes in the economy introduced by the East India Company led to madrasa education losing much of its utility. Whereas earlier, Muslim education was relevant to both religious and secular needs, it gradually became increasingly otherworldly in its focus. Hence the Muslim educated classes became divided between the modern educated and the madrasa educated. Madrasa education became economically irrelevant under the new regime, which made children of elite Muslim families opt for secular education institutions. As a result, mainly children from economically less resourceful families were left to study in the madrasas.

The madrasa system was thus forced to acquire more of the other-regarding rather than self-regarding attributes of collective action, making it critical for *ulama* (Islamic scholars) within the madrasas to further embed themselves within the community and mobilize the affluent Muslim groups to support the survival of the madrasa system out of an other-regarding impulse. Metcalf (1978) documents how the Darul Uloom Deoband—a madrasa that developed in opposition to British rule and gradually became very influential within the madrasa network in South Asia—encouraged both cash and nonmonetary gifts from those who benefited from its services, and tried to win large gifts from rich Muslims by appealing to their other-regarding concern. It was thus able to attract small donations such as books, food for the students, and household items to furnish its buildings, as well as large cash gifts from its affluent patrons.

In addition to changing the flow of resources to madrasas, British rule also exposed them to a higher degree of institutional competition. Not only did the madrasas now have to struggle to obtain funding from alternative sources in order to survive, but they also had to face stiff competition from newly established modern, Western-style educational institutions that provided more relevant degrees for securing jobs. In this changed context, a process of adaptation started within the madrasa system to make it more relevant to the needs of the time. Muslims who attended the modern educational institutions transferred the principles of these Western models to religious education in the post-1857 period, when British rule consolidated in India. For example, as a result of the Western education they received at Delhi College, some of the leaders at Darul Uloom Deoband introduced formal classes and a set syllabus to replace the old madrasa practice of flexible teaching in which the *alim* worked out different teaching arrangements for each student.

The Sufi *khankahs*, on the other hand, were relatively less affected by the loss of state patronage that resulted from the fall of the Mughal Empire. These descendants of the saints had already accumulated much land under Mughal rule because the Mughal practice of granting revenue-free land to charitable causes was particularly geared to the Sufi shrines (Sherani 1991). Conscious of the influence that the Sufi saints had on the general public, Mughal rulers had exploited that influence as an easy way to strengthen their rule. They brought the *sajjada-nishins* (the descendants of the saints) under their control by granting them large properties and by contributing to the building of the shrines. The descendants thus became representatives not only of God but also of a remote Muslim ruler. The consequence of this policy was that the descendants of the Sufi saints were more concerned with preserving their own status than with serving the community (Gilmartin 1988; Ansari 1992). Recognizing its political dividends, the British continued this policy put in place by their Muslim predecessors and made further grants to influential *pirs* (Sherani 1991). They saw the *pirs* primarily in terms of their economic and political power and treated them in essentially the same way that they treated landlords and tribal leaders (Ewing 1983).

Colonial rule curtailed the work done by traditional organizations of collective action by changing the formal rules; for instance, in 1837 Persian was replaced by English as the official language of the state, making madrasa education even less relevant. It also triggered the rise of new organizational platforms within the local population that were better suited to advancing people's interests in the changed context. These new platforms were voluntary associations with explicitly stated social objectives. They were not specific to the Muslims but rather became popular first among the Hindus. These local associations took a wide variety of forms: literary and debating societies, leagues for self-betterment, reading groups, societies for social and religious reforms, associations for *vakils* (lawyers) and teachers, and so on. Many of these groups were self-regarding but many were formed out of concern for others. Initially it was religious zeal or caste solidarity that encouraged the propensity to form associations, but during the course of the twentieth "century more of the associations in India were brought into being by groups of men united by secular interests" (Seal 1968, 194).

The associations formed during this period were products of the many socioeconomic changes that occurred under British rule. Two developments were particularly important: (1) the rise of common educational skills and functions, acquired through a common education, and common aspirations and resentments against the policies of the British Raj (Seal 1968, 202); and (2) the launching of a publishing campaign against Hinduism and Islam by Christian missionaries that generated a response within these respective religious groups. The new associations drew support from students, professional men, landlords, and merchants in a limited geographical area, but the more ambitious organizations searched for ways to work together in order to extend themselves to India as a whole; this trend culminated in the formation of the Indian National Congress (Seal 1968, 195). The changes in formal rules introduced during the colonial period thus had great influence in shaping the present profile of both self-regarding and other-regarding groups in Pakistan.

The first type of associations formed among Muslims focused on restoring and perpetuating traditional customs and institutions, such as preserving *waqf* (religiously endowed) property, collecting *zakat*, and sponsoring schools. These practices had deteriorated as a result of Muslim loss of political power and impoverishment, and in some instances had been further eroded by governmental, judicial, educational, and settlement reforms (Churchill 1974). A second type of associations aimed to enable the community to meet new political challenges. Such associations resulted from Muslims' concerns about their deteriorating sociopolitical and economic conditions. In an article published in 1888 (Churchill 1974), Muhammad Shah Din referred to the proliferation of Muslim societies in the Punjab in the preceding twenty years as evidence of the intellectual awakening of the Muslim middle class. The pressure to preserve their common interests forced them to develop new forms of associations that were distinct from mosques and madrasas. These associations were designed to promote the interests of their members under the new rules introduced by the British to regulate civic association.

These social organizations, often referred to locally as *anjumans*, relied on membership fees as well as on donations from the old elite (Churchill 1974). The support of a wealthy *nawab* (local notable) was usually sufficient to start a society and was often driven by the *nawab's* ambition to gain social or political esteem. Douglas Haynes and Chris Bayly have developed these arguments in detail in their social histories of the cities of Surat and Allahabad, respectively. Haynes (1992) argues that during the 1860s and 1870s the Sunni gentry contributed heavily to public charities. The *nawab* of Surat and a few other prominent Muslim families sought to establish themselves as advocates for their coreligionists, a supposedly backward community. They gave increasingly to Muslim educational funds, largely through local chapters of the Anjuman-i-Himayat-i-Islam and the Mohammadan Union, in order to impress the British. The same families, however, also provided funds in far larger quantities to mosques, shrines, and Muslim religious festivals, which bolstered their status among their coreligionists (Haynes 1992). In his work on Allahabad, Bayly (1971) describes similar trends and explains how involvement in philanthropic activities in the cities enabled the upper classes to become mediators between the government officials and the ordinary public. The British officials preferred to patronize these classes in return for their support in mobilizing the general public in their favor.

At the same time, these organizations also gave rise to a new class of members and donors, including up-and-coming urban professionals, government officials, and more important, the lower-middle income groups. Historical accounts of most of the key social organizations show that their financial support came from various socioeconomic classes. Metcalf's (1978) work on Darul Uloom Deoband in India, Bahadur's (1977) work on the Jama'at-i-Islami,[3] and Churchill's (1974) account of Anjuman-i-Himayat-i-Islam all refer to membership fees or small donations, the sale of hides and skins collected at *Eid* (Islamic festival), rent received from building tenants, *chutki* (flour gifts), and *zakat* and *sadaka* monies collected from middle-class Muslims as critical means of financial support. Similarly, the literature on Jama'at-i-Islami shows that membership fees and *zakat* contributions received from members and sympathizers were an important source of regular income. In addition, the Jama'at has always been able to raise millions of rupees for emergencies by running large-scale relief campaigns and gathering donations from the public (Bahadur, 1977). This is how, during colonial rule, groups of Muslim initiators and joiners cooperated to establish a significant number of associations designed to benefit disadvantaged groups or the broader community.

The British government responded to the dramatic surge in the number of these groups by introducing legislation to regulate them. In 1860 it passed the Societies Registration Act, which initially operated only in Madras, Bombay, and Calcutta. The primary motive of this act was to strictly regulate the voluntary associations, especially the cultural societies that the British government blamed for the insurrection of the *sepoys* (local soldiers) in an 1857 mutiny against the British. Next, the Trust Act passed in 1882 provided legal coverage for private acts of charity and allowed the founders of a trust fund to have tremendous powers and flexibility of operations.

---

3. Jama'at-i-Islami is the largest Islamic political party in South Asia. For details, see Nasr 1994.

After the turn of the nineteenth to the twentieth century, this associational culture became even more diversified. Young Indian men went to study in British universities and were exposed to socialist and Marxist ideologies. When they returned to India, they helped to transform some of these associations into anti-imperialist groups that aimed to expel the colonial powers. The Russian socialist revolution in 1917 acted as an explosive ideological force among the younger generation of Indians (Zeno 1994). It became a political platform through the Communist Party of India, but it also manifested itself through nonpolitical platforms such as the Progressive Writers Movement (PWM). The PWM was formed in 1935 by a group of foreign-educated Muslim writers who were unremitting satirical critics of the life of their society and passionately upheld the need for social change. In 1936, many of the group's leading members were either intrepid, ardent communists themselves or "fellow travellers" with the communists (Zeno 1994). Groups of ideologically inspired individuals like the PWM worked to advance their vision of the just society in which they wanted to live, and some also fought on behalf of the disadvantaged and marginalized in their society.

The Muslim population of the Indian subcontinent thus developed a rich array of platforms for collective action. Some were shaped entirely by Islamic humanitarian principles and practices; others were inspired by secular ideas or a combination of both. These groups either emerged in response to the incentives introduced into the civic environment under colonial rule, or they were a continuation of the madrasa system that had survived by adjusting to changing socioeconomic and political conditions. By the end of colonial rule, the Muslim population in the subcontinent thus supported three forms of other-regarding groups: the religiously oriented (madrasas and *khankahs*), the welfare oriented (*anjumans* working to provide social services to Muslims), and the politically oriented (such as the PWM and other reform groups that aimed to change the existing power structure in favor of the weaker groups).

## Incentives in the Postcolonial Environment

At the time of its partition, Pakistan inherited a decent number of groups from all three of the categories just discussed. There were many madrasas in the area that became Pakistan. Also, many *ulama* migrated to Pakistan at the time of the partition, including the famous Maulana Maududi, who had established Jama'at-i-Islami and resisted the creation of Pakistan on the grounds that it challenged the Islamic notion of *ummah*, which views Muslims as one nation, irrespective of their geographic location. Many of these *ulama* set up new madrasas. Also, many of the famous Sufi saints were from southern Punjab and Sindh.[4] Pakistan thus got a fair share of Sufi *khankahs*, which in present-day Pakistan are normally referred to as shrines or *mazaars*. The *anjumans* and other associations that during colonial rule had mushroomed in the area that now constituted Pakistan also remained active. In addition, the bloodshed and dislocation caused by the partition, which resulted in a large number of refugees, stimulated many new voluntary groups to take action. For example, the Women's Voluntary Service was established under the leadership of the wife of Prime Minister Liaquat Ali Khan soon after partition in order to organize shelter, first aid, food, and health care for the migrants. Also, ethnic groups such as the Memons in Karachi that had traditionally emphasized service within their communities started to organize their workers into associations.

The political left, however, was weak in Pakistan from the very beginning. At its peak, the Communist Party of India had approximately 3,000 members in a united Punjab (Ali 1970, 1983), but partition weakened this and other leftist organizations. In the first months after partition, many of the trade unions had to be organized anew. About one-third of union workers migrated to India, and the refugees from India who took their place were isolated from the rest of the workers and kept themselves aloof from organized militant actions for fear of losing their jobs (Gankovsky and Gordon-Polonskaya 1964). In 1984 the Communist Party of India set up the Communist Party of Pakistan and sent a number of Indian Muslim communists to lead the new organization. Sajjad Zaheer, a prominent nationalist and communist leader, distinguished writer, and founder of the Indian Progressive Writers Association who was born in 1905, became the first general secretary of the Pakistan Communist Party (Gankovsky and Gordon-Polonskaya 1964).

Yet despite the relative weakness of the left, the first decade after partition witnessed the development of a host of platforms for collective action in Pakistan. "There was a vibrant intellectual culture in the fifties. The progressive writers were very active. Also, there were college debating societies, college and university student unions, literary circles in educational institutions, and literary societies outside educational institutions," argues Fateh Malik, a prominent Urdu writer, when interviewed for this research. The progressive writers, who often were members of the Communist Party, met in tea and coffee houses to discuss the socioeconomic issues affecting the public. "There used to be a coffee house every one and a half kilometers on the Mall Road. The regular

4. For an in-depth analysis of the well-established Sufi elite in Sindh, see Ansari 1992.

writers used to come there and had fixed places where they would sit. People knew where to meet them," explains Mehdi Hasan, a product of the PWM, in an interview with the author. He added, "In those coffee houses you could get a half set of tea for 6 annas [a few cents] and you could sit with it for six hours. People received their post at these cafes. Now only Pearl Continental and Avari [the five-star hotels] on the Mall Road have tea houses."

The progressives' strongest support came from a chain of newspapers launched in 1947 by veteran leftist politician Mian Iftikhar-ud-Din. The Progressive Papers Limited provided the left with the extremely influential and highly respected *Pakistan Times* and *Ambrose*, which spread the views of the left and at the same time provided the progressive writers with a means to earn a decent income. "These papers were very particular about payments to the writers, unlike the newspapers today. I earned my college fee by translating an article from Arabic to English for publication in one of these papers. This ability to earn enough to meet one's basic needs through this chain of papers was an important factor enabling the writers to stay independent," argues Malik.

Some of the nationalist parties also supported other-regarding public action. Khan Abdul Ghaffar Khan, known as "the frontier's Gandhi," led the Khudai Khidmatgars ("servants of God"). Popularly known as the Red Shirts because of the color of their uniforms, this group founded in 1929 continued to work after partition to serve the public. Establishment of schools was one of its most important activities (Khan 1995). The Jama'at-i-Islami also maintained a welfare division that became particularly active during natural disasters, setting up emergency medical centers and doing relief work (Bahadur 1977).

These quotes from interviews with prominent activists and writers who lived through this period show that at the time of partition Pakistan inherited a dense array of groups involved in self-regarding as well as other-regarding collective action. They were driven by either religious sentiments, by a sense of moral obligation and public welfare, or by commitment to a school of secular ideals such as socialism. Pakistan's failure to establish a democratic governance structure impaired the functioning of all these groups, and of some more than others. General Ayub Khan, who imposed the first martial law in Pakistan in 1958, engaged with these groups purely on the basis of how they affected his own power rather than on the basis of their contributions to uplifting society. This meant he came down severely on voluntary leftist groups that opposed his rule.

To legitimize his military rule, Ayub Khan led an agenda of closely guided social and political development. He supported the VOs that were not political with grant-in-aid programs and set targets for them in each social sector. This support helped him strengthen his own image as a social reformer. In 1961, Ayub Khan introduced the Voluntary Social Welfare Agencies Ordinance. A social welfare department was established and opened offices in all four provinces of Pakistan. At the same time Ayub created the West Pakistan Department of Auqaf, which was entrusted with the task of managing the *waqf* (endowed) properties. Although this was done under the pretense of protecting these properties, it was politically significant because it brought most of the madrasas and shrines under state control, because most were built on *waqf* properties. Ewing (1983) has argued that the governments of Ayub Khan, Zulfiqar Ali Bhutto, and Zia-ul-Haq each adopted a similar policy toward *pirs* and the shrines whereby they used these shrines, as well as the West Pakistan Department of Auqaf, as a vehicle for modernization. Sherani (1991), however, counters Ewing's argument and claims that all three leaders preferred to nationalize these institutions in order to extend their influence over the scores of people who attached much spiritual and political value to them.

Whereas the madrasas and the shrines were exposed to subtle political maneuvering to strengthen the military regime, the leftist and nationalist organizations were exposed to blatant victimization. The first phase of the Ayub dictatorship saw the regime attempting a cleanup operation. Politicians were prosecuted and barred from political activity for several years. Trade unions and peasant organizations were banned, and students were warned against initiating or participating in any form of political activity (Ali 1970, 1983). The Progressive Papers chain of newspapers was taken over by the state on the grounds that Mian Iftikhar-ud-Din was a "foreign agent" (Ali 1970). "This was the sharpest blow against the left, depriving it of its voice and providing the new regime with newspapers under its direct control" (67). Nationalist leaders like Khan Abdul Ghaffar Khan were marginalized (Tendulkar 1967).

Tactics such as regular blacklisting, withdrawal of official advertisements, restrictions on newsprint quotas, lawsuits, and individual harassment of journalists through intelligence agencies were used to pressure editors and newspaper proprietors (Malik 1997). Where coercion failed, temptation was also used. By striking a close collaboration with leading financiers such as the Adamjees, the Saigols, and others, Ayub Khan established a number of awards and organizations with which to shower obliging Pakistani journalists, poets, and authors with attention (Malik 1997). The Pakistan Writers' Guild was formed with money obtained from such sources in order to reward pro-regime intellectuals. Explicit state oppression along with a split between pro-Soviet and pro-China groups of progressive writers led to a rapid decline of the PWM in the 1960s. The PWM was an important other-regarding group because the writers associated with it played a critical role in raising awareness of needed social reforms, and in exerting pressure on the state to undertake those reforms. They thus performed the role that present-day development discourse expects of public-interest advocacy groups.

The formal institutions of the state under Ayub Khan thus engaged with all the voluntary groups purely from his interest in how these groups related to his regime rather than from interest in the role these groups played in society. The ten years of Ayub Khan's rule effectively suppressed the leftist and nationalist groups. Mazhar Ali Khan, editor of the *Pakistan Times*, was prevented by Ayub Khan's military regime from writing for any newspaper for eleven years after he refused to support the regime. In a rare speech to the short-lived Civil Liberties Union in 1963 he said, "For too long Pakistan has become a land of great silence; a silence born of fear, of apathy, of cynicism, of ignorance; a silence so oppressive that often truth finds expression only in uncertain whispers" (Khan 1996, 6).

Zulfiqar Ali Bhutto came to power by drawing on the socialist vocabulary. His election to prime minister of Pakistan in 1971 provided some relief to the leftist workers after the long suppression under Ayub Khan. However, Bhutto disappointed many of his senior leftist supporters, who were removed from the party within months of his coming to power (Noman 1990). Bhutto's hanging in 1979 by Zia-ul-Haq proved to be the final blow to the liberal thinkers. The timing of this development was important because it matched up with important global developments and policy shifts that affected the voluntary groups in Pakistan. The development of these groups in the 1980s thus merits detailed analysis. However, before doing that, it is important to review the diverse groups identified earlier to assess whether, despite their differences, they have any common characteristics that have survived over time to justify grouping them all as traditional voluntary groups.

## The Unchanging Norm

So far, three forms of collective action platforms have been identified: religiously oriented, welfare oriented, and politically oriented. Each of these platforms inspires both self-regarding as well as other-regarding groups to take collective action. Regardless of the ends they pursued, their underlying philosophies, or their work methods, all of these groups had one key characteristic: they all received voluntary contributions from the initiators to advance the cause of the group. No claim is being made here about the motivation of the initiators; they could be driven by pure concern for the other or by some personal vested interest; however, at least apparently, initiators of all of these groups that were able to mobilize public support worked voluntarily and showed visible signs of material sacrifice. Some made this sacrifice by investing their own financial resources in the work of the group, as happened in many welfare associations; others invested their time and faced persecution from the state, as did many members of the PWM.

By looking at the madrasas, the Sufi orders, and the *qasbat* (small towns) that existed between 1803 and 1857, Farhan Nizami (1983) shows that there was a distinction between *Ulama-i-Akhirat* (other-worldly scholars) and *Ulama-i-Dunyia* (this-worldly scholars). The *Ulama-i-Dunyia* were interested in state patronage and lived comfortable lives; the *Ulama-i-Akhirat*, who were more respected and more independent minded, lived off public charity. "Their piety and erudition, combined with their poverty, enhanced their stature in the public eye," argues Nizami (1983, 132). Further, he asserts, it is the madrasas that were led by those ulama who lived a simple life that were able to survive after the demise of the Mughal Empire, whereas the madrasas led by ulama who were used to comfortable living under state patronage perished. He then concludes that although, theoretically, the social power of the ulama rested on individual voluntary submission, in reality the moral authority they built through their lifestyle and social interaction with the community was what made them far more effective and powerful. In addition, Nizami states that greater recourse to Sufi methods of organization and simple living was important in enabling the ulama to build a support base within the community. Metcalf (1978) similarly documents the simple living of the ulama of Deoband and how they pointed out the spiritual advantages of poverty in fostering unity among the personnel of the school. As Muhammad Qasim Nanotawi, one of the founders of Darul Uloom Deoband, suggested, "In matters of income and buildings . . . let there be a sort of deprivation" (Metcalf 1978, 115).

The same voluntary commitment on the part of group initiators has seemed to be critical in mobilizing the joiners of welfare-oriented organizations. Historical accounts of the evolution of some of the prominent Muslim *anjumans* and other associations, such as Anjuman-i-Himayat-i-Islam Lahore, Anjuman-Faizul-Islam, and Anjuman-i-Islamia Amritsar, show that the initiators, who were moved into action by some societal problem, came forward to invest their own time and resources for the cause. This voluntary contribution of time and money mobilized other people to support the association. Ahmed Saeed's (1986) account of the Anjuman-i-Islamia Amritsar shows that the visible commitment and sacrifice of time and money on the part of the key initiators of this *anjuman*, who were influential Kashmiri Muslims, was critical in building the credibility of the Anjuman-i-Islamia Amritsar and in mobilizing its joiners. Saeed also records that for the members of this *anjuman* it was important to give donations, to work for the development of the Anjuman-i-Islamia Amritsar, and to participate in the rallies it organized and give their opinion on the matters of concern. Emphasizing the importance of material self-sacrifice in winning the respect of the joiners, Yusaf Hasan (grandson of Sheikh Ghulam Hasan, one-time president of the Anjuman-i-Islamia Amritsar, whose family led the *anjuman* for a long period) argued in an interview conducted for this research, "I remember my father used to devote every afternoon to the affairs of the anjuman; he was not paid for any of this work. He also had many other affairs to attend to due to his involvement with the Pakistan Muslim League. But he took his commitment to the work of the anjuman very seriously, just like my grandfather did." Saeed documents that all of the key positions in this *anjuman* were honorary.

Written accounts of the functioning of nationalist and leftist groups, as well as interviews with some members of the left in Pakistan, place similar importance on voluntary commitment and material sacrifice on the part of the initiators in mobilizing joiners. The Khudai Khidmatgars were all volunteers and were driven by Khan Abdul Ghaffar Khan's pledge of selfless service (Khan 1995). "Voluntary contribution and denunciation of material goods was critical to the working of the leftist ideology. People used to walk ten-ten miles on foot. No one would ever ask for roti [bread]. And they used to do it very happily," explained Rana Shafiq ur Rehman, a member of the defunct Communist Party of Pakistan who now runs an NGO, when interviewed. He added that with the rise of NGOs, people now ask first what the food menu is. "When you get money to give a speech, and you get money to listen to the speech also, then volunteerism is over." In the same tone, Nasir Zaidi, who had once been an active worker with the Communist Party of Pakistan, explained that the student members of the party initiated a social service program for the villages in which a medical student and a political activist made a weekly visit to a village. Zaidi argued, "There was no money involved. It was all done for inner satisfaction. The feudal lords attacked us; the *maulavis* [religious preachers] also criticized us. But we carried on doing our work." He continued: "We sacrificed for this work; we also went to jails because we had conviction in our work."

Hussain Naqi, a prominent trade unionist in the 1960s and a highly respected leftist thinker and journalist associated with the Human Rights Commission of Pakistan (HRCP), similarly stated when interviewed that a voluntary spirit on the part of key leaders is very important for voluntary groups. "The reason HRCP is different from other NGOs is that I. A. Rehman [a prominent journalist and leader of the former Communist Party of Pakistan] from the very beginning emphasized the importance of voluntary spirit if one wants to work for a cause."

Regardless of the values that gave birth to a voluntary group and regardless of the method adopted to produce the desired good, the one characteristic that thus appears to be common to the collective action platforms mapped in this chapter is the existence of a core group of initiators who are willing to contribute voluntarily and to make material sacrifices to advance the objectives of the group. Because this important characteristic can be traced to the very first types of altruistic groups that emerged within the Muslim population on the subcontinent, as well as to the welfare-oriented *anjumans* and hard-core socialist groups that arose under colonial rule and were inherited by the newly created state of Pakistan, it can be argued that group members' demand that the leader of the group demonstrate signs of material sacrifice in order to advance the cause of the group has remained an unstated institutional norm regulating collective action within voluntary groups in Pakistan. This rule governing voluntary cooperation becomes all the more important given that studies of NGOs that raise concerns about NGOs' inability to mobilize joiners also document the high salaries of NGO professionals (Henderson 2002). Even the policy documents of many international donors hint at this issue: "civil society is the arena in which people come together to pursue the interests they hold in common—not for profit or the exercise of political power, but because they care enough about something to take collective action" (World Bank 2000a, 5). The next section looks at the rise of NGOs, the new players in Pakistan's civic space that began to emerge in the 1980s.

## Violating the Established Norm

The six years of Zulfiqar Ali Bhutto's regime had a significant impact on other-regarding voluntary groups; following a socialist agenda, Bhutto nationalized many of the schools led by VOs. He also, however, promoted the policies of the previous regime vis-à-vis the shrines and the madrasas (Ewing 1983, Sherani 1991). The left, meanwhile, had weakened further. Another military coup in 1977 brought an end to Pakistan's first engagement with democracy. The timing of this shift was significant because it coincided with important international events: Afghan jihad, the weakening of the Soviet Union, the rising international influence of neoliberal thinking through the influence of Bretton Woods institutions, and the influx of international development aid into developing countries through NGOs rather than through the state. All of these factors played important roles in shaping the voluntary sector in Pakistan.

It was in the early 1980s that Pakistan registered the birth of voluntary groups called NGOs. These organizations claimed to work for the benefit of disadvantaged groups just as traditional voluntary groups did, and they were registered under the same voluntary welfare association laws as the other groups. However, there was one big difference between them: the NGOs relied on external sources of financing in the form of international development aid whereas the traditional voluntary groups depended on domestic donations. The NGOs also provided generous salaries for their initiators. NGOs claimed to be professional organizations. They promoted the idea that social reformers and activists do not have to undertake this work voluntarily but can be paid for it. The fact that NGOs operate differently than traditional voluntary groups is noted in interviews with many members of the left. "I came across the term *NGO* for the first time in 1982 in the *Dawn* newspaper. I called up a friend in the government ministry to ask what this really means," said Muhammad Tahseen, who was once a leftist worker and today runs one of the biggest NGOs in Pakistan. "The term *NGO* came to Pakistan after the 1970s. It came to Pakistan in *lunda* [secondhand items such as clothes and shoes sent to the developing countries from the West]," argued Munnoo Bhai, a prominent public intellectual and columnist, when interviewed. Also, many writers have argued that in the first decade of the existence of these groups, the main NGOs were set up by people from the left. A look at the ten biggest NGOs from the late 1970s and the 1980s—such as the Aurat Foundation, SAP-PK, and Shirkat Gah—supports this claim in that the initiators of all of these groups came from the left.

Interviews with and journalistic writings of prominent activists and thinkers in Pakistan indicate that Zia ul Haq's repression of the left as well as internal weakening of the leftist groups due to the Sino-Soviet split and the gradual decline of the Soviet Union were important factors in this shift from traditional voluntary groups to NGOs. After the dissolution of the Soviet Union, many prominent members of the left joined NGOs, argued Mehdi Hasan when interviewed. Some intellectuals had become disillusioned; others had left the country. Arguing that many senior communist intellectuals in Pakistan idealized the Soviet Union model so much that they were completely demobilized after its fall, Hasan added, "I often argued with them that the failure of the Soviet Union does not mean that the socialist philosophy is wrong." Interviews further suggest that a general trend toward commercialization had set in. "Before, a writer who wanted to wear a broken shoe could do so. But by the eighties, status was calculated purely in terms of material progress and not intellectual growth," added Hasan.

The internal weakening of the left due to internal and external factors co-incided with the influx of aid for NGOs through international development organizations. "The donors were looking for individuals who talked of public concerns and the left was most trained in that jargon," claimed Rana Shafiq ur Rehman when interviewed. To the people from the left who were tired of internal political repression and slightly disillusioned with the socialist ideol-ogy, the idea of getting funds to set up organizations through which they could do the work they wanted to do was very tempting. "Many leftist leaders joined the NGOs because they realized that it is difficult to mobilize people purely on the basis of ideas; it is much easier to build a relationship when you go to them with a school and a dispensary. Many therefore opted for NGOs," argued Dr. Nayyer, a prominent physicist and activist in Pakistan, when interviewed.

All of these observers also note, however, that this shift to NGOs led to a change in the way these people worked. When talking about their former left-ist colleagues who had joined NGOs, people often mentioned the high salaries drawn by the heads of NGOs. They repeatedly identified individuals whom they had seen acquire a lot of wealth by initiating NGOs. A common critique was, "I have seen him build his house within years of setting up the NGO. I know where he lived before. Before, he used to walk with us for miles for the cause; now he only moves in a four-wheel drive."

The influx of donor aid to NGOs thus led to the rise of a new form of collective action platform in Pakistan, a platform that violated the core institutional norm that had traditionally regulated the work of self-regarding and other-regarding groups in Pakistan: voluntary material sacrifice on the part of the initiator of a group in order to advance the group's cause. The initiators of the NGOs did not have to make any material sacrifices to undertake their work; on the contrary, they could earn a very comfortable living from it. In other words, they no longer did this work as volunteers; they instead became professionals.

As aid has continued to flow to Pakistan, the NGO sector has expanded steadily, as it has in other countries, and it is no longer the exclusive domain of ex-leftists. Today there are four prominent categories of NGOs in Paki-stan—categories based on the group's scale: national, provincial, city based, and village based. Some NGOs focus exclusively on advocacy or service deliv-ery; others combine the two. The rapid increase in their number has also led to the formation of the Pakistan NGO Forum, a voluntary body that represents the collective interests of NGOs. Each province has its own provincial NGO forum that links to the national forum. The density of the NGO population varies from province to province. Punjab, the most densely populated province of Pakistan, hosts the largest number of NGOs and voluntary groups, followed by Sindh (NGO Resource Center, 2003b). The government estimated that the total number of registered VOs in Pakistan in 2001 was 44,000 (Pakistan Centre for Philanthropy 2002).

The 1990s also saw numerous state experiments with the NGO sector in Pakistan. A critical emergence was the establishment of rural support programs (RSPs). Inspired by the success of the Aga Khan RSP, a project of the Aga Khan Foundation, in the northern areas of Pakistan, the government has sought to emulate the program by creating a national RSP plus four provincial RSPs with the help of grants from bilateral and multilateral donors. RSPs act as semi-autonomous bodies and are often referred to as GONGOs (government NGOs). Another occurrence of the 1990s was the evolution of NGO support organizations, such as the Strengthening Participatory Organization, South Asia Partnership Pakistan, the NGO Resource Centre, and the Frontier Resource Centre. Themselves registered as NGOs, these organizations provided training in capacity building to smaller NGOs.

## Conclusion

The analysis offered in this chapter has illustrated how organizations that were established initially in response to intrinsically driven religious incentives within the Muslim community on the Indian subcontinent strategically reshaped how they worked in order to survive under the changed economic and political institutions of the colonial and postcolonial context. In addition, new forms of organizations emerged within the same Muslim population to advance the interests of the community. Madrasas adapted their organizational form and their curricula in order to survive under colonial rule, and *anjumans* and socialist platforms such as the PWM arose to benefit from the changed context. By the end of colonial rule there were three forms of such altruistic groups: the religiously oriented, the welfare oriented, and the politically oriented.

In the newly created state of Pakistan these groups were exposed to constant manipulation by the state. The decade of General Ayub Khan's rule effectively suppressed the progressive groups—a process that was repeated during General Zia ul Haq's regime from 1977 onward. Domestic and international political developments during the 1960s and 1980s were critical in shaping the voluntary groups in Pakistan. NGOs rose as a phenomenon in the 1980s in response to oppressive military rule, Afghan jihad, the weakening of the Soviet Union, the rising international influence of neoliberal thinking, and the influx of international development aid to such organizations in developing countries rather than to the state.

The central argument advanced by tracing the evolution of the different forms of collective action platforms that have marked the civic sphere in Pakistan is that despite changes in strategies for surviving in the face of adversity and competition, one institutional norm that traditionally has been central to regulating collective action platforms in Pakistan is material sacrifice on the part of the leader of the group in order to advance its cause. NGOs are the only collective action platform that has violated this norm. Could this be why the NGOs have been unable to mobilize members, as was noted in detail in this book's introductory chapter? If yes, then why is this simple informal rule so critical to sustaining collective action? To answer these questions it is important to start by understanding the decision-making processes of the initiators and joiners, and their motives for forming other-regarding or self-regarding groups.

# 3 Why Cooperate?

Motives and Decisions of Initiators and Joiners
in Other-Regarding Groups

*Yet formal rules, in even the most developed economy, make up a small
(although very important) part of the sum of constraints that shape choices;
a moment's reflection should suggest to us the pervasiveness of informal
constraints.*

**Douglass North, *Institutions, Institutional Change,
and Economic Performance*, 1990, 36**

*Signals are the stuff of purposive communication. Signals are any observable
features of an agent that are intentionally displayed for the purpose of alter-
ing the probability the receiver assigns to a certain state of affairs or "events."
This event can be anything. And the "features" of an agent that make up a
signal can be anything too: they include parts or aspects of his body, his behaviour, and his appurtenances.*

**Diego Gambetta, *Codes of the Underworld*, 2009, xv**

WHAT MOTIVATES INDIVIDUALS to cooperate to produce a good that benefits a group
other than themselves? What motivates the initiators—the individuals who
start an initiative—to initiate? What motivates the joiners—those who decide
to support the initiators by giving of either their money or their time to make
the initiative viable—to join? Why do joiners join one set of initiators from
among the various groups of initiators demanding their cooperation? This
chapter studies three locally funded other-regarding groups in Pakistan in
order to address these questions; the next chapter examines the same questions
with reference to self-regarding groups. The focus is on understanding group

behavior by studying individual action. Is cooperation the result of conscious calculations? Or is it mainly a product of diverse and disparate cultural and historical factors? This distinction is important because it will have differing implications for policies that might be recommended to enhance cooperation. At the same time, the analysis provided here is sensitive to the development literature's rising interest in the question, If it is culture that influences public action, then what is the actual process by which this happens?

## The Three Cases

A prominent case was selected from each of the three main categories of other-regarding groups identified in Chapter 2: religiously oriented, welfare oriented, and politically oriented. The purpose was to see whether, despite the groups' differences, any commonalities would emerge from among the three groups that could help explain why initiators and joiners collaborate to form other-regarding groups. Because it would provide better means to understand cooperative decisions, an organization with a large number of joiners was selected from each of the three categories: the Edhi Foundation (the largest welfare organization in Pakistan), Jamiat ul Uloom al-Shariah (a madrasa that provides a free Islamic education to four hundred students), and the People's Rights Movement (a radical organization that aims to strengthen social movements in Pakistan). During a year of fieldwork with these three groups that involved repeated interviews with their initiators, their staff, and their joiners; observation of their routine activities; and study of their organizational documents, clear commonalities in the institutional norms regulating cooperative behavior emerged, despite their different ideological outlooks.

### The Edhi Foundation

The Abdul Sattar Edhi International Foundation is the largest welfare-oriented VO in Pakistan,[1] making it a very attractive case for a study aimed at understanding the decision-making processes of joiners. Named after its founder, Abdul Sattar Edhi International Foundation was started in 1951 in an eight-foot-square dispensary in Mithadar, a low-income area in Karachi—the former capital of Pakistan. From that humble beginning, the Foundation has expanded

---

1. Given the lack of systematic data on VOs, there is no official ranking that identifies the Edhi Foundation as the largest welfare organization. However, in terms of geographical coverage, no other VO matches its scale. Also, in terms of public recognition, the Edhi Foundation is the most prominent organization of its kind in Pakistan. During the survey interviews, founder Abdul Sattar Edhi was one person whose work was quoted by people across the country.

into a multiservice network across the country, with international offices in six countries. It has been recorded in the *Guinness Book of World Records* as the largest free ambulance service provider in Pakistan. Abdul Sattar Edhi has won numerous awards and honors, and in 1996, Themina Durrani (2001), a prominent personality and ex-wife of a former politician, penned his biography.

From its beginning, the Edhi Foundation has combined welfare with emergency relief. Within one year of opening the Foundation's first dispensary, Edhi purchased an old van and since then the emergency work has gone hand in hand with the dispensary work. The Foundation's emergency services include providing field ambulances, air ambulances, marine and coastal services, and emergency checkposts along the main highways of Pakistan. Also referred to as the Twenty-Five Kilometer Project, these checkposts are situated at twenty-five-kilometer intervals and connecting roads that link Punjab with Sindh and Balochistan and go beyond the Khyber Pass to the Siachin Glacier. A wireless service connects the checkposts to each other and to the central location that controls the ambulance service, to ensure quick ambulance provision in emergencies. The ambulance service also maintains an active presence within the cities, where it responds to individual calls as well as to emergencies caused by accidents.

The Foundation's primary welfare service is the provision of free goods and services, but it also has a component of activities aimed at supporting income generation. The key function of the six international branches of the Edhi Foundation is fundraising, especially among expatriate Pakistanis. In Pakistan, the Foundation runs welfare centers and homes for individuals who are destitute, acts as an information exchange for those searching for missing persons, provides graveyard services and aid to prisoners, and runs a "cradle scheme" to give shelter to abandoned, unwanted newborn babies, who are then given in adoption to married couples; more than twenty thousand babies have been saved in this way. The Edhi Foundation is also active in emergency relief efforts during international calamities. In five major cities of Pakistan there are fifteen Edhi Foundation homes, called *Apna Ghar* ("our home"), that take in destitute women and men as well as youngsters and adults who have run away from home, and mentally handicapped people. More than one million children have been delivered in ten Edhi Foundation maternity homes. The Foundation also runs nursing schools in Karachi that provide basic training courses, through which it claims to have made more than forty thousand women economically independent. And it employs many of the abandoned and runaway children who are brought to the *Apna Ghar* and end up staying because their families cannot be located.

In addition to the thirty free dispensaries that operate in various cities, there are eight Edhi Foundation hospitals in four provinces that provide free medical facilities. Since 2000, the Foundation has constructed a huge Edhi village that covers sixty-five acres of land along the Super Highway in Karachi. The Foundation supplies rations to refugee camps and distributes mutton for consumption by patients at government hospitals and sanitariums, feeding a thousand patients daily at these hospitals in addition to running public kitchens that provide free food. The Foundation also maintains graveyards in six major cities.

The management of the Edhi Foundation is in transition. Abdul Sattar Edhi, the sole initiator of this nationwide phenomenon, is growing old and weak. There is a debate within the Foundation about whether it will be able to sustain its vast number of joiners after Edhi is gone. Edhi has been gradually transferring the management of the organization to his eldest son, Faisal Edhi. The ambulance service is already entirely under Faisal's control. In terms of organizational philosophy, Edhi strongly maintains that the organization believes in promoting self-sufficiency as a nation and in enhancing a sense of responsibility toward fellow human beings at the individual level. The Foundation therefore charges those who can afford to pay for the use of its ambulance service. This enables it to recover the basic cost of running the ambulance service. Meanwhile, those who cannot afford to pay and emergency cases are covered for free. The welfare services, however, including the *Apna Ghar*, are completely free for all users.

As a policy, Edhi Foundation does not accept any monetary aid from international donors. Durrani's (2001) biography of Edhi maintains that the reason for this is his belief in the importance of self-sufficiency for a nation. In the words of Edhi's son Faisal, "When the public is giving, then why should we accept external interference? When we can do this work ourselves, then why should we take from international donors?" The Edhi Foundation does, however, at times accept gifts in kind from international donors. For example, some of the helicopters in its air ambulance service were gifted by the United States Agency for International Development, or USAID.

### Jamiat ul Uloom al-Shariah

Jamiat ul Uloom al-Shariah, a madrasa of the Sunni Muslim sect, is the second case to be studied and analyzed in this chapter. Jamiat ul Uloom al-Shariah is located in the lower-income periphery of an affluent area of Rawalpindi. It was established in 1970 and upgraded in 1980 when the Imam (religious scholar) of a local *masjid* (mosque) who is now head of Jamiat ul Uloom al-Shariah mobilized enough resources to fulfill his long-harbored desire to establish a madrasa next to his mosque. The Imam took charge of the mosque in 1965 on the advice of one of his teachers, when he was only a twenty-year-old student. At the time it was just a small place for prayer, built by a local industrialist; the Imam was the only employee. Today the mosque has a grand building with a fine interior. It can accommodate more than seven hundred men for prayer, and the madrasa has more than four hundred students. Until the introduction of restrictions on allowing foreign students to enroll in madrasas, it also hosted students from East Asia. The rapid expansion of the mosque and the subsequent establishment of the madrasa are all to the Imam's credit. When he took over, the mosque was being run as a *waqf* property. Per the legal requirements, a board of governors regulated its functions. The board still exists but its role in the functioning of the madrasa has become increasingly marginal as the Imam has taken on more responsibility. This shift in authority began soon after the Imam's arrival, when he put forward a plan to expand the mosque and build a decent residence for himself. None of the board members was in a position to help financially. Instead they gave the Imam the authority to shape the place as he wanted, provided he could mobilize the funds himself.

From that point on the Imam was more or less on his own. He then had the authority to expand the mosque and build a place for himself to stay rather than continuing to make a bed for himself in the veranda of the mosque every night, but had no resources to exercise that authority. Thus started a long, hard struggle to mobilize resources from the public. The state helped by providing the land. Recalling the initial phase of the process, the Imam narrates that it was not easy. Even after the construction had started there were periods of extreme tension and stress. Fluctuation in the inflow of funds made it impossible to pay the constructor on time. The constructor's religious belief played a key role in sustaining work on the project during these barren periods. The initial expansion project was eventually completed when a benefactor donated a large amount. Since then the mosque–madrasa complex has steadily expanded through public support.

Work on the madrasa followed the expansion of the mosque. Named Darul Alum Tadreesul Quran, it was opened in 1970. In the first ten years the focus of teaching remained the elementary Islamic books, *Nazra* (reading of the Holy Quran), and *Hifz* (memorization of the Holy Quran). Sustained work over this period helped build the madrasa a good reputation. Students gradually enrolled from all over the country. This led to expansion of the madrasa; in 1980, formal teaching began for *Dars-i-Nizami* (scholarly degrees in Islamic studies).

At this time the name was changed to reflect the enhanced scholarly status of the madrasa. A quarter of a century later, the madrasa now issues seven different degrees in Islamic studies (the highest degree is accredited by the Pakistan Ministry of Education as a master's degree); it houses and feeds four hundred students, stocks nine thousand books on Islam (some quite rare), and provides a decent living space for the Imam and his family. In addition, it houses a free clinic and operating theater for basic surgeries. A benefactor's recent donation of two computers has led to the initiation of computer training programs for the students. Being a Sunni madrasa, it follows the school of thought of Hazrat Shah Walliullah and Ulama-i-Deoband, the dominant school of thought in Sunni madrasas in South Asia.[2] It is associated with the Wafaq-ul-Madaris-al-Arabia Pakistan (the official board of Deobandi madrasas).

The madrasa does not see its role as purely educational; it also claims a space among welfare-oriented organizations. Its brochure states that its purpose is threefold: to produce scholars of Islam, to spread the teachings of Islam to the broader society, and to carry out welfare programs for the needy. The welfare element of any madrasa is that the students are charged no fee and are provided free boarding and lodging. In addition to this usual service, Jamiat ul Uloom al-Shariah has also been running a free medical clinic since 1993. Renowned specialists from Rawalpindi and Islamabad volunteer their services at this clinic on a regular basis. Days and times are fixed for various specialists throughout the week, and the timetable is displayed in the clinic's main entrance hall. On any given day there are from 30 to 150 patients. The death of a student at the madrasa after a fatal fall from the rooftop led to the establishment of the operating theater, which is now a fully functioning part of the clinic but is used mainly for emergencies. The presence of this pool of highly skilled and specialized volunteer doctors made this madrasa all the more interesting for the purpose of this book; it provided an additional pool of joiners who were cooperating with the Imam to use the madrasa platform to produce a good that benefited a group other than themselves.

The Imam does not acknowledge receiving any foreign financial support for the working of the madrasa, and he absolutely denies receiving any money from the Pakistani government or from any international donor.[3] In the Imam's

2. The Deobandi movement, which emerged in late-nineteenth-century colonial India, stresses a renewed commitment to hadith and sacred laws as the basis of a "reformed" and reinvigorated Islamic identity (Zaman 2002).

3. Any debate on the funding of madrasas in Pakistan often gets embroiled in the contentious issue of Saudi money. It is argued that Saudi money given to promote the wahabi agenda

words, "As a rule the madrasa does not take money from any country's government or an influential person. When governments help, they do so to promote their own agenda. If those agendas are not met they will stop giving to you. In the poor man's giving there is sincerity, and *barkat* (God's approval); the poor man's motivation is right. All madrasas run with the support of poor or middle-class people." The Imam does, however, expect the government to provide land for expansion of the madrasa.

### The People's Rights Movement

The final case analyzed in this chapter draws on the third prominent strand of organized civil society within Pakistan, as discussed in Chapter 2: the politically oriented organization driven by talk of rights and power redistribution in society. Selecting this case proved more demanding than selection of the other two cases because it transpired that those who spoke the language of rights and empowerment relied mainly on international development aid. A few organizations in this category did work without international development aid, but interestingly, all of them spoke the language of politics and change instead of the development jargon of "beneficiaries and empowerment." Inspired by Marxist and Leninist thought, these international-aid-free organizations, which constitute a very small percentage of civil society groups compared to those that do rely on international development aid, questioned the notion of development and the legitimacy of the international development system itself.

The case selected for study out of this small pool was the People's Rights Movement (PRM). Intentionally unregistered, the PRM aims to act as an umbrella organization for supporting and strengthening indigenous resistance movements across the country. It supports social and political movements, but the PRM itself is not a movement. It is an organization in which a group of initiators and joiners are trying to produce a good for groups other than themselves. At the heart of the PRM are six core members whose voluntary, monetary, and time contributions sustain the PRM's activities. The organization does undertake local fundraising, though it is quite limited and event specific. Also, integral to the PRM's work is the mobilization of voluntary activists, who provided a pool of joiners for this study.

---

abroad gets channeled through the madrasas. It was never the concern of this research to test this, however. The focus here is on understanding why those individuals who do support the madrasa do so. The issue of Saudi money would merit attention only if the givers were to list it as a factor affecting their decision to join a given madrasa.

The six core team members are distinct and powerful personalities, but one individual is clearly most critical to the organization: Akhtar Sheikh, a Yale graduate who, admittedly inspired by Marxist thought, returned to Pakistan with the clear intent of working to bring about change in society. Juxtaposed against Akhtar's affluent background, however, are two members of the core team whose training ground has been much more humble than Akhtar's Yale education, but much more rigorous. They have learned the ropes of activism as trade union workers, and one of them gained valuable experience by dealing with the day-to-day struggle of living in a *katchi abadi* (slum dwelling). Their real-life experiences were channeled into hardcore activism when both imbibed Marxist and Leninist revolutionary ideas while participating in the literary circles of the seventies (which were run by the now-defunct Communist Party of Pakistan). The wife of one of these trade union leaders, who was very active in the slum dwellers' struggles herself, is another member of the core team. Another member brings to the team years of experience working with a high-profile local advocacy NGO, which he eventually quit, and inspiration gained from Gandhi's ideas and the thinking of Muslim Sufis rather than from the Marxist leanings of the other team members. The other member of the the core team is a young woman educated in the United States and Britain. All six members are very strong individuals who differ on issues and approaches; but beyond their differences of opinion on the mechanisms of change, they have a consensus on the need for change.

As noted earlier, the PRM's main objective is to act as an umbrella organization for various indigenous social movements in the country. Its intentions are twofold: to strengthen each of these movements, and to make their members politically conscious so that they rise above their individual struggles and join hands with each other to work toward broad change in society. The PRM gained attention mainly because of the success of two of the movements it has supported: the Katchi Abadi Movement (slum dwellers movement), and the Okara Military Farm Movement, which is now represented through the Anjuman Mazareen-i-Punjab (association of the farmers of Punjab). Unlike the other two organizations studied in this chapter, the PRM does not provide material services to its beneficiaries; it works under a very different philosophy. Whereas the other two groups studied believe in providing a service to the needy, regardless of how the state operates, the PRM focuses on mobilizing people to defend their rights from an oppressor, especially when the oppressor is the state itself.

The PRM therefore does not provide a free service of any kind. Rather, it demands active participation by and contributions from the affected communities toward the effort to attain their rights. The methods employed by the PRM range from planning active media campaigns and undertaking strategic lobbying with parliamentarians to staging peaceful rallies and entering into violent confrontation with state agencies. Members of the PRM are clear that the PRM's aim is not to initiate movements but to support existing ones. It deals with movements for which an acknowledged leadership already exists within the community that is mobilizing people to resist the oppression. The PRM enters the movement through this leadership, but then forms direct links with the community members themselves.

The PRM has no paid staff member. The core team of six is very clear that all staff members should have other sources of income. They agree that the PRM cannot be a source of income; instead it is a platform on which they come together to work voluntarily for a cause they believe in and for which they cannot be paid. All six—although some more than the others—spend extensive amounts of time visiting various movements all across Pakistan. The members' other professional commitments plus their long visits to the communities that they support entail that the PRM's office does not maintain a nine-to-five, five-days-a-week routine. Instead the team members come to the office whenever the need arises. They can meet in the evening, in the middle of the night, or during the day, depending on the nature of the activity that is at the top of the agenda at any given time. When there are no core team members in the office, all visitors and phone calls are entertained by two boys from a local slum dwelling, who get living space in the office in return for providing security coverage.

After interviewing these six members, it is clear that there is no hierarchy within the organization. All of the members feel free to think as they like, to voice their opinions, and to mold the actions of the organization. No one is treated as the head, but some members clearly invest more time or money in the organization, and all members acknowledge that without Akhtar, the PRM would not survive in this form for very long. All of the core members worked for various causes before the PRM's platform came into existence in 1999, and they will continue to do so even without this platform, which owes its existence mainly to Akhtar. One reason for Akhtar's influential role was initially viewed to be his relatively affluent background and bachelor lifestyle, which enabled him to make heavy time and money investments in the PRM. However, things have not changed since he got married. The other reason is that he places a much greater value on the PRM than any of the other members.

The core team of six is very clear that it won't accept money from any international development donor. The PRM's members argue that money comes with its own agenda. They believe that if they accept international aid, they will have to accept the agenda of the donor. In Akhtar's words, "When you take money from the same system, then how can you criticize that system? It places very serious constraints on the policy decisions that one can take. An organization like ours is based on a constituency; we have to be responsive to that constituency. By the same token, those who take money from international donors have to be responsive to the donors; the donors are their constituency."

## Why Do Initiators Initiate?

So why would some individuals initiate an activity that will lead to no material gain for them? Why would Edhi commit his life to providing a welfare service across the length and breadth of Pakistan instead of concentrating his energies on accruing more material comfort for himself and his children? Why would the Imam of the madrasa take on the added stress and financial pressure of establishing a madrasa when he could earn his living just by leading the prayers at the mosque? Why would a Yale graduate choose to leave a financially promising career in favor of austere living and invest his own time and money to set up a platform to support the indigenous movements of deprived communities? What is the rationale behind their decisions? The ensuing analysis focuses primarily on the key initiator in each of the three case studies presented here. However, it also draws on in-depth interviews with five of the co-initiators on the PRM's core team, plus initiators of twenty traditional VOs interviewed for a survey presented in Chapter 5 of this book.

Seen through the public's eyes, the three initiators introduced in this chapter come across as altruistic, philanthropic, self-sacrificing individuals whose actions are driven by concern for other individuals rather than for themselves. For all three initiators, enhancing the well-being of other individuals seems to have become more important than their own material well-being. The image of Edhi—always dressed in his standard grey *shalwar kameez* (traditional Pakistani attire) made of cheap cotton, along with his equally humbly dressed wife—personally washing days-old decaying and deformed corpses for burial presents a picture of a man who epitomizes self-sacrifice out of love for humanity. So does the fact that his children's speech and presence convey humble living and state schooling while the foundation he single-handedly controls has an annual turnover in the billions of rupees. The Imam's stories of unrelenting struggle to sustain the madrasa when sudden drops in donations made it impossible to pay the teachers for seven months and caused insecurity about the food supply for the students reflect a similar selflessness, as does Akhtar's decision to leave a financially promising career in favor of investing his own resources in grass-roots movements.

In-depth interviews with the initiators in all three case studies make it very clear, however, that even behind these apparently altruistic actions, the primary motive is self-interest. Analysis of interviews with the three initiators strongly indicates that all three of them act on the basis of rational calculations of how to maximize their own satisfaction. What is altogether different about their calculations, however, is the source of their satisfaction. During the course of the fieldwork, I spent a lot of time in repeated interviews and discussions with the key initiators. Questions about their motivation for undertaking their volunteer work always generated responses about what the work did for them rather than what it did for the beneficiaries of their work. None of the initiators explained their work to me in terms of concern for the poor; they all explained it to me in terms of its importance for themselves. Contrary to popular as-sumptions about philanthropic actions, none of these initiators claimed that they started this work out of benevolent love for their fellow human beings; rather, they all explained that their work was as an outcome of their strong be-lief in the value of the work itself. Undertaking this work made their lives more rewarding and more meaningful. A particular incident or some pressing public need might have triggered them into initiating the work, but the reason for re-sponding to that public need clearly rested in certain values they possessed, and promoting those values increased their own satisfaction.

Neither Edhi nor the Imam nor Akhtar do this work at the cost of their own well-being, as they understand it; none of them think they are becoming worse off by doing this work. All three do it because it makes them feel better. I repeatedly asked Akhtar why he chooses to undertake this work rather than investing his energies in building his career. His standard response was, "For me there is no question of whether to do it or not. There is no choice. It is an addic-tive lifestyle; it is about your own survival. Other things become meaningless."

For Edhi the value that is of prime importance is service to humanity, for the Imam it is promoting a social order in line with Islamic teaching, and for Akhtar it is the establishment of a just social order. All three are working to promote a vision that is very dear to them—dearer than any monetary and eco-nomic gains. Edhi was passionate in his interviews about the value of serving humanity. His biography repeatedly highlights his belief in serving others. He claims that this is the purpose of life. For the Imam, forming a more virtuous society is the main purpose of life. For Akhtar, leading revolutionary struggles that change the existing social order is the essence of life. It is their ardent belief in the significance of these values and the satisfaction they attain by perpetuating these values that motivates these three initiators. All three are very ambitious about their respective visions. They work strategically to excel over others in their field in doing what they are doing. Their motivation is thus very self-interested, but their notion of self-interest is value oriented rather than material oriented.

It can be argued that viewing altruistic action as self-interested is analytically unhelpful because it confuses side effects of the action with the main motive. In this view, the individual serves others primarily because his religious or political values maintain that such action is better than just looking after one's own interests and not primarily because it makes one feel good or brings spiritual rewards. This is of course a very fine distinction. However, the data from these three case studies argues overwhelmingly that the primary motive of engaging in altruistic action is to attain psychosocial rewards. Helping others is an outcome of the human need for nonmonetary rewards rather than purely driven by a concern for others. What is being argued here is summed up well in a quote from Gandhi: "If I found myself entirely absorbed in the service of the community, the reason behind it was my desire for self-realisation. I had made the religion of service my own, as I felt that God could be realised only through service" (1958, 19).

This outcome of the interviews then raises the question, What factors shape the preferences of these initiators? How do they develop preferences that make their notion of self-interest value oriented rather than material oriented? Two levels of analysis are needed here. The first level is based on the initiators' own understanding of the factors influencing their preferences; the second level requires identifying possible socioeconomic material gains that could serve as hidden incentives for undertaking this work. The interviews and observations of the three initiators demonstrate that parental influence and religious and moral training are key factors in shaping the preferences of the initiators. Edhi's biography, for example, emphasizes greatly his mother's role in inculcating the value of charity in him. Edhi credits to his mother's teaching his commitment to his work. When he was still a child, his mother made bundles of foodstuffs to be dropped through the windows of poor people's houses. Edhi says in his biography that his mother always told him that "it is charity only when your left hand does not know what the right has given, when the respect of the receiver is foremost." He adds that "the priority she gave to social work was to be the foundation of my future" (Durrani 2001, 27). He also acknowledges the training provided by his father, who always told him that no kind of labor is an insult; even the lowest form is dignified and worthy of respect.

In the case of the Imam, because his father was also an Imam in the village where they lived when he was a child, the preference for religious values was inculcated in his family. The Imam's father exposed his children to religious education from early childhood and emphasized to them the importance of religious belief.

Akhtar himself did not mention any role of his family in shaping his preference for the work he is doing. One of the other members of the PRM, while talking about the sources of funding for the organization, however, mentioned the donations made by Akhtar's family due to their religious belief. The influence of parental training in shaping these initiators' preferences for the work they do was borne out further by the survey that is presented in Chapter 5 of this book. Twenty traditional VOs were surveyed, and in eighteen cases initiators identified parental influence as a key factor in making them undertake their work.

Given that all three of the initiators profiled in this chapter have siblings who opted for standard professional roles, one cannot help but wonder if some people just have a propensity for being attracted to certain values. Explaining any phenomenon as human propensity or instinct does not explain much, however. For example, in *The Logic of Collective Action*, Olson (1971) is critical about placing too much emphasis on "instinct" or "tendency" to explain why people form and join associations, because, he argues, this theory adds nothing to our knowledge. The concept of the instinct to belong, for example, merely adds a word to our vocabulary, not an explanation of the phenomenon under study. Although I agree with the limitations of an analysis based on individual propensity, I would argue that when trying to understand why individuals prefer certain values over others, it is impossible not to allow for the propensities of individuals. If nothing else, they highlight that it is difficult to explain fully the process of human preference formation.

Despite the belief systems and consequent home environments that Edhi and the Imam shared with their siblings, those siblings did not take up the work that these two men chose to do. The Imam has a brother who dropped out of religious education despite the initial guidance they both received from their father. Edhi talks similarly about his brother, who does not have much appreciation for Edhi's work. Both cases highlight the propensity of individuals to be attracted to some values more than to others. The role of individual propensity in shaping preferences seems all the more pronounced when analyzing the case of Akhtar, who identified one very early experience that made him identify his priorities. At the age of ten, while on a drive with his parents, he saw a poor boy dressed in dirty rags walking along the roadside with his father, which made him think, what if he was in that child's place or that child in his? According to Akhtar, "Ever since I realized that it is all potluck, I thought there is a need to do something about it."

Parental training and personal propensity thus appear to be important factors in shaping the preferences of individuals so that their notion of self-interest becomes value oriented rather than material oriented. Yet although these could be genuine explanations for such preferences, it is important not to lose sight of other possible socioeconomic or psychological factors that could be the reasons for undertaking this work. One such factor could be termed *strategic choice*, the other could be called *long-term ambition*. Seen critically, the strategic choice element could be applied to Edhi and the Imam, and long-term ambition can be applied to Akhtar. From one vantage point, Edhi, who had a sparse formal education and limited economic means, had little chance of success in other fields. The same could be said of the Imam—that because of his religious training he had little chance of success in other professions. Seen in this light, both men chose to work toward goals that are unprofitable in economic terms but that, if seen strategically, presented them with greater chances to excel.

It cannot be said that Akhtar, with his privileged education, chose this field as a strategic option; he has all the formal credentials to make a mark within a professional field. However, long-term ambition clearly could have played a role in shaping his preference for this work. This ambition could be as explicit as gaining access to political power through mass movements, or just reaching the status of martyr or visionary. At one level, these are very harsh interpretations of the factors that could be influencing the initiators' preferences. The reason for discussing them here, however, is to explore all of the explanations that could possibly have motivated the initiators to start such initiatives. Such critical examination is essential because only by identifying the multiplicity of motives that can shape an individual's decision to initiate other-regarding groups can we hope to understand why aid ends up eroding cooperation within those groups.

As important as explaining why initiators initiate is identifying the factors that are critical to sustaining the initiators' work even in the face of rising stress or outright resistance. Psychosocial rewards, including public recognition, the ensuing respect and encouragement, and the sense of achievement over having done what was thought impossible at one time, are critical in sustaining the morale of the initiators. Such an emphasis on psychosocial rewards for both starting and sustaining altruistic action, or any action that helps others but promises no material gain, finds support within the literature of economics and psychology that recognizes the diverse nature and importance of nonmonetary rewards in shaping social action.

Some prominent studies that explore this line of reasoning include Scitovsky's *The Joyless Economy* (1976), which discusses our continual pursuit of novelty and our need for stimulating activity; Hardin's (1982) evaluation of a broad class of "extra-rational" motivations, which include both moral and participatory goals; Margolis's (1982) examination of three types of "non-contingent" benefits: demonstration benefits, consumption benefits, and psychic or moral benefits; and Elster's (1985) consideration of "process-oriented motivations for cooperation." Hirschman (1985) has also studied noninstrumental activities such as the pursuit of truth, beauty, justice, liberty, community, friendship, love, and salvation. He argues that costs normally attributed to participation should instead be regarded as part of the benefits. The motivation behind political activism, he contends, lies in the special nature of the cost-benefit calculus. While questioning whether it is possible to have a genuinely unilateral transfer—a quid for which there is no quo, not now, not in the future, nor in the past—Kenneth E. Boulding (1962) asks whether a blind man should give something in return if someone drops a dime in his cup. He suggests that "we feel a certain glow of emotional virtues, and it is this we receive for our dime. Looked at from the point of view of the recipient, we might suppose that the blind man gives out a commodity or service, which consists in being pitiable" (57–58).

Edhi, the Imam, and Akhtar all acknowledged the role of public encouragement and appreciation for the work they are doing in increasing their zeal to do even more. Also, by looking at how they are perceived by their joiners and by observing their interactions with the communities with which they work it became clear that all three men command great respect, and all three are well aware of this fact. Edhi and his family are invited to speak on many TV talk shows and he has been awarded numerous national and international awards. The Imam mentioned that people in distant cities know of his work. Akhtar has also been invited to TV talk shows to represent some of the communities with which the PRM works, and he has been invited to national-level consultation meetings between international donors and government representatives. The Imam is invited to all community social gatherings. In his words, "It is not a matter of money; there is a lot of respect in it. Even the biggest military general comes to us when he has a problem." Similarly, one of the PRM's members said, "You feel that you are contributing something to people's lives, which yields inner satisfaction. If today we go to a Pakistan People's Party rally, the leaders get up to meet us." This respect becomes a source of reward in itself. It raises one's pride in oneself; it inflates one's ego.

This awareness that one is respected is in turn linked to a sense of achievement, which is also a critical factor in sustaining the motivation of the initiators, even against all odds and challenges. The feeling that one has achieved what once seemed very difficult, or even impossible, seems to play a critical role, and brings with it a strong ambition and desire to excel at what one is doing. It is also a source of psychological reward in that it brings inner satisfaction. These effects highlight the importance of nonmonetary psychosocial rewards in shaping social action.

In summary, it thus appears that all three of these initiators are indeed motivated by self-interest, and the reason for this preference is their strong conviction about a certain value system or ideals. Parental influence and a propensity to be attracted to these values help shape this preference, but seen critically, it could also be an outcome of strategic choice or long-term ambition. Nonmonetary psychosocial rewards are instrumental in motivating the initiators both to start the work and to sustain their commitment to it, which in turn brings a sense of achievement that seems to play a key psychological role in strengthening the initiators' morale and motivation to carry on.

## Why Do Joiners Join?

Why do joiners join? And why do they choose to join a particular set of initiators from among the available options? Answering these questions requires asking people why they give and volunteer to advance the cause of a group, and why they choose one group of initiators over others who claim to be doing the same work. For example, why do people who give to the Edhi Foundation choose to join the Edhi Foundation rather than another welfare organization? Why do the supporters of Jamiat ul Uloom al-Shariah choose to support this particular madrasa over the others? Why do those who give to and volunteer with the PRM choose to help strengthen this platform rather than other civil society organizations?

### The Joiner: The Giver

Why people would give away something of their own for economic gain has long been a question of interest to social scientists in all disciplines. Interviews and open-ended discussions with givers in this chapter's three case studies highlight that, just like for the initiators, all giving is eventually driven by the search for inner satisfaction, if not by the outright expectation of a reward in this life and in the hereafter. Religious values were the reason most commonly given for giving; moral values were the other stated source of inspiration. The interviews show that most people give out of an internal compulsion to give, which brings its own reward, rather than purely as a response to the conditions of the needy. This internal compulsion to give appears to be stronger in religious giving than in giving based on purely secular reasons.

The givers to the madrasa and to the Edhi Foundation explained their motivation to give in purely religious terms. There was, however, a distinction between the two in that those who gave to the Edhi Foundation paid more attention to the Islamic notion of *Haqooq-ul-Abad* (the rights of people) whereas those who gave mainly to the madrasa seemed to find *Haqooq-ul-Allah* (the rights of God) more important. Islamic teaching places equal emphasis on both of these rights. There are clear instructions on the duties of one individual to other people, just as there are clearly defined individual responsibilities to God. Givers in both categories were giving because Islam promises explicit reward for every penny spent. These rewards vary from explicit material gains and protection from bad luck in this world to enhanced status in the life hereafter. The action of giving to and taking care of the poor is emphasized through the reward it brings to the individual giver himself.[4] During the interviews with those who give to the Edhi Foundation and the madrasa, the scriptural and jurisprudential understanding of giving provided by Islam, discussed in Chapter 2, repeatedly came up. These principles shape these givers' decisions about who, when, and how to give. Whether they chose the Edhi Foundation or the madrasa, how frequently they gave, and the kinds of things they were giving were all normally explained in terms of the understanding they had of *zakat*, *sadaka*, and *khayraat*.

Endearing oneself to God so that one is saved from punishment in the grave and from torture in the hereafter and instead is placed among the believers in heaven was clearly one of the key factors in people's decisions to give. In

---

4. Here it is interesting to note that in *Democracy in America* ([(1835] 1994), while commenting on the notion of enlightened self-interest that makes individuals cooperate in causes that demand a material sacrifice, Tocqueville argues along similar lines: "The founders of almost all religions have used very much the same language. The way they point out to man is the same; only the goal is farther off; instead of putting in this world the reward for sacrifices demanded, they transpose it to the next" (528). He adds, "I do not think that interest is the only driving force behind men of religion. But I do think that interest is the chief means used by religions themselves to guide men, and I have no doubt that that is how they work on the crowd and become popular" (529).

response to questions about motivation, this answer repeatedly came up: We do so much for this world, why can't we do something for the life after? A volunteer with the Edhi Foundation summed it up well when he said: *Maqsad ha Keesi Tharhan Ranjha Razzi Hoo Jai* ("the objective is that the beloved be won over one way or the other"). At a deeper level, however, for many givers it was not the actual place in heaven that was so real but the spiritual satisfaction of being close to the entity who in their view created them and provides for them. Islam places a lot of emphasis on showing gratitude to God for all he has given. For many of the people interviewed, their own giving expressed this gratitude, and the hope that his kindness will continue in the future.

An additional, equally powerful motive was the promise of reward and protection from evil in the present world. To fend off evil was one of the main reasons mentioned for giving *sadaka*. One of the givers to the Edhi Foundation, whom I had come across while sitting in one of the Foundation's donation collection offices, explained that the money I had just watched her donate was a *sadaka* to protect her daughter who had been ill for some time. For this woman, by giving that money she had given her daughter the protection of Allah, who according to the faith is the only one capable of protecting a person from bad luck. Having a bad dream about oneself or someone dear also often translates into the giving of *sadaka* to stop the dream from coming true. Similarly, for many givers, the hope of continued protection and enhancement of their wealth translated into the giving of *khayraat*.

This discussion should not be interpreted as meaning that initiators and receivers had absolutely no concern for other people. When asked why they give, many who donate to the Edhi Foundation at first said they appreciate the concept of service to humanity. In answer to the same question, many people who give to the madrasa said that poor children get food, shelter, and education there. However, when the interview questions probed deeper, all respondents said that although they feel concern for the beneficiaries of these organizations, their real motivation was the rewards these actions brought. They all acknowledged that they give because it makes them feel better. Those with faith in God hoped for the rewards explicitly promised by God for this act; others gained the moral satisfaction of having done a good deed, which made them feel humanly superior and virtuous.

Given the secular orientation of the PRM, it is not surprising that none of its givers mentioned religious belief as their reason for giving. In this case, giving seemed guided by a vision of what the society the giver lives in should be like. The sense of contributing to attaining that vision was critical in people's decision to give. Seen narrowly, the act of giving to the PRM was aimed at supporting deprived communities. Seen more broadly, however, this giving was directed at establishing a just society that would benefit the givers as well as future generations.

In-depth interviews and discussions with the givers in all three case studies have thus made it clear that people give because doing so makes them feel better. At the minimum, they get the satisfaction of having done a good deed; at the maximum, they get explicitly promised rewards in the form of enhanced wealth in the present world or protection from any impending misfortunes. However, by comparing the givers in these three cases, an issue that emerges is the need to distinguish between compulsory and optional giving. Compulsory giving is that in which the giver has to give because of an internal compulsion that comes largely from religious faith. For example, the woman who was giving to the Edhi Foundation because her daughter was sick was giving out of an internal compulsion because her faith told her that doing so would make her daughter well. She gave to the Edhi Foundation, but in its absence she would have been driven to give to someone else. Optional giving, on the other hand, is giving that occurs in response to a particular demand, in the absence of which the giver might not have given at all. Those who give in response to a particular fundraising demand of the Edhi Foundation, the madrasa, or the PRM fit into this category.

The interviews and observations done for the three case studies show that for both categories the motives for giving are the same. Nevertheless, it is useful to develop this distinction because, as is elaborated later in this chapter, compulsory giving becomes at times less discerning of the authenticity of the recipient because of the givers' internal need to give. This can have implications for the givers as joiners in deciding which initiators to join.

## The Joiner: The Doer

Why would people give freely of their time to work for a cause that does not bear any direct benefit for them? Interviews with the volunteers in the three case studies led to the same answers as those obtained from the givers. Self-satisfaction is the key reason for undertaking volunteer work, whether the goal is to earn a reward from God or just to feel that one has done a morally good deed. The more important issue, however, in studies focusing on volunteers is the definition of what constitutes a volunteer.

As Emmett D. Carson (1999) highlights, the word *amateur* is often closely associated with the notion of *volunteer*, thus leading to the image of a volunteer as a person who is not as accomplished or professional as other people. Along with the influx of international development aid to NGOs has come a great emphasis on professionalizing the voluntary sector, which has led to increasing pay scales within NGOs and indicates a clear lack of faith in voluntarism. Implicit in the policies of the international donors is the unstated assumption that volunteers are individuals with limited options who are often amateur and unprofessional and thus largely incompetent and unproductive.

In all three of the organizations studied, volunteers gave freely of their time without any economic gain. Analyzing their professional backgrounds, their contribution to the work of the organization, and their motivation for doing the work seriously challenges the notions of volunteers that are currently in vogue in development policy and practice. Unlike the image portrayed in development discourse of the passive volunteer who takes on welfare work due to lack of options in the marketplace, the volunteers interviewed in the three case studies were extremely dynamic individuals. All of them had strong professional backgrounds and were doing volunteer work not because they lacked options or because they didn't have anything better to do, but in addition to their paid professional work. Still, it is important to untangle fully the various categories of volunteers and identify the most critical type: the one who becomes a joiner to enhance the work of the initiators.

There were in fact differences among the volunteers: some were regular (that is, they had permanent responsibility within the organization); others were irregular (that is, they offered their services to the organization occasionally, on the basis of need and their own availability). The Edhi Foundation and the PRM both had regular as well as irregular volunteers. In the Edhi Foundation, regular volunteers had maintained full-time managerial positions for many years. Irregular volunteers, on the other hand, were available only on selected occasions, for example, to collect animal hides during *Eid*, to facilitate some emergency work, or to help set up health camps. The Edhi Foundation maintains a register of such volunteers, whom it calls on when the need arises, while remaining cognizant that there is no guarantee these people will be available. Discussion with the staff member who coordinated these volunteers revealed that they hailed from diverse backgrounds and disparate social statuses. They included students, shopkeepers, retired officials, and others.

The list of irregular volunteers ran into the hundreds in the Edhi Foundation's Islamabad office alone. The regular volunteers in that office, on the other hand, numbered only fifteen. These were people who had for years— some for over a decade—initiated, managed, and expanded the work of the

Edhi Foundation in Islamabad and the surrounding areas. These people did not necessarily sit at the Foundation office from nine to five; rather, they managed the programs and were on call twenty-four hours a day. These were the critical volunteers, the joiners of the Edhi Foundation. Because of their importance to the organization, this study focuses on these regular volunteers rather than on the irregular ones. The volunteers interviewed were all men between forty and seventy years of age, and all were financially well-to-do. A few had retired from positions as senior government or military officials, and some owned private businesses. They had come to the Foundation in the late 1980s when it was trying to expand its services in Rawalpindi and Islamabad. All of them worked for the Edhi Foundation in addition to their other professional and business commitments.

The same categories of regular and irregular volunteers exist in the PRM. The irregular volunteers are those who come out for protests or walks in response to a call from the PRM. They also come to the regular PRM meetings to help shape the organization's future work plan and agenda. The regular volunteers, on the other hand, are the six members of the core team introduced earlier. It is these volunteers who will be focused on in this section. At the madrasa, the number of irregular volunteers was insignificant. The key volunteers were the specialist doctors who volunteered a fixed number of hours at the madrasa clinic. The PRM's regular volunteers and the volunteer doctors at the madrasa clinic were thus professionally employed individuals who were carrying out this work in addition to their regular professional commitments, which for the medical specialists at the clinic were particularly intense.

These regular volunteers in all three organizations had clearly defined roles and responsibilities. Interestingly, in none of the cases did any organizational personnel monitor the activities of the volunteers. The volunteers were responsible for getting the work done. All three organizations had only the volunteers they needed and with the skills to carry out their designated roles. In all three cases, the reason these volunteers were volunteering was their strong belief in the value of the work, and thus the strong accompanying feeling of satisfaction. Some volunteered purely for religious reasons, some did it out of a sense of moral duty, but they all agreed that they were volunteering because it had its own rewards. Parental training and inculcation of certain values during their childhood shaped their appreciation for these values, but as with the initiators, some space has to be left in the analysis for the natural propensity of individuals to volunteer. In the words of one of the volunteers with the Edhi Foundation, "All volunteers have a virus. Before joining Edhi I worked with a small organization. Even during my school-going years I had a small cabinet in which I kept medicine and first-aid materials, with which I helped my neighbors when they were in need."

All the individuals who volunteered for the Edhi Foundation at a senior managerial level did so because their religious values held that serving humanity is a good deed that will endear them to God. The same intention motivated the doctors at the clinic. Islam emphasizes good conduct toward one's fellow human beings just as much as the act of giving itself. A saying often found in Islamic books is this: "Where one has nothing tangible to give, one can still utter a kind word." Good conduct is frequently termed *sadaka* in the Prophet Mohammad's sayings. Actions that benefit others, such as planting something that a person, bird, or animal later eats, count as *sadaka jariya.* So, rather than claiming to help others, the majority of volunteers at the Edhi Foundation and the madrasa responded that it is their good fortune to have found this platform and to do this work. One of the Edhi Foundation volunteers said, "I often told Mr. Edhi that we are using your platform to fulfill our own desires." Similarly, one of the specialists at the clinic said, "I feel lucky that God has chosen me to serve on this platform. He could have chosen someone else for it too." For the PRM volunteers, conviction about a secular intellectual idea replaced religious belief, but the motive remained self-satisfaction. In the words of a PRM member, "I do it because I believe that the world should be a certain way. I want to live my life accordingly."

Although conviction about the values of an organization was the joiners' primary motivation to join, public recognition and a sense of achievement, though not consciously sought, did play a role in sustaining the work of volunteers. They often responded that "money is not the only thing that matters; appreciation and respect from people can be extremely encouraging." During my field visits it was very easy to see that this respect marked the relations between the volunteers and the beneficiaries of the work. As part of the daily routine at the madrasa clinic, for example, there were many moving scenes in which patients would thank the doctors for providing this great service. In fact, most patients left the clinic murmuring loud prayers for the doctors: "We cannot pay you for this service, but God will reward you for this work." Such sentiments were often heard in this atmosphere.

Similar respect and gratitude marked the relationship between volunteers and the beneficiaries of the Edhi Foundation. The communities with whom the PRM works were equally expressive of their respect for the PRM members. Constant interaction has developed deep personal contacts between these communities and the PRM members and volunteers. PRM members are invited to weddings and other special social events, and if the members come, the community expresses their pride over their association with these members. Similarly, in all three cases the sense of achievement stemming from past success played a key role in keeping up the volunteers' momentum. In the words of an Edhi Foundation volunteer, "As you do more work, there comes a *jazba* [a passion] that even one chance of doing good should not go to waste."

Thus we see at play in these volunteers the same self-interest that we saw in the initiators and the givers. However, as current economic theory fully recognizes, it is a self-interest shaped by conviction in certain values rather than by the prospect of material gain (Becker 1993). The main distinction between initiators and joiners, however, is that for initiators, ideal self-interest becomes more dominant than material self-interest, and the work becomes their primary purpose in life. For the joiners, however, ideal self-interest coexists as a secondary force with a clear material self-interest, which leaves only limited time and energy for pursuing ideal self-interest.

In contrast to this distinction between initiators and volunteers, the key distinction between volunteers and givers is that the volunteers' involvement in and commitment to the cause are greater than the involvement and commitment of givers. The three case studies show that the same ideals shape the actions of both volunteers and givers, but in practice, volunteering requires more devotion and dedication than giving. Some givers simply do not have a very strong devotion to the organization's stated ideals. Others are constrained from volunteering by time and money considerations. During the interviews, the givers often expressed great admiration for the actual value of doing the work that the initiators and volunteers do. Many givers expressed the desire to do what the initiators and volunteers do, but either the tough nature of the work or other professional and social commitments restricted them from doing so.

The analysis developed here thus supports the dual conception of self-interest: ideal and material. It is important to mention that other authors have also argued for developing a distinct notion of self-interest based on material sacrifice. Howard Margolis (1982) has suggested that individuals have two types of utility functions—those that favor group-oriented preferences and those that favor selfish preferences—and that they make trade-offs between the two. The analysis in this chapter also contends that each of the two forms of self-interest, ideal and material, has its own distinct reward mechanisms. Whereas it is the prospect of material gains that shapes material self-interest, for ideal self-interest the potential rewards are nonmonetary, psychosocial, and spiritual, all of which rest in the very denial of material gains. The next important question that needs to be answered to understand the rise of other-regarding groups is, Why do joiners cooperate with a particular initiator? That is, how do joiners decide which group of initiators to cooperate with from among the many groups seeking their cooperation?

## Why Join a Particular Initiator?

The three case studies show that joiners do have inherent preferences for specific values, and of the numerous organizations claiming to advance those particular values, they join the one where the initiator reduces the transaction costs involved in joining a group, that is, the costs of gathering information about and monitoring the activities of the group. Initiators who display material sacrifice help to reduce these costs and thereby are more successful in mobilizing other-regarding collective action.

### Values

Shared ideals or conviction about certain values, whether they originate from religion, an innate sense of morality, or secular ideologies such as socialism, are fundamental to cooperation between initiators and joiners. In all three of the case studies it became clear that individuals choose to support organizations that promote the values they believe in. In the Edhi Foundation, the primary value, shaped by both religion and morality, is service to humanity. For the Imam, the primary value—a value deeply rooted in religious faith—is the establishment of a religiously virtuous society. For the PRM initiators, particularly Akhtar, it is the pursuit of establishing a just social order, a value drawn from the secular ideology of socialism.

When I asked joiners of the Edhi Foundation why they had joined this particular organization, I repeatedly got the answer, "We agree with the basic value of the foundation, which is to help other human beings in need." They mentioned with admiration the kind of work the Edhi Foundation does, and their appreciation for the values that shape the Edhi Foundation's work was critical to their decision to support it. People often mentioned the numerous ways the Foundation serves people. They spoke of how the Foundation buries the dead who have no claimants, how it feeds people who do not have enough to eat, how it provides a home to children and the destitute who have no place else to go, and so on and so forth. For most people, this value is rooted in the Islamic religious training that emphasizes *Haqooq-ul-Abad*, which is one of the main teachings of Islam. For others it stems from a general sense of morality. The ability to relate to the values that shaped the Edhi Foundation's work was thus critical to joiners' decision to join.

The situation at the madrasa was no different. Individuals giving to Jamiat ul Uloom believe in the virtue of producing scholars of Islam who can promote religious values in society and maintain the purity of Islamic rituals, which mark people's lives at the times of joy as well as the times of sorrow. It is important to mention here that many joiners were skeptical about the ability of a madrasa (not Jamiat ul Uloom in particular but madrasas in general) to actually produce scholars of Islam given the gradual decline in the quality of madrasa education over the decades. Nevertheless, they still strongly appreciated the value of Quran being recited, and the fact that children (often from economically less privileged backgrounds) were being given food and lodging as they learned the teachings of God. Thus belief in the values for which a madrasa stands was critical to these joiners' decision to cooperate.

The same reasons held true for joiners of the PRM. The PRM's appreciation for the value of social justice, for which it claims to be working and which often emanates from secular ideologies like socialism and Marxism, was critical to joiners' decision to join. The PRM supporters I interviewed spoke of how they appreciate the thinking that drives PRM's work. In contrast to joiners of the Edhi Foundation and the madrasa, rather than mention the immediate, tangible gains of supporting the PRM's work, joiners highlighted the importance of political mobilization and public empowerment work for effecting long-term change. This conviction about the value of a just social order in which there is no exploitation was thus critical to their decision to give time and money.

It is important to mention here that preference for a particular value does not have to be exclusive or exclusionary. Interviews with joiners in all three case studies revealed that most givers to the Edhi Foundation might also give to a madrasa, and joiners of the PRM might also support the Edhi Foundation, because they valued its welfare work. Some of the supporters of the PRM, however, appeared to have a strong resistance to supporting madrasa-type organizations, which they perceived as promoting sectarian divisions within society; but others' preferences were not so exclusionary; indeed, some supporters of the PRM acknowledged that they also supported a madrasa in their area.

This analysis thus demonstrates the importance of ideals in shaping individual preferences. It also argues that individuals can appreciate a variety of values simultaneously. It does not, however, explain how individuals choose a particular representative organization over other organizations claiming to advance the same preference. A preference for certain values, however, does not explain why joiners choose to join one set of initiators over the many other initiators who claim to be working for the same values. Shared ideals explain why some joiners prefer to contribute to a madrasa whereas others prefer to contribute to a welfare-oriented or activist organization, but it cannot explain why those who have a preference for madrasas join Jamiat ul Uloom rather than another madrasa in the same region, or why the Edhi Foundation has completely outshone other welfare organizations in the number of joiners, or why the PRM has established a pool of joiners while many other activist organizations have failed. Is the beneficiary of their cooperation just randomly picked? Or is there an identifiable, rationally calculated logic behind joiners' choices? The cases presented here show that cooperation between initiators and joiners is an outcome of rational calculations on the part of the joiner about the efficiency and motivation of the initiators. Furthermore, these cases suggest that the initiator is equally aware of these calculations and therefore shapes his actions to meet those calculations and thereby reduces the transaction costs that underlie the exchange between initiators and joiners.

## Monitoring Efficiency and Commitment

My interviews with the joiners, initiators, and staff members of these organizations plus my observations of the organizations themselves overwhelmingly suggest that a joiner's decision to cooperate is based on her conviction that the initiator is committed to the cause and has the ability to deliver what he promises. Joiners want to know that the initiator is actually delivering what he is claiming to, that he is efficient, and that he is spending the funds he collects on the cause and not on himself; in other words, he is committed and his motivation is sincere. One possible hypothesis could be that joiners expected to be shown financial audits of receipts of donations and expenditures as proof of the efficiency and motivation of the initiators, much as the stakeholders of a business firm expect. The three case studies quickly set aside any possibility of this hypothesis being valid, however.

The main reason that joiners don't rely on receipts became clear in the very first interview when a giver to the Edhi Foundation said, "Paperwork and reports have no meaning for me; receipts can be forged, accounts can be fudged. I do take receipts from the staff at the collection desk so that money gets to Edhi, but I tear it up as soon as I am out of his sight." This same expression of distrust about formal paperwork and accounting systems recurred throughout the interviews, reflecting a complete lack of trust in the machinery of the state and any central accounting system. Receipts and audit reports were meaningless for the majority of givers. This complete lack of trust in the state was emphasized by one of the givers to the Edhi Foundation when he said, "The government also collects *zakat,* but it is all paperwork. The public does not even know which ones of the state departments handle *zakat* money. Edhi, on the other hand, gives its own number. Even in remote places that we can't reach ourselves, Edhi is working." This general and pervasive lack of trust was thus central in shaping alternative mechanisms for monitoring the sincerity and competence of the initiators.

It must be added, however, that although the authorities that controlled centralized accounting systems, such as the state and private auditors, were not trusted, there was recognition of the benefit of having a receipt system if it was used properly. The giving of a receipt indicated to most givers that the organization had a well-developed management system. It reflected that the initiator kept track of the money coming in and going out, and signified that the money they would give would get to the initiator and not be embezzled by staff members. In other words, the receipt was not a means of monitoring the initiators, because givers realized that because of the corrupt state system, a formal accounting system could be manipulated easily if the initiator wanted it to be. Instead the receipt acted as a monitor of the employee. It was important to the joiner to know that the money he gave to a member of the organization would get to the initiator. This concern was borne out in cross-case analysis. The Edhi Foundation had donation collection offices scattered across the country. There joiners' contributions were not put directly into the hands of the initiators, and the receipt system was very complex. The giver was given multiple copies of the receipt, one of which he was asked to mail to the organization's main office in a pre-paid envelope provided with the receipt. Most of the Edhi Foundation givers I interviewed assured me that they took the receipt, for the reasons just discussed.

The PRM, which maintains only one office and undertakes limited fundraising, has no receipt system. This is not, however, an issue for joiners, because they put their contributions directly into the hands of the initiators rather than giving them to paid staff members. The madrasa, on the other hand, does have a receipt system and the Imam encourages givers to take a receipt for every donation, but because givers often give their gifts directly to the Imam, receipts were, it seemed, insignificant for most of them. This dual role of the receipt highlights that in itself the receipt does not mean much; rather, it is the giver's trust or mistrust of the system or of the individual issuing the receipt that determines its significance. Also, a well-developed receipt and accounting system is very important for internal management as an organization expands. Both Abdul

Sattar Edhi and the Imam were convinced that without a well-developed receipt and accounting system, management would be impossible.

In the absence of a meaningful accounting and auditing system, the logical means of monitoring the efficiency of initiators can be hypothesized to be direct physical contact with and inspection of the initiators' projects that the giver is considering supporting. The following analysis demonstrates, however, that only for a core group of givers is direct interaction important. The majority of givers do not have the time or energy to visit the organization to meet the beneficiaries of its work or to look through its accounts, even if the initiators allow them access to these. Because the time investment and physical exertion necessary for such direct monitoring are high for the givers, rationally calculated indirect means of monitoring the initiators become more useful.

During the interviews, when respondents said they support the initiators because they are convinced of the value of the organization's work, I questioned them about how they know whether the initiators are actually delivering what they say they do. I asked whether they actually visited the office to see the organization's work. The answer I repeatedly got was "No, I don't have time to visit an organization to evaluate its work." However, they all also said that they wanted to ensure that their money is being used for the purpose for which it was given. When asked how, in the absence of financial audit reports and direct physical inspections of the organization's projects, they become convinced of the efficiency of the organization, the common answer was, "We trust it." The word *trust*, which currently is of much interest to social scientists, was actually used many times by the interviewees. What this study contributes to existing theoretical debates on trust is dealt with in the book's final chapter; for now, the following section looks at what *trust* means to joiners.

When the concept of trust is untangled, what joiners trusted turns out to be a combination of four cost-effective, rationally calculated means of monitoring and measuring the efficiency and one rationally calculated means of assessing the motivation of an initiator. The four mechanisms for monitoring efficiency are *visibility of work, firsthand experience, reference and recommendation from someone trusted,* and *duration of work*; the one mechanism for assessing motivation is *signs of material sacrifice on the part of the initiator.* As is elaborated on later, the latter three mechanisms can easily be bracketed within the existing concepts of *networks, reputation,* and *norms.* The reason for not using these terms here is to help the reader refrain from quickly drawing one conclusion or the other on the basis of a preconceived understanding of these often complex and contentious notions.

*Visibility of Work*

Seeing is believing! This axiom was true for the joiners in all three case studies in making the decision to trust the initiators. In all of the interviews, one of the first things that people said when explaining the reasons they chose to trust an initiator was that they could see his work. The Edhi Foundation has a very visible presence on the ground. Its offices are located across the country on main highways and in low-budget but central city areas; its ambulances are often seen darting through the streets; its free-food provision centers, which are often situated on main city roads, are heavily packed at the times of food distribution. As one giver said, "I can see the work of Edhi. When I go to donate money, I can see the phone ringing, people coming and going, the cars moving. When I am on the road, I observe Edhi offices, Edhi cars. Trust is based on the work that I see on the ground." Throughout the interviews, people said that the Edhi Foundation ambulances played a key role in convincing them of Abdul Sattar Edhi's performance. Others highlighted that the Foundation ambulances are the first to get to accidents. As one of the long-term volunteers with the Foundation said, "Without the visibility attained through the ambulance service, donations to the Edhi Foundation would never have reached this scale."

A similar visibility marks the work of Jamiat ul Uloom al-Shariah. Four hundred students live and study in the madrasa building at any given time. As part of their daily routine, these students mingle with the local community, including the shopkeepers and the children at the playground. They also interact daily with people who come to the mosque to pray. This constant presence of the students makes the work of the madrasa very visible. Everyone can see that a certain number of children are being fed and taught in the madrasa. Potential givers do not know the exact amount of donations coming into the madrasa or how much it costs to support a child. They also have no means of checking whether each penny collected is being honestly spent on the cause for which it was collected. Nevertheless, the physical presence of the students and the close interaction that the students and the Imam have with the community convinces them that worthwhile work is going on here.

The issue of the visibility of the PRM's work was equally important to its supporters. However, the significantly different nature of the PRM's work compared to the work of the Edhi Foundation and of Jamiat ul Uloom al-Shariah (in that the beneficiaries of its work are often in remote communities) requires a deliberate strategy for gaining visibility. One of the key elements of the PRM's work strategy is thus to maintain a presence in the media. The team actively engages with the journalist community to ensure that the protests and rallies that the PRM stages get prominent space in newspapers, ideally with photographs. If a reporter fails to turn up at an event, the team members pursue newspapers with press releases. This active media presence is the primary means by which it makes its work visible to potential joiners living in the bigger cities, which often are very distant from the actual place of the PRM's work. This media coverage is therefore very important in convincing joiners of PRM's worth.

In addition to the conscious effort that PRM members make to get their work covered, the media on their own have ended up covering the PRM's activities extensively because of the role it played in the success of two of Pakistan's most prominent grassroots movements, which became the focus of attention for national as well as international human rights groups. The active role that the PRM plays in these two movements and the coverage of this role in the press has been critical in convincing joiners of PRM's worth. Akhtar has often been interviewed on popular shows on the electronic media as a representative of these movements. It is thus clear that the visibility of the initiator's work is one of the indirect monitoring mechanisms that joiners in all three case studies used to test the efficiency of the initiators.

### Direct Contact: Firsthand Experience

Firsthand experience of either benefiting from the work of an organization or seeing someone else benefit from it—also called direct contact—is another indirect mechanism that joiners use to develop trust in the efficiency of the work of an initiator. The very nature of the work of the three organizations under study involves contact with various groups within society. For example, because one of the specialized services of the Edhi Foundation is burying the dead and dealing with emergencies and accidents, during the process of identifying joiners for interviews, I came across a large number of doctors who donate to Edhi. The main reason they gave for doing this was that they had seen his ambulance service always deliver when others failed to. These professionals with firsthand exposure to the work of the Foundation constitute the core group of joiners.

Direct contact was also at work in the madrasa. As mentioned earlier, the Imam as well as the teachers and students at the madrasa are in direct contact with the community. The Imam is an important part of the community. He is present in people's daily lives and is an integral part of important occasions in their lives, such as births, marriages, and deaths. In explaining the reasons that people respond to his call for support, the Imam placed a lot of emphasis on the importance of the direct contact he has with people, including his involvement in sensitive matters, such as mediating to salvage a marriage that was otherwise heading for divorce. In addition, senior students from the madrasa often teach the Quran to children in the neighboring houses. This interaction gives people in the community a fairly good idea about who the Imam is; and it helps the joiners judge the personality, calibre, and knowledge of the Imam.

Along with this knowledge comes a sense of differentiation. That is, many of the respondents explained that they differentiate among Imams on the basis of the quality of the *Khutba* (sermon) they give, and by seeing whether they practice what they preach. Moreover, when people consult the Imam on religious issues affecting their daily lives, they get to know a lot about the "capacity and capability of the Imam," as some respondents commented. This sense of differentiation that is established through direct contact is also demonstrated by the fact that the madrasas that expand dramatically have Imams who are formally trained and qualified or who come from established religious families.

Most of the joiners of the PRM had firsthand experience of participating in some of the planning meetings of the initiators, or they knew the initiators previously, as colleagues, relatives, or friends. Some had worked closely with the initiators in previous jobs and thus had firsthand experience of their capabilities as well as their credibility.

Another form of direct contact is when a joiner has personally benefited from the initiator's work. During the interviews it became clear that among the core group of supporters of the Edhi Foundation there were some who themselves had benefited from the Edhi Foundation's work at some stage. A letter from a Pakistani based in the United Kingdom, shared with me by one of the senior staff members of the Edhi Foundation, explained that the personal experience of his family affected his decision to donate a new ambulance to the foundation: "My uncle/father-in-law passed away a few years ago suffering heart attack. In an emergency, he was taken to Rawalpindi Hospital from Gujar Khan via your ambulance, as the Civil Hospital did not have one available. It is with this background that we as a family have decided to donate an ambulance to serve other needy people of Gujar Khan."

The experience of another supporter of the Edhi Foundation reflected the same sentiment: "When my father died I could not find any ambulance in the hospital except Edhi's. Similarly, once my husband got very delayed on an intercity travel. This raised serious concerns about the possibility of an accident. At that time of extreme tension, in the entire world there was only Edhi Foundation's emergency service that I could rely on to get information about my husband's well-being." The madrasa also had some joiners who were direct beneficiaries of its work. One of the respondents from the local community, when probed for his reasons for supporting the madrasa, explained that his own children and those of some of his colleagues study in the madrasa. He said that their personal experience makes it clear to them that real work is going on there. There were also joiners who supported the PRM's operations because PRM work was being carried out in their own community.

What we see, therefore, is the importance of two forms of direct contact in building joiners' trust in the efficiency of the initiators. In the first form, the joiner has personally seen someone else benefit from the initiator's work. In the second form, the joiner himself has benefited at some stage from the work of the initiator. For joiners, these two forms of direct contact replace the need for formal monitoring and inspection of the work.

### Recommendation of a Trusted Person: The Role of Networks

In addition to direct contact, social networks—that is, the people with whom one is connected—also play a critical role in convincing a joiner to trust an initiator. Networks seem to serve a dual purpose across the three cases studied: (1) they bridge the information gap by spreading the word about the existence of the organization, and (2) they act as promoters (through recommendation) of the work of the initiators. Many of the interviewees became convinced of the efficiency of the work of an initiator because a close friend, relative, or colleague whose judgment they trusted said something good about the organization. It was also clear, however, that joiners took recommendations with a measure of caution and acted on them mainly if they were convinced that the person making the recommendation had real knowledge of the organization's work. In most cases, the people whose recommendations were trusted were those who had worked with or through the organization, had personally benefited from the initiator's work, or were known to have personal or professional interest in or knowledge of the initiator's field of activity.

Across the case studies, givers who were interviewed said the recommendation of individuals whose judgment they trusted was an important means of judging the efficiency of initiators. An interviewee who gives to the Edhi Foundation commented that she gives to this organization because her friend who had worked with the Edhi Foundation and found it very satisfying had recommended it. Another interviewee mentioned the experience of his friend's father, who was in the military and had seen the Edhi Foundation handle casualties at the Indo-Pakistan border. Similarly, people who supported PRM without having any direct contact with it said they did so because of the recommendation of a trusted friend, colleague, or acquaintance. Again, those whose recommendation mattered were those known to have professional or personal knowledge of the field in which the organization worked. Many of those who gave to the PRM mentioned the names of prominent activists whom they personally knew who had recommended the PRM to them.

Analysis of the role of networks in building joiners' trust in initiators is made more nuanced by the madrasa case study. For the madrasa joiners, the role of social networks became secondary to a general sense of association with one's community, the area in which one lives, and the sense of responsibility one feels toward making that community better. Unlike VOs, such as the Edhi Foundation, that raise donations across the country, madrasas generally rely on resources acquired from the catchment area of the community they serve. The madrasa appears to have two categories of givers and each category seems to have its own distinct perception of the madrasa. The first category, which seems to be the majority, views the madrasa as a place where poor students get to memorize the Quran. This view does not really see the madrasa as a place of scholarly learning; instead it sees it as a place where some good is being done by teaching poor children God's word.

The interviews with the givers revealed that not only the supporters of Jamiat ul Uloom but also those who give to the Edhi Foundation or the PRM feel associated with the madrasa in their area. This feeling of ownership stems partly from their social interaction with the Imam and the students of the madrasa, and partly from the Islamic emphasis on taking responsibility for the less well-off in one's own community. For most givers, the local madrasa, regardless of its performance, was thus eligible for some of their help, because of their inner compulsion to give. Many respondents said that the *sadaka* they believed they had to give in order to ward off bad luck was often channeled through a madrasa in their area. They reasoned that however poor the quality of education in the madrasa might be, poor students at least get to learn the Quran there. Overall, this was considered to be a good thing; by supporting a madrasa one would be supporting these poor children, as well as earning a reward in the afterlife. This sense of responsibility and preference for giving to a madrasa in one's own area rather than to one more distant madrasa seems to reduce the role that social networks play in madrasa joiners' selection process. As one female giver to the madrasa said:

> I give my main donation to Jamiat ul Uloom because I know the Imam there is knowledgeable. But I also make a small donation to the smaller madrasa. I know the Imam in this smaller madrasa lacks proper training. Also, his com-

mitment to his work at times appears questionable, especially when he sends out messengers with sorrowful pleas to collect funds for the madrasa. But despite all of this, I feel that since God's name is being recited in that place, and relatively poor children are studying there, I should donate at least a small amount to it.

This one response, which reflects the reaction of many other interviewees, upholds a number of the arguments developed in this chapter. First, it indicates that when the internal compulsion to give is very strong, the giver is willing to compromise on the efficiency of the initiator. Second, it shows that giving within one's own community reduces the role of social networks and the importance of the recommendation of trusted people, because the giver is in direct contact with the initiator. Third, it upholds the argument that even in the case of madrasas, where at times the internal compulsion to give reduces the efficiency standards expected by joiners, there is indeed recognition for those Imams who on the basis of direct contact are assessed as performing better. Ultimately it is the efficient Imams who draw more joiners and attract bigger donations; indeed, the interviews show that most of the donations that were made only on the basis of the internal compulsion to give were relatively small.

In contrast to givers driven by internal compulsion, there also seems to be a category of givers who choose to give to madrasas because they genuinely perceive them to be critical for producing Islamic scholars. What they perceive is close to what Imams claim they actually do in madrasas. Donors who make big contributions to madrasas appear to be those who believe in this image of the madrasa. Often these are people who are more religiously inclined than others and make an active effort to identify good madrasas. For them, giving is not tied to the madrasa in their area. They contribute to Jamiat ul Uloom, for example, not because it is in their locality but because they have the knowledge and access needed to compare the efficiency and performance of various madrasas and have concluded that this particular one is better than others.

In an interview with one such donor, the reason given for supporting Jamiat ul Uloom was that it had a good reputation within religious circles. What this indicates is that although the general public has only a limited capacity to judge the efficiency of the madrasa, those who are more religiously inclined hold clear criteria for differentiation. These individuals explore various madrasas, meet like-minded people with whom they share interests, attend social ceremonies at these madrasas, read the Imams' published work, and make informed decisions about the efficiency of these madrasas. They thus become part of a network through which the reputation of good madrasas gets established, and big donors more often than not come from this group. When it comes to choosing a madrasa to support, rather than giving out of internal compulsion, the recommendation of a trusted individual with specialized information is therefore as important in influencing a joiner's decision as it is for individuals considering whether to support the Edhi Foundation or the PRM.

Looking across the three case studies, it appears that these specialized networks develop among people who are deeply interested in a particular activity. Individuals who are interested in a particular issue gather information about that issue, as well as about other people who are working on the issue. This process gives them access to specialized knowledge on the issue; as a result, people start to associate that issue with them. One of the interviewees whose family I was familiar with mentioned various relatives who she thought could give reliable information on the performance of a welfare organization, such as the Edhi Foundation, or a religious place, such as a madrasa. The female relative who she thought could give a reliable assessment of a welfare organization was a young doctor who often volunteers for welfare activities or sets up free medical camps for patients. Similarly, the relative she thought was reliable to consult about the reputation of a madrasa was an elderly uncle whose religious devoutness and patronage of many religious institutions and madrasas is well known in their family. The respondent gave their names instantly in response to my question, without having to make any deep calculations, but when I probed, she gave the reasons just provided as the basis for her choices.

It is therefore individuals with special interest and expertise in an area who often act as connectors between the initiators and the joiners. In all three of the case studies, the trusted friend, relative, or acquaintance upon whose recommendation a joiner decided to support a particular initiator was someone the joiner knew to be well-informed about the issue addressed by the initiator.

### Duration of Work: The Role of Reputation

The longer an initiator has been working, the easier it becomes for the joiner to trust him. In all three case studies it is clear that the duration of an initiator's work is an important sign to joiners of the initiator's efficiency. Whereas Abdul Sattar Edhi and the Imam have been working for decades, the PRM is only a few years old, and this clearly has an impact on the number of its joiners. And the fact that the Edhi Foundation has survived for so long is what has convinced many people of its efficiency. Thus duration of service seems to play the most critical role in the decision making of those givers who either have had no direct contact with the organization or who had no one in their social network interested in or knowledgeable enough about the relevant issue to recommend an organization.

Among interviewees who did not know someone who had directly benefited from or observed the Edhi Foundation's work the most common response to the question about the basis of their conviction was this: "If the Foundation has been working for so long and people have been supporting it for so long, then it must have been doing good work." This response shows the tendency to trust something if so many others have been supporting and participating in it for a long period. The understanding implied is that not all of them can be wrong; if an organization has survived people's scrutiny for a long time, then it must have some good elements. This response also indicates the role of collective trust, which can be called reputation and which helps initiators make the transition from going out to seek joiners to having joiners come to them. In the latter stage, the role of reputation is significant; the organization moves from having to convince people to support the work to having joiners themselves want to associate with it. At this point, by receiving their money or providing them with a platform for volunteering, the organization is actually doing them a service. In some ways, the Edhi Foundation, with its established reputation, is doing just that by making it easy for them to carry out their obligations to give and volunteer without having to spend a lot of time identifying a deserving initiator.

Duration of work in itself thus becomes a mechanism the joiner can use to monitor the efficiency of the initiator. It coexists with direct contact and recommendations by trusted individuals, but in the absence of these two other monitoring mechanisms it becomes the key criterion, along with visibility of work, for monitoring the efficiency of initiators.

## Monitoring Commitment

As was discussed in the introduction to this chapter, the joiner's decision to join a particular organization is facilitated by an organization giving clear signals that help reduce the monitoring costs for the joiner. Although signs of efficiency are important for the joiner in assessing whether the initiator can actually deliver what he promises, clear signals of the initiator's commitment to a cause are important in building joiners' trust that an initiator is actually spending all of the collected funds on the cause and not on himself. Analysis of the three case studies demonstrates overwhelmingly that there is one signal that acts as the biggest proof of the motivation of the initiator. This one mechanism becomes critical to the joiner's decision to join an initiator, even overtaking at times the need for mechanisms to measure efficiency: clear signs of material self-sacrifice on the part of the initiator.

It is clear from the three case studies that material self-sacrifice on the part of the initiator is critical to generating and sustaining cooperation between initiators and joiners. In all three cases it was important to givers to feel that their donations were not being spent to benefit the initiators themselves. Because monitoring this is either simply impossible or would cost joiners heavily in terms of time, observing evidence of material self-sacrifice on the part of the initiators becomes the convenient means for monitoring them. If we define *norms* as "rules of the game," then self-sacrifice on the part of initiators becomes the norm that regulates cooperation between initiators and joiners. It is self-sacrifice that gives initiators the power to mobilize joiners.

Interviews with givers to the Edhi Foundation reflect that the conviction that money given to the Edhi Foundation is not being used to benefit Abdul Sattar Edhi himself was critical to the decision to give. Abdul Sattar Edhi is a very simple man. He has lived his entire adult life clothed in two gray *shalwar kameez* and with a wife who has maintained an equally simple outlook. His simple lifestyle convinces people that he is not making any personal gain out of the money being given to the Foundation. In the words of one interviewee who supports the Foundation: "In Edhi's case, self-sacrifice is visible. His living tells it. If you come in a Mercedes, then I will think that you are spending the money on yourself. If you are simple and the organization is performing well, then there will be trust that you are spending the money on the cause and not on yourself." All of the volunteers interviewed said that Abdul Edhi inspired them by his simplicity and devotion. One of them commented, "An individual does all the work due to a *jazba*. There should be the courage to sacrifice."

Abdul Sattar Edhi himself documents the importance of self-sacrifice in mobilizing joiners. While talking to me he said, "I decided that I will wear very simple clothes so that the thief and the beggar also say that he is even simpler than us. I impressed people by my service and simplicity. I drove the ambulance myself." Similarly, during an interview with Faisal Edhi, the son who is taking over for Abdul Sattar Edhi, when I commented on his extremely simple office that had only a fan for relief from the hot Karachi summer, he smiled and replied, "Simplicity is critical for success. The office is simple; you noticed that. Tomorrow when you give to Edhi, you won't question where the money is going. Sacrifice and dedication are essential for this work. If you collect money for yourself, you will become an ordinary man but not a personality."

The key here is not the simple living but the conviction that the initiator is committed to the work that he is claiming to do, that his motivation is sincere, and the way joiners test that motivation is by observing the initiator's material sacrifice for that cause. All of the interviewees who gave to the Edhi Foundation said that giving to the Foundation because of Abdul Sattar Edhi's simplicity does not mean they will give only to someone who lives in two pairs of clothing like Abdul Sattar Edhi does. Most of them mentioned Imran Khan, former Pakistani cricket star, and his cancer hospital, and said they would give to Imran Khan too, despite his comfortable lifestyle. They explained that this is because they know he too is committed to his work because he has sacrificed his own time and money to establish the hospital. One giver commented:

> Edhi's personality does not mean much in my decision. It could be Imran Khan with all his flamboyance. I will still give to him because of the work being done at the hospital and the fact that he himself has invested heavily in it. However, if I came to know that he is enjoying an extravagant lifestyle because of the donations I am giving to that organization, then it would be a different story.

Self-sacrifice as proof of the commitment and motivation of initiators came up in all the interviews with the joiners of the PRM. Explaining their reasons for supporting the PRM's work, one person said:

> I give to PRM because I saw that all the people here were committed people. I determined that they are committed because I see these people work day and night. I see these people, who have many other alternatives available to them which could bring them money and fame, but they have chosen to do this work. Commitment is evident when they are putting in their own money. They are doing it because they feel it is something important that needs to be done. Jobs are secondary to them.

The same simplicity that marks the Edhi Foundation's offices marks the PRM's office. The organization operates with a minimum of infrastructure. It is housed in a small, three-room office on the third floor of a building in a middle-income area of Rawalpindi. It is surrounded by workshops and low-income businesses—a venue in stark contrast to where a person with Akhtar's qualifications would be expected to be working. There is simply nothing posh about the office. The main room is barely furnished, with two old tables and chairs, and otherwise appears relatively barren. The only carpeted room in the office serves the dual purpose of hosting big meetings and accommodating representatives from the communities that PRM supports when they need to stay in Islamabad overnight for work. There is only one computer and one telephone. The third room serves as a bedroom for two boys from the local slum dwelling who, in return for the accommodation, provide security for the office.

The same approach was taken to the Imam. It was important to joiners that he have the appearance of a simple man. As discussed earlier, because of the religious obligation to give, people at times give even if they are not fully convinced of the work of a madrasa. When, however, they give to a madrasa out of choice, it is important to them that the Imam not come across as living a lavish life on their donations. According to the Imam himself, "The *maulavi*'s living is within the public. The public surrounds him from all four sides. The *maulavi* goes to their homes and people come to his house. They know where their money is being spent. They can see the mosque and the madrasa. If I change cars every day, they will question it in their minds."

All joiners cooperating with initiators highlighted that they got involved because the initiators inspired them through their material sacrifice. One volunteer said, "A true volunteer will sacrifice. If he can't sacrifice, he will always be doing calculations about what he is gaining or losing by doing this." To quote Abdul Sattar Edhi again: "Luxury and commitment to welfare cannot coexist. The merging of the two is impossible without one affecting the other. It is impossible for the committed to live two lives." This analysis thus highlights that material sacrifice is an institutional norm that not only becomes the symbol of the commitment of the initiator, but also lends credibility to the efficiency of the initiator. Krebs (1982) makes a similar argument in his paper "Psychological Approaches to Altruism: An Evaluation." Asking why the intentions behind one's actions are so important to others, he argues that it "surely relates to the fact that the intentions behind an act may supply a better basis for predicting subsequent behavior than the act itself. Another reason relates to the credit and blame observers seek to attribute to the people who perform the helping acts. It is not as much behaviour that observers are interested in as the [internal] personality or character of the people who initiate it" (450).

## Conclusion

This analysis of the three case studies highlights that perception of initiators' efficiency and motivation is critical to joiners' decisions about which initiator to join. However, given that direct monitoring of initiators is very costly for joiners, even if it is possible, joiners develop indirect monitoring mechanisms—signals—to gauge the efficiency and commitment of initiators. Furthermore, this analysis establishes that although visibility of work, direct contact, networks, and reputation build joiners' trust that initiators deliver what they claim, it is material sacrifice on the part of the initiators that builds the trust that every penny given to the organization is actually being spent for the cause.

Review of indirect mechanisms developed to monitor the efficiency as well as the motivation of initiators suggests that rational thinking is central to an individual's decision-making process. Respondents across the three case studies demonstrated such rational explanations as relying on visibility of work, direct contact, recommendations, and reputation to be mechanisms for monitoring the initiators. Decisions about initiators' efficiency were made not on the basis of hearsay but in response to signs or direct experience of their work. Recommendations were taken not from anyone in one's own social network but from people who had established interest in and knowledge of the organization's area of work. Duration of the initiator's work mattered not because it established familiarity but because it reflected that the initiator had survived the suspicions of many other joiners.

Rational calculations even more explicitly marked the process of monitoring the motivation of initiators. It is clear from all three case studies that the importance of material sacrifice in gaining the trust of joiners cannot be attributed merely to a culture or tradition that teaches joiners to revere self-sacrifice. Material self-sacrifice on the part of the initiator was important because for the joiner it is the rationally appealing signal that the initiator is sincere. When the initiator himself is making visible sacrifices for the work he is asking others to join, then it is rational for the joiner to conclude that the initiator is unlikely to be putting the money of the givers to personal use. This is the only way that the joiner can overcome the need to monitor every penny that comes the initiator's way.

Moreover, the analysis highlights that although ideal self-interest does exist, it is an exception rather than the norm. Individuals expect others to behave on the basis of material self-interest. They make predictions about the actions of other individuals, which in turn shape their own actions, on the basis of the assumption that all individuals will try to maximize their own material self-interest. Joiners therefore find it difficult to trust initiators blindly, because they are suspicious of individuals who claim to work toward an end that does not hold any material gain for themselves. It is for this reason that individuals demand signs of material self-sacrifice from those who claim to work for an end that promises them no economic gain. Evidence of material self-sacrifice thus becomes the norm by reasoning individuals to regulate their charity work.

Again, the fact that individuals expect material self-interest to be the most dominant motivation for social action is the reason that once they identify someone who demonstrates credibly that she or he has overcome material self-interest, they tend to respect and revere that person. Most individuals' respect for material sacrifice as a virtue is due to religious or moral training, but they also realize that it is very unnatural and difficult to act this way, because individuals have a natural inclination to maximize their own material comfort. Most individuals are therefore initially suspicious of those who claim to be engaging in materially self-sacrificing work, but if they become convinced that a person is indeed sacrificing, they develop a deep respect for that person precisely because they understand how difficult it is to act that way. Chapter 6 analyzes how both distinguishing between ideal and material self-interest and the emphasis on material sacrifice in mobilizing members help explain the negative impact of aid on traditional institutions of collective action. The next chapter tests these findings with reference to self-regarding groups.

# 4 Why Cooperate?

## Motives and Decisions of Initiators and Joiners in Self-Regarding Groups

*The investment in institutional change was not made in a single step. Rather, the process of institutional change in all basins involved many small steps that had low initial costs. . . . Because the process was incremental and sequential and early successes were achieved, intermediate benefits from the initial investments were realized before anyone needed to make larger investments. Each institutional change transformed the structure of incentives within which future strategic decisions would be made.*

**Elinor Ostrom, *Governing the Commons*, 1990, 137**

*This means that the peasants' subjective estimates of the would-be entrepreneur's capability and credibility will directly influence the entrepreneur's ability to organize peasants, and that,* ceteris paribus, *a situation with more credible organizers is likely to be a situation with more effective organizations.*

**Samuel L. Popkin, *The Rational Peasant*, 1979, 251**

THE PREVIOUS CHAPTER ANALYZED the motivations and decision-making processes of initiators and joiners in cooperating to produce a good that benefits a group other than themselves, that is, to join in other-regarding collective action. This chapter expands that analysis to study cooperation in a group in which the initiators are driven by ideals but the joiners—unlike the joiners in other-regarding groups, who gain no material benefit for their contribution—do want personal gains from this cooperation. This chapter addresses the following questions: Why do those who are affected by an organization's work join the initiators who claim to work for their interests? What processes shape the decisions of joiners in self-regarding groups about whether or not to join a set of initiators who are claiming to work for them, given that the decision to join involves high costs (in time, money, and risk) and at times leads to loss of life itself? Is this decision an outcome of blind faith in anyone who claims to work for them, an instinctive or emotional response to the given scenario, or a product of rationally calculated decision making? Especially when there are multiple initiators claiming to work to protect their interests, how do joiners select one set of initiators over others?

This chapter studies the relationship of the People's Rights Movement (PRM), one of the three case studies discussed in the previous chapter, with one of the grassroots movements it has supported—the Anjuman Mazareen-i-Punjab, an association of tenant farmers—in order to explore how the PRM was able to facilitate collective action within a community affected by a common problem. The motivation of the initiators of the PRM has already been analyzed as being the search for psychosocial rewards. This chapter studies the motivation of the joiners to cooperate in producing the desired good, and analyzes the process by which members of a community faced with a common challenge made decisions to cooperate with the PRM rather than with the various other initiators seeking their cooperation. Self-regarding groups have been the primary focus of a rich literature on collective action and social movements. Within the dense literature on the origins of social movements there is significant work that highlights the importance of leadership in such movements. This literature also documents the characteristics of these leaders. However, studies that aim to understand the processes through which joiners decide who to accept and follow as a leader are rare. The analysis in this chapter contributes to the theoretical understanding of the decision-making processes that joiners engage in to decide who to follow as a leader in a social movement.

The chapter draws on open-ended interviews, group discussions, and informal conversations with members of the PRM, officeholders of the Anjuman Mazareen-i-Punjab, and the tenant farmers who constitute this movement. It also draws on observations of the interaction between PRM and the Anjuman Mazareen-i-Punjab members. Extensive interviews were conducted with PRM members. In addition, fieldwork was conducted with tenants at Okara Military Farms, the heartland of the tenant farmers movement. During this period I fully immersed myself in the company of the local tenants, sharing the women's sleeping space, where my discussions with them lasted late into the night. Equally useful was my silent observation of interactions among community members as I accompanied the Anjuman's officeholders on their routine visits to the various households, where they provided updates on the movement, brainstormed about future courses of action, and shared community gossip and family updates over cups of tea. These interactions were a very important means of observing the relationships among the members of the movement and the movement's relationship with the PRM. I am personally indebted to three female officeholders of the Anjuman, who were designated to coordinate my stay and accompany me to meetings in all the villages. Finally, documentary records, including copies of First Information Reports (which are filed with the police), newspaper clippings, and video recordings of TV shows in which the PRM represented the movement, were consulted. Reports on the movement by international human rights groups, such as Human Rights Watch (HRW), were another useful source of information.

## The PRM's Organizational Details

The PRM is a VO that acts as an umbrella organization to support and strengthen indigenous resistance movements across Pakistan. Its aim is two-fold: (1) to support individual resistance movements and (2) to link different resistance movements to one another and increase communication and collaboration among them. The ultimate objective is to help empower these movements to challenge the broad power imbalances in society rather than just focus on their individual struggles targeting specific causes. Imbued mainly with Marxist ideology, with a sprinkling of Sufi and Gandhian philosophy thrown in, the PRM core team of six members aims to mobilize marginalized communities by talking with them about political empowerment and rights. Although the PRM supports movements, it is not a movement itself. Its members work to produce a good for groups other than themselves. The backgrounds of the core members of the team, their motivation to engage in this work, and their relationships with *horizontal joiners*—that is, those who do not directly benefit from the PRM's work but support its activities through donations of time and money—are covered in the previous chapter. This chapter focuses on the PRM's relationship with *vertical joiners*—those who are simultaneously direct beneficiaries as well as participants in its work.

The PRM's work strategy is to undertake mass mobilization among communities caught in a struggle to defend their rights against the state or any other powerful lobby. As one of the members said, "We spend hours and hours sitting with people trying to build what we call class-consciousness." The PRM does not, however, instigate new movements; it simply works to support existing indigenous movements that already have leadership within the local community that is mobilizing people to resist oppression. The PRM's members are clear that the purpose of their work is not to distribute patronage; they detest the use of the term *beneficiary* for the communities with which they work. They believe in equality. They consider all participants to be "comrades" or partners in the struggle, with individual members of the community having as much say in all matters as do the PRM members. According to one member, "We spend most of the time telling people that we can't do anything for them and that they have to get justice for themselves." The two members mentioned in Chapter 3 who imbibed Marxist teaching in the literary circles of the now defunct Communist Party of Pakistan excel in making ideologically charged speeches.

The numerous grassroots movements with which the PRM was involved at the time of my fieldwork included, in addition to the Anjuman Mazareen-i-Punjab, the All Pakistan Alliance Baray Katchi Abadi, the Pakistan Fishers Folk Forum, and the Association of People Affected by the Big Projects. It also has ties with teachers' and students' movements, with the All Pakistan Power Looms Association, and with labor associations. As mentioned in Chapter 3, however, out of all the work it does it is the phenomenal success of two of the movements it has supported that has established the PRM as a force within Pakistani activism circles: the Katchi Abadi (slum dwellers) Movement, and the Okara Military Farm Movement, now known as the Anjuman Mazareen-i-Punjab. The PRM's relationships with these movements provided good opportunities for exploring the questions posed in this chapter. The Anjuman Mazareen-i-Punjab was selected for this study for two reasons: first, not only has it been one of the most prominent indigenous movements in Pakistan but it has also gained international attention; and second, it has been one of the most radical movements in the country because it has directly taken on the Pakistani military, a confrontation between the army rangers and the community that has resulted in the death of a number of tenant farmers.

## Anjuman Mazareen-i-Punjab: A Brief History

In 2000 in south central Punjab, the most fertile land of Pakistan, a movement against Pakistan's military authorities took hold. At the heart of the struggle is conflict over ownership of the land. More than 150,000 largely illiterate farmers whose families for the past three generations had been ploughing state land under a tenancy agreement took on the Pakistani military, which currently controls this land, with the slogan *Maliki ya Mout* (ownership or death). The movement has caught the attention of domestic as well as international media and human rights groups. Its existence has perplexed everyone because the movement sets one of the weakest groups in Pakistani society—tenant farmers—against the most powerful institution in the country—the Pakistani armed forces. It has also been a surprise because it is situated in southern Punjab, a region where the people are renowned in public folklore for their passive acceptance of those in power.

The land that is the basis of this dispute has a long history. Canal-irrigated agriculture was introduced under the British Raj, which, along with the promise that ownership rights would be granted to those who made the land arable, motivated many settlers of eastern Punjab to move to western Punjab. This promise was never kept, however, because the cultivated land, which included areas of Okara, Sahiwal, Khanewal, and Sargodha, turned out to be the most fertile land in the region. In 1913 the government of Punjab, the legal owner of the land, leased parts of the land, especially in Okara district, to the British Indian Army for cultivation under a twenty-year lease agreement. The military, however, retained hold of the land even after the expiration of the lease. The arrangement was handed down to the Pakistani state; the military thus retained possession of the land and the government of Punjab continued to be its legal owner.

The relationship between the military and the tenant farmers tilling the land was governed from the start under the Punjab Tenancy Act of 1887. This act divides tenants into two categories: *occupancy tenants*, who have a statutory right to occupy the land, and *simple tenants*, who occupy the land on the basis of a contract with their landlord. A simple tenant can be evicted from the land when his contract with his landlord expires or for other reasons set out in the Tenancy Act. Occupancy tenants and farmers can be evicted only by court decree. At the Okara Military Farms, where the Anjuman Mazareen-i-Punjab movement started, the estimated population of 150,000 tenants had worked there as occupancy tenants for three generations. In return for this land security, the tenants had been giving more than 50 percent of their annual harvest to the management of these farms.

This generations-old relationship became adversarial, however, when in early 2000 the management rolled out a plan to replace the tenancy system with a rent arrangement. The new system gave the tenants the freedom to grow what they wanted rather than take dictation from management as they had been doing. In return, however, it took away their tenancy rights. Now the tenants could be evicted from the land if management so desired. Within a month of this announcement, the Anjuman Mazareen-i-Okara arose among the tenants to resist this move. It then expanded across Punjab and took the title Anjuman

Mazareen-i-Punjab. The tenants of Okara Military Farms claim that they are the lawful and rightful tenants of the land and are governed by the Punjab Tenancy Act of 1887. The military maintains that they are just lessees. If the military stance is correct, there ought to be a lease agreement between the military farm authorities and the tenants. Reports from independent human rights groups, however, maintain that no such lease agreement exists.

This resistance has by no means been costless for the tenant farmers. Their refusal to sign documents enforcing the change in contract resulted in heavy state oppression. The farm's management called in the military rangers, who initially barred the tenants from carrying out their daily activities, such as collecting wood, and later resorted to aggression.[1] The relationship between the two sides kept deteriorating. On January 9, 2002, the first death of the movement took place: a tenant injured when the military rangers fired at a group of tenants succumbed to his injuries. The death of another tenant followed on May 20, 2002. Many other organs of the state machinery were also used to harass the tenants. Numerous court cases were filed against the tenants, particularly against the leadership of the Anjuman. The key leaders were also exposed to torture in custody. Against this rising pressure, the movement almost broke down after a major attack by the rangers on August 18, 2002, which resulted in the death of one more tenant and left two tenants permanently disabled. The movement regained its momentum, however, within the next few weeks, although another tenant did lose his life during protests on May 3, 2003. Since the spring of 2004, the movement has held strong; the tenants do not pay any share of their harvest to the farm authorities, and the latter refrain from using force.

The success of this movement raises multiple questions. What made the military halt its aggression? What enabled this illiterate and socially and politically disenfranchised group to resist the most resourceful organ of the state? What motivated these tenants to cooperate in order to resist the military? How did the community organize itself to work toward this end? That is, were there distinct groups of initiators and joiners among the tenants? If so, then what were the characteristics of the initiators? As an outside group of initiators, did the PRM play an important role in mobilizing the tenants as joiners in this movement? If so, then why was there room for outside help among the local

1. Nationally, military farms fall under the jurisdiction of Pakistan's Federal Ministry of Defense and, hence, the army's General Headquarters (GHQ) in Rawalpindi. The Okara Military Farms are managed on behalf of the army by the Remount Veterinary and Farms Corps and the Army Welfare Trust. It is this joint management team, in consultation with the GHQ, that has been making decisions about how to deal with the resistance from local tenants.

initiators? Finally, were other groups of initiators competing with the PRM to support the movement? If so, then how did the community respond to them and what differentiated the PRM from the rest? Extensive interaction was undertaken with the tenant farmers and with PRM members to explore the answers to these questions.

## Mobilization of the Tenants: The Role of Local Initiators

To the onlooker, the Anjuman Mazareen-i-Punjab is a movement that has steadily expanded from an unknown collection of a hundred farmers on Okara Military Farms to a provincewide phenomenon. It has been prominently covered in the national media and occasionally in the international press. Were all the individuals who constitute this community of tenants across the diverse villages of Punjab wholly convinced from the beginning of the need for resistance? And did they all play an equally important role in the rise of the Anjuman? Close examination shows that this was not the case. In the absence of a small group of tenants from the Okara Military Farms who mobilized the broader community to resist the proposed change in their ownership status, there would not have been such a movement.

Unable to read and write and possessing limited understanding of legal acts, the majority of the farmers initially welcomed the rent system; they did not realize the legal consequences of the new contract for their tenancy rights. When the farm's management promised them, in exchange for a fixed rent, the freedom to grow the crops of their choice without having to share the produce with the management, the majority of tenants thought it was a good deal. Just a handful of tenants realized the implications. It was this small group of individuals, who were slightly educated or had worked in the cities for some time and had some awareness of the legal consequences of this change, who issued the initial call to resist it. It was this group that initiated and led the movement.

Thus, from the beginning of this movement we see a distinct group of initiators. However, the existence of initiators within a community does not necessarily mean they will be able to mobilize joiners. The initiators of the Anjuman Mazareen-i-Okara initially found it difficult to do so. In the words of Mehr, the leader of the Anjuman Mazareen-i-Punjab, "On 29 June 2000, in the director general's *Darbar* [court], the farm authorities announced the implementation of the contract system. A group of us realized its negative consequences and explained them to the other community members. We gave a call to the community members to come to the *chowk* [corner] to protest against the implementation of this system, but no one came."

What, then, helped move the community away from this apathy? This chapter shows that this movement followed many of the design principles that Ostrom (1990) noted are important in mobilizing and sustaining collective action. However, it also illustrates that the role of the initiators, and their apparently self-sacrificing behavior, is a critical factor in sustaining collective action. Material sacrifice on the part of the initiators of other-regarding groups in facilitating collective action—witnessed in the cases analyzed in the previous chapter—was an equally critical factor in initiating and sustaining cooperation among the tenants.

## Pushed to the Limit

Analysis of the sequence of events and of interviews with the tenant farmers and local initiators shows that the threat of losing the land was not enough motivation; it was the actual experience of losing it that convinced the tenants to join the initiators in resisting the proposed system change. Within ten days of initiating the new plan, the farm authorities notified the tenants occupying the land around one of its dairies to vacate ten acres of that land. It was this command that made the tenants realize that their very right to the land was at stake and there was no option but to resist the new rent system. In Mehr's words, "After no response from the community despite repeated calls, we stopped attempting to mobilize the tenants. But people panicked when the army took over the land. They then came to us themselves. We started with corner meetings in each village and involved older people in whom community members had trust. This time there was a great response from the tenants due to the ten acres taken away."

Following these Okara village meetings, members from across the villages were called to attend a big meeting, where the Anjuman Mazareen-i-Okara was launched. An informal, unregistered body of local farmers, its sole objective was to prevent the farm's management from changing the tenancy system to a rent system. Although at this point most of the community members had joined the movement, the majority doubted the Anjuman's ability to resist management. The skewed power distribution between the tenants and the Pakistani armed forces was visible to everyone. How this uncertain gathering of a hundred farmers expanded to become an aggressive provincewide movement—the Anjuman Mazareen-i-Punjab—constitutes an interesting case for analysis. Were the local initiators able to advance the cause of the Anjuman Mazareen-i-Punjab and lead it to its success entirely on their own?

Newspaper records and historical accounts of the movement show that the answer is no. Interviews with the current leadership of the Anjuman, corroborated by observations made during field visits, uphold this assertion. Although the local initiators clearly took pride in the success of their movement and attributed it to their own efforts, even their accounts highlight that on their own they were having great difficulty making their voices heard. To begin with, their access to the media—which eventually played a critical role in spreading awareness of the movement—was very limited, and their access to foreign embassies and political parties—both of which have played an important role in increasing pressure on the military to refrain from aggression—was almost nonexistent. While narrating the problems they confronted in the initial days of the movement, the local initiators frequently commented on the resistance they faced from the local media. Reluctant to strain their relationship with the military, the local media outlets refused to give extensive coverage to the movement. Attempts to win support from the national media bore equally limited success.

Yet ultimately the success of the movement rested in its ability to mobilize support among the media, the foreign embassies, the national political parties, and international and national human rights groups. Eventually, due to rising support for this movement from embassies and international human rights groups, the military government's fear of negative publicity in the West halted the oppression. An analysis of the factors that enabled local initiators to develop this support despite initial failures makes the role of outside intervention in strengthening this movement very clear.

During the field visits, I personally witnessed the limitations of the local initiators in dealing with international media and embassies. For instance, during one of the meetings, the key local initiator mentioned in passing to the other members that a British journalist recently sent by the PRM had called to ask permission to release a story about the movement. This local initiator, as well as most of the members present at the meeting, had met the journalist, but none of them remembered his name or the organization he represented, even though the strength of the movement depended on cultivating these links. Even the most educated of the local initiators had very limited English language skills. Similarly, even the wealthiest of the tenants had no access to local or national political elites.

The need for support from an external body in strengthening the local struggle was thus very clear. The PRM was one organization among others that could have played that part, but its ability had to be proved rather than assumed. By 2002 many national and international NGOs were visiting the Anjuman Mazareen-i-Punjab and issuing media statements in its defense. What finally established the unique role of PRM in this movement? The answer to this question lies both in what the community had to say and in my own observations of the interactions among the community, the movement's local leadership, and the PRM.

One measure of the PRM's role in the movement is the fact that many NGOs and media groups in Pakistani society associated PRM with the tenant farmers' movement. As mentioned in Chapter 3, Akhtar Sheikh, the driving force behind PRM, was invited to represent the movement on TV talk shows, and the whole PRM team had been quite visible in the media coverage of the movement. A major report on the movement published by Human Rights Watch (2004) extended special thanks to Akhtar Sheikh for his assistance in studying the tension between the military and the tenants.

Conversations with community members also indicated that there was a close relationship between the tenants and the core members of the PRM. When they realized that I had come from Islamabad, most community members immediately asked me about four of the core members of the PRM team who had been active in the movement. In contrast, the community members did not remember the names of any of the NGOs that had visited them or what they had done to support the tenant farmers' movement. The only other outside body that came up during our discussions was the Labour Party.

The community members were very clear about the PRM's contribution to the tenants' struggle. Many of them explained that the PRM team had mobilized the community with their ideologically charged speeches. They also repeatedly acknowledged that PRM members had actually fought alongside the community members when military rangers launched an aggressive assault. Some tenants told how they once had to plan a dramatic escape for two of the PRM members in the middle of the night due to rising pressure from the rangers to hand them over. Also, during chance visits to the PRM office in Islamabad, I twice ended up meeting senior members of the Anjuman—one of them the president of the movement himself. The purpose of both the senior members' visits had been to plan future strategies, because after a lull of a few months, the military was expected to increase the pressure once again, at the time of the forthcoming harvest. All of these details reveal an intense relationship between the PRM and the tenants. None of the other NGOs that had engaged with the movement could claim anything close to this association.

One final indication of the PRM's heavy influence over the struggle was the conscious refusal of the tenants to take international development aid to support the movement. This was a major decision. Initially a core group of local initiators had accepted aid from an international NGO. The tenants, however, later returned the money. The decision to steer clear of any foreign aid, even when it has come through development organizations, has played a key role in sustaining the movement in its current form. As mentioned by one of the key leaders of the Anjuman, this policy was a direct outcome of the PRM's intervention.

What was the impact of international development aid on the tenant farmers' movement? And why did the tenants agree with the PRM to return the money and stay away from international aid? These questions are critical to this book, but to retain the clarity of this chapter's analysis, they will be discussed in Chapter 6. This chapter remains concerned with understanding the processes through which the tenants made the decision to follow the PRM rather than another of the various external groups that offered support to their movement. Prior to addressing this question, however, another question demands attention: Why was there a need for outsiders to strengthen this movement that had been started by local initiators?

## The Role of Outside Initiators

The reason there was a clear role for outside initiators in the tenant farmers' movement, despite the presence of a group of local initiators, is that on their own the tenants did not have the resources to make their voices heard. Although the local initiators were slightly more aware than the rest of the tenants of the implications of the changed contract offered by the armed forces, in resisting this change they too were crippled by the same limitations. These limitations can be grouped into two distinct categories: (1) lack of exposure to the working of the armed forces and capacity to design an effective strategy to run the movement, and (2) lack of access to socioeconomic and political means to implement a strategy. Close study of the Anjuman and its relationship with the PRM reveals that although education, exposure to international political debates, and ideological training are critical in designing a strategy for a movement, influential social networks are essential for implementing the strategy.

Analysis of the factors that created the need for the PRM's involvement in the movement shows that formal schooling, especially a university education, plays a key role in strengthening grassroots movements. During the interviews and discussions, the tenants repeatedly highlighted the importance of education in running their movement; and while I was in the field I often heard tenants say that what differentiated the local initiators from the local joiners was a formal education, because it indicated to community members that these individuals knew the ways of the world. They often referred to the education qualifications of the main local initiator, who holds a bachelor of science degree from the University of Agriculture, Faisalabad. In a "league table" of universities in Pakistan, this university would be ranked relatively low, but for uneducated farmers, a degree from there was a big achievement. Formal education thus generated confidence among the tenants in the capabilities of their local initiators; however, at the same time, their own lack of education diminished their confidence in their own capabilities. Both the male and the female tenants argued that without this core group of educated members they would not have been able to build the movement. They highlighted that innumerable human capabilities are contingent on education: the ability to approach the media and government officials and to acquire knowledge about the legal issues involved, and above all the confidence to deal with the world outside the village community. As one of the older farmers said, "We have been used to putting our thumb impressions on the paper without being able to read what is written. We cannot challenge the authorities." Access to education was thus critical not only for dealing with the social structures and institutions outside their own villages, but also for acquiring knowledge about their legal rights.

Education and the exposure it facilitates was also the key to the movement's need for outside initiators. The sophisticated formal qualifications of some of the PRM members, such as their fluency in English, their familiarity with the Internet and other modern communication technologies, and their ability to understand complex legal issues and produce press releases on short notice were critical to the design and implementation of the movement. The importance of educated individuals in movements like this is also highlighted by Akhtar's importance to the core PRM team. As one of the co-initiators of the PRM said, "We cannot do the work that Akhtar does. He can speak in English, write e-mails, use the computer. He can talk to the embassies." In a country where English is a sign of status and affluence, formal education is associated with the ability to speak English well. The outside initiators' command of the English language, especially Akhtar's foreign accent, which he had acquired while growing up in the United States, thus played an important role in strengthening the movement. The local initiators, with their limited English, found it very difficult to access those in power in the media, the international embassies, and the human rights groups. Akhtar himself jokingly explained that his foreign accent is a big asset. Many times it had enabled him to get tenants released from the police station by making a simple phone call and pretending to be from a foreign embassy.

Another reason that outside initiators were necessary in shaping this movement was their access to more influential social networks than the community had on its own. The tenants lacked not only education but also political af-filiation and the economic means to connect to influential social groups. Even those local initiators who were educated had gone to non-elite state schools and universities, which did not help them develop such networks. This lack of connections at least partially explains the problems these local initiators faced in convincing the local and national media to cover the movement. In contrast, the relatively elite family background of two of the PRM's core members en-abled them to bring contacts to the table who were economically, socially, and politically influential. These social networks greatly contributed to the develop-ment of the tenant farmers' movement.

So did the PRM members' previous experiences of activism, which made their access to members of the political parties relatively easy. They either al-ready had contacts within the main political parties or knew how to cultivate them in parties with whom they had no prior interaction. If a PRM member did not personally know a particular politician or authority, someone in his or her social circle did. Living and working in Islamabad, the capital of Pakistan, and having a dense network of family and friends in influential positions en-sured easy access to the media and to staff in the diplomatic missions. It also dramatically increased the organization's fundraising potential, because there were more wealthy individuals with money to spare in the social networks of PRM members than in those of the tenants. This dramatic expansion of social network access was thus critical in making space in the tenant farmers' move-ment for a body of outside initiators.

Another critical factor in creating a role for outside initiators in grassroots movements is exposure to international scenarios and other domestic strug-gles, coupled with training in political activism. Both of these issues were quite critical to the success of the PRM. As mentioned earlier, one of its members who played a key role in the tenant farmers' movement was trained in the 1970s in the literary circles of the now defunct Communist Party of Pakistan. He was also later sent to Russia to study political activism. His ideologically charged speeches played a key role in mobilizing the tenants and sustaining their mo-mentum, and his prior experience of activism helped shape the movement's strategy. These speeches were particularly important in sustaining the move-ment after the initial attack in August 2002 by military rangers in which two tenants succumbed to the rangers' bullets. At the same time, PRM members were also more aware of the complexities of sustaining these struggles because of their prior involvement in other domestic struggles and their exposure to both international political movements and grassroots movements in other countries. Their knowledge of these movements and of the strategies that were used to advance their struggles was very helpful in designing the strategy for the tenant farmers' movement, and sharing their knowledge of the success of these other movements was important in building the morale of the tenants.

The final reason that outside initiators are important in grassroots movements is the need within such movements for external encouragement. The word of an outside party that does not have any stake in the movement is more encouraging to the affected community's members than the reassurances given by the local initiators. The outsiders' words about the legitimacy of the claims being made and their assessment of the possibility of the movement's success carry more credibility than the encouragements of local initiators. This issue came up in many of my discussions with tenants but was particularly pointed out to me by one of the female tenants while she tried to explain to me the role of the PRM in the movement and the reasons the community responded to it—which brings us to the key question of this chapter: How do individuals make decisions about whether or not to follow outside initiators?

## Creating Demand for Outside Initiators

The Anjuman Mazareen-i-Punjab case makes clear that the fact that an outside group of initiators would be helpful does not automatically translate into local initiators and joiners choosing to follow just any group of outside initiators. As the movement gained media attention, an increasing number of NGOs tried to build alliances with it. Many made media statements emphasizing the need to protect the interests of the tenants. Some also offered international development aid. As was noted earlier, the local initiators did accept one such offer of international aid, from Action Aid Pakistan. The community, however, soon decided to return the money. Neither ActionAid nor any of the other NGOs were able to develop a long-term relationship with the movement.

On what basis did the tenants decide to join PRM rather than the other NGOs? Did they make a conscious effort to assess the potential initiators, or did they just blindly trust anyone claiming to work for the tenants' interests? The analysis of this case highlights that joiners are very suspicious of anyone who claims to work for their cause without having anything to gain from it. They expect all individuals to work for their own material interests. They therefore join groups whose leaders help reduce the costs of information gathering and monitoring by giving signals that demonstrate their commitment and efficiency, as witnessed in the other-regarding groups analyzed in the previous chapter.

From talking to the joiners—the tenants in this case—it was clear that for them the motivation of the local initiators for undertaking this work remained a constant concern. They repeatedly mentioned that they were conscious that those who lead often have either monetary or political motives. They also mentioned being fully aware that leaders, especially local ones, often build a struggle only to enhance their bargaining power with the authorities, and these joiners were of the view that the local leaders let their communities down by negotiating personal contracts with the authorities when the struggle is at its peak. They were similarly suspicious of all outside initiators who claimed to be working for them for no benefit of their own. "Why would anyone work for something with no interest of their own? There is always some monetary or political motive involved," said one of the senior tenants who is also a member of one of the local committees of the Anjuman. Despite expressing appreciation for the PRM's work in strengthening the movement, he still questioned the motives of some of its core members: "We know that Akhtar comes from a well-off family so maybe he does not need money, but Shahid [another core member of the team] has no regular income; why would he work with us unless he has taken some money for it?" Joiners, therefore, are very conscious of and watchful for any ulterior motives that could possibly be driving the initiators of their movement; and clear signs of material sacrifice and efficiency on the part of initiators are critical for mobilizing joiners.

## Monitoring Efficiency

Interviews with the tenants and analysis of the sequence of events leading to the rise of this movement show that joiners judge initiators' ability to meet their stated goals in a number of ways, including by referring to their past experience. By the time the PRM approached the Anjuman Mazareen-i-Okara, the PRM had already been involved in a few other movements across the country. The most prominent of these was the Katchi Abadi Movement, which had succeeded in extracting important concessions from the state. The local initiators of the Anjuman Mazareen-i-Okara were aware of this success and for this reason they took seriously the PRM members who first approached them.

An important component of the PRM's work strategy was to maintain a collection of clippings of the media coverage of all its rallies and press statements. In addition to serving as a record of the group's activities, these press clippings become an important mobilization tool. Each new community that the PRM approached got to see this evidence of the PRM's successes. One of the PRM's members explained to me that these clippings served a dual purpose: "One, they provide proof of PRM's prior engagements and success, which makes the communities feel that they should engage with us. Two, they act as a mobilization tool, as they show the communities that they are not the only victims." The realization that they are not alone and that other oppressed communities have been able to defend their rights is very empowering for the communities involved in such struggles. Copies of *Ashiyana* ("Home"), a one-page weekly newsletter produced by the PRM that contains all of the media reports of the PRM's activities in a given week, were circulated among the tenants when the PRM first established contact with them. During the early days of their interaction, when proposing strategies for action, PRM members referred repeatedly to the success of the same strategies in the slum dwellers' movement. Thus the previous successes of the PRM acted for the joiners as a key measure of the efficiency of the PRM's members.

Joiners also based their decision to join a movement on visible signs of the competence of the individual initiators. The high qualifications of the PRM's members, including the fluent English of some of them; their knowledge of the Internet, computers, and international politics; their capacity to approach embassies and the international and national press; plus their ability to mobilize the public were not lost on either the local initiators or the tenants in general. As discussed earlier, the tenants were also very clear about their need for educated people to strengthen the movement. They were quick to identify these characteristics in the PRM's members.

Looking at the relationship between the tenants and the PRM's members it is also clear that development of a strong association between the two groups has been a gradual process. What the tenants were willing to sacrifice at the suggestion of the initiators at the end of six months they were not willing to let go of in the first month. The joiners thus increased their own stakes in the struggle and showed their willingness to take greater risks, but only when they saw the success of less risky options suggested by the outside initiators. The success of each step of the proposed strategy was critical in getting the joiners to contemplate following the next suggestion. Many tenants explained to me that the success of individual moves and their coverage in the newspapers were discussed the next day with great pride among the members and motivated them to go one step further in their struggle. This case thus shows that winning the confidence of joiners is a gradual process, because joiners constantly try to evaluate the value of initiators' guidance, and they take personal risks only in proportion to the confidence they have in the success of the initiator's strategy.

## Monitoring Commitment

Just as joiners make conscious, rational calculations to judge the efficacy of initiators, they also make equally rational calculations to monitor initiators' motivation. As mentioned earlier, the motivation of the initiators of the tenant farmers movement was a constant concern for the movement's joiners. The tenants were suspicious that the initiators might have hidden ulterior motives for undertaking the work. Also, despite accepting the PRM's intervention, some of the local initiators remained suspicious of the motives of the PRM's members. How then do joiners monitor the motivation of initiators? The answer lies in two important characteristics of outside initiators: material self-sacrifice and deep personal involvement.

The tenants had no reliable means to check whether the outside initiators were gaining monetarily by getting involved with their movement. Nonetheless, their means of gauging these initiators' motivation was to observe the willingness of the PRM's members to stand alongside the tenant communities in the face of all their challenges. In response to my questions about their ability to mobilize joiners, PRM members emphasized that they were with the tenants in all their protests and rallies. They highlighted that they were in the front rows even when the army rangers opened fire. Their willingness to put their own lives in danger was thus critical to establishing their credibility among the joiners. Also, given the privileged background of some of the initiators, just their decision to live among the tenants for weeks at a time was a sacrifice. It was easy to judge during the fieldwork that for some of the PRM initiators the decision to live within the tenants' communities was not an easy one. Comfortable beds with fresh linens were replaced by simple *charpais* with used bed sheets; simple toilets with no running water replaced marble-floor bathrooms; and gourmet food was replaced by simple village cooking. Although this sacrifice was not openly acknowledged by the tenants, they did realize and appreciate it.

The issue of material sacrifice came up repeatedly in discussions with the tenants about the local leadership. They kept referring to the commitment of the key local initiator by telling me that he would inherit only two acres of land after the distribution of his family's holdings among his siblings and cousins. This was, for them, an indicator that this initiator was not involved in the movement purely for monetary gain. They also repeatedly mentioned that with his qualifications he could easily get a good job in the city, but he had chosen to work for the movement in order to benefit the tenant community. Such sacrifice on the part of local initiators was important to joiners because it was the measure of the initiators' motivation and commitment to the cause. Clearly the tenants were making decisions about the motivation of both outside and local initiators on the basis of their calculation of how materially motivated individuals would behave. Self-sacrifice on the part of the initiators was thus the only means for the joiners to judge the sincerity of the initiators' claims. Conviction about the sincerity of the motivation of the initiator was very important in turning a tenant into a joiner.

Constant contact and the resulting social relationships between the PRM members and the tenants were the other critical means for the joiners to measure the motivation of the outside initiators. PRM members stayed in the homes of tenants, and representatives of the Anjuman stayed in the homes of PRM members when they went to Islamabad for rallies. Deep personal friendships were formed in the process. When I was among the tenants it was easy to see that some of the young girls had developed personal friendships with the female members of the PRM. Similarly, the male tenants expressed that they had formed close affiliations with some of the male members of the PRM. One of the senior members said, "Akhtar is our *yaar* [very close friend]; we won't let him go." There was a wedding in one of the villages one weekend that I was there. The girls from the villages were keenly waiting for some of the PRM members, who had been invited, to turn up. In the words of one of the PRM members, "After some time, with most people we form personal relationships. They come and stay at our homes; we go and stay at their place. When we meet we do not have to talk about the movement all the time. We talk about them, their personal issues, and their families. We have deeper dealings."

There was also regular contact between PRM members and the local leadership. PRM members made regular phone calls to the local initiators, even when there was a lull in the farm management's activity. PRM members argued that this frequent contact with the tenant communities was critical to building and sustaining the movement. Similarly, the Anjuman's leaders regularly updated the PRM members, and every few weeks they visited the PRM's Islamabad office for a few days to chalk out future work strategies and visit political parties and media outlets. Twice I met unexpectedly with the Anjuman's members during my chance visits to the PRM office.

What we see, then, is that just like the joiners of other-regarding groups, whose decision-making processes were analyzed in the previous chapter, the joiners of self-regarding groups also base their decision to cooperate with an initiator on calculated reasoning about the initiator's efficiency and motivation. However, we also see that due to their personal stakes in the success of the movement, the joiners of self-regarding groups will at times cooperate even if they know that the initiator is making a personal gain out of their cause—although this holds true only while the initiator demands no major contributions to the cause from the joiners. Once the initiator does demand major contributions—whether in time, money, or risk—the joiners base their decision to cooperate on what they calculate to be the likely success of the initiator's strategy, as well as on their assessment of the sincerity of the initiator's motivation.

This chapter's empirically driven analysis bears striking similarities to some of the conclusions of Samuel Popkin (1979) in his famous debates with James Scott (1976) about the character of peasant protest and society in Southeast Asia. In *The Rational Peasant*, Popkin (1979) argues that when a peasant makes his personal cost-benefit calculations about the returns expected on his own inputs to the collective resistance, he is making subjective estimates of the credibility and capability of the organizer, "the political entrepreneur" (259), to deliver. Popkin argues that in order to get contributions from the peasants, the leader must use terms and symbols that his targets understand, he should be able to design the struggle in a way that it yields immediate payoffs, and he must denounce material wealth. Popkin maintains (261):

> It can be argued that a major factor in the credibility of both the Communist and religious movements over the century, in contrast to the failed bourgeois organizations, was the self-abnegation of the leadership. The self-denial of Communist organizers, the celibacy of missionary priests, the scorn of conspicuous consumption by Hoa Hao organizers, were striking demonstrations to peasants that these men were less interested in self-aggrandizement than were the visibly less self-denying organizers from other groups. Thus, another way to raise the peasant's subjective estimate of the credibility and capability of an entrepreneur is to increase the probability that he is actually going to use the resources for common rather than selfish purposes.

This chapter's findings are completely in line with this analysis. What remains is for us to analyze the factors that help sustain a movement.

## Factors That Helped Sustain the Tenant Farmers' Movement

This study shows that the explicit economic gains acquired through resistance make it easier to sustain a movement. Economic incentives played a very visible role in sustaining the Anjuman Mazareen-i-Punjab. Ever since the start of direct confrontation between the military rangers and the tenants, the community's members have been keeping the entire harvest rather than following the traditional practice of giving more than half of it to the farm's management.

This direct economic gain has been a key factor in sustaining the movement despite rising pressure from the military. By the time I started my fieldwork, the community had already been reaping this benefit for two years. The tenants themselves acknowledged that these economics benefits were very important in boosting the morale of the people. As one of the tenants in the community, said, "We won't give up now. We all know that we have been eating for the last two years now due to this movement." When I shared the findings of this research with PRM members, Akhtar Sheikh also highlighted the importance of economic gains in building and sustaining a movement. He said that in his experience with various movements across the country, he has seen that those in which members experienced immediate economic gains were more resilient than those where members did not.

Another factor that seems to have helped build and sustain the tenants' movement is the relative lack of inequality of land ownership among the farmers. Almost all of the tenants of the Okara Military Farms have small farms. The maximum land holding per family is six acres. For this reason there was no major clash of interests within the community that could lead to internal conflict. All of the participants expected similar gains from the movement. As some of the community members mentioned, the relatively equal distribution of land ensured that no one feared that one or two big landowners were going to gain more than the rest of the farmers from the success of the movement. The feeling that others will gain much more from a resistance than oneself can have a negative impact on commitment to contribute to a cause.

This study of the Anjuman Mazareen-i-Punjab also shows that a community's awareness of the legal standing of its demand further strengthens its resolve to fight. Only toward the end of the first year of the struggle did the tenants realize that the land they were farming did not legally belong to the military but was still owned by the government of Punjab. Consultation with legal experts who reassured the local initiators and tenants that their claim was legitimate did much to help raise the morale of the community. Even small achievements in making their voices heard are important in strengthening a movement. For the members of the Anjuman, such things as media coverage of their rallies or a visit from a foreign dignitary helped raise tenants' morale. They felt that if they had come this far, they could go even further.

This study also shows that at some point in the movement, the community's losses, rather than being a deterrent, collectively become a source of strength. During one of my first conversations with one of the female hosts I was told, "Once we had seen death of our members, the fear was over." During the interviews the tenants kept saying that they had seen the worst. They kept saying they had lived through everything they had feared the most at the outset of the movement. They felt that for this reason they could now cope with anything. "People have been jailed for months. All kinds of violent tactics have been used during their interrogation. Four people have also been killed. Due to the oppression of the military we have gotten stronger," said a very determined member of the Anjuman.

This study also demonstrates that any social movement brings with it many unintentional changes to the social structure and leads to new institutional rules of social organization. There were, for example, two significant changes in the social structure of the tenants' village communities: changes in gender roles and a deepening of social relations both within and across the villages. The spread of the movement dramatically changed the relationship between the genders within the community. Before the movement started there was strict gender segregation. Female tenants told stories of how in the past it was not easy to get permission from the male members of their households to visit even female friends; now these women are active members and officeholders of the Anjuman. They participate in the group's planning meetings and confidently greet their menfolk on the street. Furthermore, the men openly attribute the success of the movement to the resilience of their womenfolk.

Part of this new recognition of women stems from their participation in the movement's demonstrations and rallies. This participation was an outcome of necessity as well as choice. It became a necessity when the military took many of the local initiators into custody. This action forced the women to come out to protest. It became a matter of conscious choice when in the face of rising aggression from the military the PRM members suggested that women should lead the protests because they are less likely to be physically assaulted. This combination of factors provided women the opportunity to show their strength to their menfolk. The men in turn learned to respect them for it. Now, not only do the men openly appreciate the contributions made by the women, but the women themselves have also become very conscious of their power.

The other outcome of the movement has been the deepening of social ties among tenants within and across the villages. The Anjuman has a very detailed organizational structure. Each village has its own committee. The village committees report to a central committee. Interaction between the tenants and the committee members plus interaction between committee members from different villages has enhanced social relations and obligations manifold. The officeholders of the Anjuman, especially the top leadership, are invited to all the weddings in the area. They feel it is critical to respond to these social calls in order to sustain the momentum of the movement. While I was in the field, Mehr, the primary local initiator, was constantly on the move. He had to travel from one village to another to record his presence at the various occasions to which he had been invited. During the course of one day he had to participate in a wedding, join a funeral, accompany me to one of the village meetings, and settle a dispute between two tenants. This networking was also critical to ensuring that any feuds between the tenants stay subdued. During the discussions Mehr mentioned that when the external threat was slightly reduced, the internal feuds among the tenants increased. He explained that it is important for him to fulfil his social obligations because doing so enables him to act as a mediator in settling these feuds.

## Conclusion

The analysis of the Anjuman Mazareen-i-Punjab presented in this chapter supports many of the factors identified by Ostrom (1990), in particular the often incremental self-transforming nature of institutional change, which is critical to the rise of collective action. It is clear that over time the tenant farmers developed a sense of responsibility to the collective that they did not have in the beginning, because they came to know that some had died for the cause and others had suffered much torture in prison for it. Through this process a sense of obligation to the group developed that was not there at the outset and that became an internal check on free-riding. Neither the tenants nor the initiators of the movement said their ethnic, religious, or political identity affected either the initiation or cohesion of the movement. Both Muslim and Christian tenants were involved in the struggle. Also, until the start of the movement the tenants were completely nonpolitical. This is evident from the fact that they had great difficulty accessing the members of the national or provincial assemblies that represented their constituencies. Similarly, the PRM members came from various ethnic and political backgrounds and did not share any strong collective identity. With the success of the movement, the tenants developed a sense of identity they had never had before. Blunt statements by the president of the Anjuman on one of the TV talk shows in which he participated were very important for raising the morale of the tenants. His harsh critique of the military's spokesman raised the tenants' image of themselves. The fact that as a group they were publicly challenging powers they had never dared challenge before was in itself an empowering thought. Their collective identity became more important for the tenants as the movement progressed, although this identity was a product of the success of the movement rather than the cause of it. Once this identity developed, it did contribute to sustaining the morale of the movement. Thus the success of the movement and its collective identity became mutually reinforcing.

The dense social networks resulting from these repeat interactions also made free-riding very costly socially. The formal organization of subcommittees within each village made the individual contributions of all the tenants very noticeable. The members of each committee visited all of the residents of their village in their homes. They collected contributions from all residents for the movement's activities. These contributions were meticulously recorded. All of this direct contact made it very difficult for individual members of the movement to shirk their contributions. This effect supports Olson's (1971) argument that the free-rider problem is overcome by organizing a movement's members into relatively small multitier units that make possible direct contact with all members and build close social networks. In addition, the severity of the problem being addressed by the movement also reduces the desire of individuals to free-ride. For the tenants, the failure of their struggle would mean an utter collapse of their economic as well as social order. Both the fear of losing everything and the immediate economic benefits of the struggle played a role in making free-riding less attractive to the tenants. The cost of failure was too high.

This case also clearly demonstrates that in order to generate and sustain collective action among a movement's joiners, the initiators have to provide proof of their efficiency as well as their commitment. The tenants constantly monitored the initiators on both of these fronts and increased their contributions to the collective action only after the initiators demonstrated their efficiency and commitment. Proof of efficiency and commitment involves practical demonstration of material sacrifice on the part of the initiators, which is the only means the joiners have to judge the initiators' motivation. To be on call whenever the community needs you, to live for weeks with them, to stand by them during demonstrations and face bullets—all of this constitutes material sacrifice on the part of initiators.

The issue not addressed in this chapter is this movement's experience with other NGOs. Why did the tenants decide to return the international aid that a group of local initiators had taken? Did international aid affect cooperation between the local initiators and the tenants? This chapter also did not fully analyze why community members did not join other NGOs. Did it have something to do with those NGOs' inability to take up radical causes that explicitly confront the state? Also, could paid NGO professionals rationally engage with the community in the way the ideologically charged volunteer workers of the PRM did? These questions are the focus of Chapter 6. Meanwhile, given the importance placed on the behavior of the leaders in mobilizing and sustaining collective action in both self-regarding and other-regarding groups, Chapter 5 presents the results of two nationwide surveys that were used to test the emerging hypothesis that aid breaks down cooperation within civil society groups because it offers incentives that encourage the leaders of these groups to pursue their own material interest, which negatively impacts their performance and their ability to mobilize members.

# 5 Does Aid Break Down Cooperation?

*Although there are various additional factors which affect the creation and destruction of social capital, only one broad class of these is especially important. This is the class of factors which make persons less dependent on one another. . . . When, because of affluence, government aid, or some other factor, persons need each other less, less social capital is generated.*

**James Coleman, *Foundations of Social Theory*, 1990, 321**

*We can celebrate the civic-mindedness of wealthy individuals and families who give so much, yet at the same time realize that their largesse brings attenuated democratic responsiveness—as the public fisc subsidizes ever more top-down civic funding, which in turn exempts increasing numbers of nonprofit and voluntary endeavours from the need to amass widespread popular support.*

**Theda Skocpol, *Diminished Democracy*, 2003, 231**

In the literature on cooperation and related notions of trust and social capital, the role of a force external to the parties directly involved in an action in either enhancing or breaking down cooperation has attracted much attention. Although some argue for the beneficial impact of the external force, others point to its destructive potential. For instance, seventeenth-century English philosopher Thomas Hobbes ([1651] 2010) found that an external force in the form of a Leviathan was necessary for bringing about civic order. Similarly, the extensive literature of economics on the problems of collective action—as captured in the Prisoner's Dilemma, Hardin's (1968) "Tragedy of the Commons," and

Olson's (1971) *Logic of Collective Action*—argues for third-party intervention through state imposition of private property rights as a solution to problems of cooperation. On the other hand, James Coleman (1990), the key theorist on social capital, argues that external intervention that makes people less dependent on each other breaks down social capital. He conceptualizes government aid in times of need as one such intervention that, by making people less dependent on each other, often reduces social capital. This chapter is concerned with the impact of one such outside force—international development aid—on cooperation between initiators and joiners. It addresses two interrelated questions: (1) Does international development aid restrict cooperation between initiators and joiners and break it down where it already exists? (2) Does this shift occur because international development aid provides material incentives that lead to material rather than ideal motivation in the initiator, thereby reducing the initiator's efficacy and efficiency?

## Methodology

To address these questions, a countrywide survey was designed that compared twenty voluntary groups whose initiators take international development aid, that is, NGOs, with twenty of those whose initiators rely mainly on contributions from local joiners, that is, VOs (see Map 5.1). The rationale for undertaking this comparative analysis was that controlling for the source of funding would help identify trends emerging in response to international development aid. If we find clear differences on three attributes (ability to mobilize joiners, motivation, and performance) in the two types of organizations under study—NGOs and VOs—then we can establish some correlation between these trends and the availability of international development aid.

Organizations selected within both categories served constituencies external to themselves, that is, they were other-regarding groups; the difference between the two, however, was their source of funding. Drawing on the literature on aid and NGOs reviewed in Chapter 1, the term *NGO* was used for those civil society organizations that choose to rely primarily on development aid to execute their program. This did not rule out the possibility that some of them might also mobilize funds domestically. The term *VO*, on the other hand, was used for organizations outside the donor-funded chain who choose to rely primarily on public donations and volunteers to advance their cause. Because these donors and volunteers are of different kinds (regular and irregular), the term *members* was used to cover all categories of supporters who facilitate the working of VOs.

**Map 5.1** Pakistan: Main Cities Covered in the Survey

The sample was developed on the basis of purposive and maximum variation sampling because it helped capture maximum variation within the NGOs and VOs in terms of scale, geographic distribution, and sector variation (see Table 5.1). This method made it possible to test whether the issues being studied are sensitive to these variations. It also meant that the NGOs selected could be funded by any kind of Western donor—multilateral, bilateral, or international NGO. The approach was to select the most prominent cases—determined by their scale of operation, annual budgets, funding levels, and reputation among donors, government officials, media, and research institutes. The logic was that if the best examples from the two types of organizations failed on a specific indicator, it would then be reasonable to suspect that the less established organizations stood even less of a chance of performing better. Carroll (1992) used a similar logic in his study by selecting thirty NGOs that were identified as "well-performing" in some respect by the concerned donor agency.

The organizations were identified in discussions with staff members of seventeen prominent international donor agencies operating in Pakistan, by consulting their annual funding reports, and by analyzing previous surveys and reports on NGOs in Pakistan (Aga Khan Development Network 2000; Leadership for Environment and Development 2002; Pakistan Centre for Philanthropy 2002; NGO Resource Centre 2003a, 2003b). Thus the survey included the most prominent and largest NGOs and VOs in the selected categories across Pakistan. A sample size of forty was selected to enable me to conduct all the interviews personally; this allowed consistency in data collection while allowing space for covering maximum variations within each category. It also enabled me to observe the locations, physical infrastructures, and organizational cultures of the surveyed groups.

A semi-structured questionnaire was administered to the chief executive of each organization. It was designed to measure three factors: the ability to mobilize members, the motivation of the leaders, and the organization's performance. A correlation was suspected among these factors given that the NGO literature noting lack of members also refers to high salaries of NGO leaders and questionable performance (Tvedt 1998; Henderson 2002). Where possible, brief discussions also took place with some of the staff members and volunteers. Organizations' publications, such as annual reports, introductory brochures, and weekly or monthly newsletters, were also analyzed. Taking cues from Putnam and Tocqueville, two indicators were developed to measure each organization's ability to mobilize collective action: the presence of local donors and the presence of volunteers who contribute freely of their time to advance the work of the organization for no material gain.

Economic anthropologist Jean Ensminger's (1992, 10) reasoning—"How else can we be confident with any degree of scientific certainty that an ideological commitment exists except in terms of what people are prepared to forgo for its service?"—helped to develop indicators to measure the motivation and ideological commitment of the leaders of the organizations. Measuring performance was more complex. The survey was designed to test organizational, not project, performance. It therefore examined the organization's ability to survive and stay focused on its stated vision rather than measuring specific outcomes of the projects implemented by the organization. Table 5.2 lists the key indicators developed to measure the three factors.

**Table 5.1** Sample Selection

| Selection Criteria | NGOs | VOs |
|---|---|---|
| Sector Variation | 9 education<br>5 health and sanitation<br>2 child rights<br>2 purely advocacy based<br>2 microcredit (6 others did microcredit in additon to their core programs)<br>100% claimed gender and governance as cross-cutting themes; 3 focused exclusively on women's rights | 9 education<br>7 health<br>2 legal aid<br>2 purely advocacy based |
| Scale[1] | 25% nationwide<br>30% provincewide<br>40% districtwide<br>5% CBOs | 30% nationwide<br>30% provincewide<br>35% districtwide<br>5% CBOs |
| Geographic[2] Distribution | 5 Punjab<br>5 Sindh<br>4 federal capital<br>5 Khyber Pakhtunkhwa<br>1 Baluchistan | 7 Punjab<br>8 Sindh<br>1 federal capital<br>3 Khyber Pakhtunkhwa<br>1 Baluchistan |

1. Nationwide organizations have a main office in the capital and regional offices in the provincial capitals; provincewide organizations have a main office in the provincial capital and field offices at various locations in the province; districtwide organizations focus on a district; CBOs operate within certain areas of a city or at the village level.

2. The sample represented the varying density of voluntary organizations across the four provinces in Pakistan; Sindh and Punjab have the largest concentrations of voluntary organizations and Baluchistan has the smallest (NGO Resource Centre 2003b).

**Table 5.2** Indicators

| Factors | Indicators | Subindicators |
|---|---|---|
| Ability to Mobilize Collective Action | Presence of local givers<br>Presence of volunteers | <br>Direct and indirect volunteers |
| Motivation and Ideological Commitment | Material sacrifice<br><br>Origin of the organization<br>Commitment to beneficiaries<br>Material comfort | Leader's salary<br>Initial investment<br><br><br>Organizational spending |
| Organizational Performance | Empowerment vs. dependence<br>Advocacy vs. service delivery<br>Agenda setting vs. agenda following<br>Sustainability vs. fluctuations<br>Elite representation vs. grassroots representation | <br><br><br>Annual budgets; stable objectives<br>Socioeconomic background of leaders |

The data gathered through the survey was triangulated against the findings of a survey of public perceptions of these organizations. Because all individuals in a given society can potentially be joiners of an NGO, this book argues that public[1] perception of NGOs' commitment, performance, and ability to mobilize joiners carries much analytical weight.[2] Methodologically, this approach is said to take inspiration from the Participatory Assessment tools, which draw from the broad participatory research methods led by Robert Chambers (1997). It emphasizes the need to involve the perspectives of those who are affected by a particular intervention. *Voices of the Poor*, a four-volume series produced by the World Bank (Narayan-Parker 2000) that documents the poor's perspective on what poverty is relative to the perspective of those who are working to remove poverty, relies on the Participatory Poverty Assessment method. Given that in the development literature the term *NGO* is defined mostly in terms of what the experts and international aid agencies view it to mean, it was considered important to gauge what the term means to the general public. Therefore, during the course of my fieldwork I asked all respondents about their familiarity with the term *NGO*—what it means to them and what they think of international donors' funding of civil society organizations.

This question became a regular feature of my fieldwork. At the same time, this soliciting of views from the general public was supplemented by the views of certain groups that come into direct contact with NGOs. Important among these groups were the international aid agencies that fund NGOs; the media, which cover NGO events and comment on the work that NGOs do; the bureaucrats and politicians whose work, or lack thereof, is often the target of NGOs' critique; and the *maulavis* in the mosques, who are often presented as heavily opposed to NGOs because of the latter's liberal outlook. Unlike the general public, these specialized groups, because of their direct involvement with NGOs, could have vested interests in promoting one image of NGOs over another. For this reason it was considered necessary to solicit their views specifically, in order to see how much those views would add to our knowledge of NGOs' ability to mobilize joiners, their commitment, and their performance.

1. The term *public,* as used here, includes everyone who is a citizen of the country under study. This is a loose categorization, but it is used here so that the views of all sections of the society can be included. Ordinary citizens as well as government officials, journalists, and others were all interviewed in their capacity as individual members of the society rather than as representatives of the positions they held.

2. For detailed coverage of the public perceptions of the term *NGO* in Pakistan, see Bano (2008a).

## Mobilizing Collective Action:
## Evidence on Membership Structures

The survey revealed a marked difference in the ability of the two types of organizations to mobilize members: all twenty of the VOs included in the survey relied on indigenous donations as opposed to only three NGOs. Even for the three NGOs, the amounts of the local contributions were insignificant and consisted of corporate rather than individual donations, so all of the NGOs relied almost exclusively on development aid. As for volunteers, although both types of organizations reported difficulty harnessing a big number, 100 percent of the VOs reported having a core pool of volunteers, whereas none of the NGOs did. There were two types of arrangements with volunteers: 80 percent of the VOs had paid staff members while volunteers provided specialized services, and 20 percent of the VOs were run entirely by volunteer members. Service and Development, a women-run organization, had a core group of six volunteers that supported the leader in the management and running of the organization. Similarly, Irtiqa, an organization of university professors and thinkers in Karachi that worked to promote freethinking, relied on the voluntary time investment of four core members.

All of the VOs with paid staff had at the same time volunteers who provided their professional services free of charge to promote the organization's mission. All of the VOs that ran schools or orphanages mentioned having an understanding with prominent doctors and dentists who provided free services to the children served by the VO. Among the NGOs, on the other hand, the only "volunteers" were the interns—young students or recent graduates who joined the organization with the explicit intention of gaining a job in the development sector.

However, even many of the VOs recorded difficulty retaining volunteers or inducting new ones from the younger generation, and most of them attributed this difficulty to the rise of the "NGO culture." The president of the All Pakistan Women's Association (APWA), the oldest women's rights organization in Pakistan, held the view that younger females often volunteer with other intentions: "Once trained, they quickly move on to set up their own NGOs where they can make good money."

In addition to the regular volunteers, the VOs also had a big pool of indirect volunteers. The initiators of the VOs as well as the regular volunteers mentioned that they were always able to get concessions on purchases and professional services. For example, volunteers at Service and Development explained that they were able to keep their costs low because they could get large discounts from shop owners. "We tell them that it is for a good deed. We say to them, you make so much profit; by giving this concession you will become part of this good deed too," explained one of the members. The members of Service and Development were confident that individuals respond favorably when they are convinced that the work is being undertaken for a good cause and that the person undertaking the work is not making a personal profit from it. This issue arose repeatedly in interviews with members of the VOs. Such support seemed to be a critical means of keeping the costs of their work very low. None of the NGO members interviewed, however, demonstrated the ability to mobilize such support.

At the same time, four VOs that had started to draw on international development aid reported problems. The Maternity and Child Welfare Association, a VO that in the last decade had started taking international aid, reported serious problems due to this move. The organization almost collapsed with the influx of such aid. "The real volunteers got disheartened. The really genuine worker leaves when he sees money come into play. The people who are more interested in personal gains start getting attracted to the organization," said the current president of the organization. In the case of a small CBO another negative effect of accepting international aid was that people refused to pay even the small membership fee they used to pay before. As one respondent said, "They now say that you are gaining profit out of this work. They say that in fact you are hiding away the money."

The survey thus indicates a clear absence of joiners, as both givers and volunteers, from NGOs (see Table 5.3). The question, then, is, Is it a matter of choice or of inability on the part of the NGOs? The survey results show it is true that NGOs in general do not work to mobilize local joiners because they prefer to focus their energies on international donors who provide big donations. At the same time, the survey shows that NGOs are unable to mobilize members even when they need them, and a few examples show that even those organizations that had members prior to taking development aid lost them upon receipt of aid.

Ninety percent of the NGOs surveyed acknowledged their inability to mobilize local joiners. Many said that fluctuations in aid flows in response to the political developments in Pakistan have made them think about exploring in-

**Table 5.3** Mobilizing Collective Action

| Collective Action | NGOs | VOs |
|---|---|---|
| Presence of local givers | 15% | 100% |
| Presence of volunteers | 0% | 100% |

digenous funds, but so far they have not been able to figure out how to do that. The inability of NGOs to mobilize joiners was also visible in a public account-ability drive launched by the bigger NGOs in Quetta, the capital of Baluchi-stan province. The Baluchistan Citizen Sector Self-Regulation Initiative—2003 Code of Conduct campaign requires its participants to become more trans-parent in their activities and accounts in order to improve their public image. The inability to mobilize members as donors and volunteers was also the most striking aspect of NGOs in the survey of public perceptions of NGOs. The cri-tiques of NGOs were overwhelming.

The term *NGO* was instantly linked in the public's mind to international development aid and conjured up consistently negative images. Except for a few staff members in international development agencies, all respondents ex-pressed concern about NGOs' agendas, motivations, impacts, and representa-tive natures. Even those staff members of international donor agencies who supported the NGOs acknowledged that the public image of NGOs is negative. Most interesting of all is that even a majority of the staff members of NGOs interviewed accused other NGOs of inappropriate behavior. Given that in the literature on NGOs, public perceptions of NGOs are rarely covered, the follow-ing section draws on the public perception survey to give a taste of views on NGOs held on the ground. However, in order not to distract from the objective analysis of the survey, which focused on forty organizations, only a few of the quotes from the public perception survey are provided here.[3]

Across the various socioeconomic and professional groups surveyed, NGOs were critiqued for their lack of performance as well as for their lack of commit-ment. Within activist circles a common critique was that NGOs have depoliti-cized society. In a country where continued military intervention has suppressed political parties and political activism, NGOs have helped to attract the political

3. One small exception to the analysis presented here is found in Hunza, one of the six northern districts of Pakistan. Hunza was the only place where the local population did not associate negative connotations with the term *NGO*. In their experience, the term *NGO* was closely linked to the Aga Khan Foundation, which had been the main development player in the region. This is an exceptional scenario, for two reasons. First, although the Aga Khan Foun-dation has in the last two decades become heavily involved with development projects funded by international donors, it is not an NGO in the sense defined in this study; it is primarily a re-ligious platform that has moved into development work. Second, although many small CBOs have mushroomed in this area under the patronage of the Aga Khan Foundation, there is still no NGO culture in the area like the one seen in the rest of the country. The importance of reli-gious values in building a favorable relationship between communities and the Aga Khan Foun-dation is also reflected in the fact that the population of Hunza is overwhelmingly Ismaili—that is, they are followers of Aga Khan.

activist away from politics. These critics argue that by promoting the concept of self-help, NGOs are shifting responsibility away from the state and in the process depoliticizing society. According to Akhtar Sheikh, the key initiator of the People's Rights Movement (PRM), one of the cases analyzed in Chapter 3, "The NGOs' negative impact is that social change has become a business. The assumption is that you can do a job and also bring a change." In his view, the idea of paid activists has changed the very culture of activism. "The issue is that once an activist gets used to the comfortable lifestyle of an NGO, then the primary focus becomes the survival of the NGO, which is his means of income, rather than the work itself," he added. His experience was that if you hold a protest after 5:00 p.m. or on a Saturday, the NGOs' staff members do not come.

Other members of the PRM had similar concerns. "An organization like ours is based on a constituency. We have to be responsive to them. By the same token, the NGOs have to be responsive to their donors. These donors are their constituency," explained one donor. He added, "PRM is different from an NGO because we do not see if money is coming for the work that needs to be done. We just do it. There is *zameen-asman* [earth-sky] difference in the work of NGOs and PRM. No NGO picks up issues that we pick up." Another member, who has more than ten years' experience of working with a high-profile local NGO on advocacy issues, said the reason he eventually left was that his work showed him "when it comes to critical issues, NGOs cannot resist the donor and government pressure."

A representative of a highly reputed VO that consists of senior academics and intellectuals in Karachi argued, "NGOs are being used as gospels of globalization. We hate to be called an NGO because the general impression is that NGOs are funded by foreign money." He elaborated, "We are not drawing big salaries; we are a dedicated group of friends. All intellectuals appreciate this platform. The late Hamza Alavi was with us. We are in the fifteenth or sixteenth year of our existence." The female head of a very radical women's rights organization that operates more like a provincewide movement said, "These NGOs need us. They come to us when they need people to demonstrate and show public power. They give money to cover the cost of our members' participation." Commenting that these NGOs are run on the basis of money, she said, "The NGOs are good for providing jobs; they are not the *rasta* [road] to *najat* [salvation]." She mentioned that her organization's own work had been affected by the arrival of development aid because many younger members had been tempted into opening NGOs rather than working on this group's voluntary platform. "These NGOs have come from where? They are an outcome of a deliberate policy to make our workers give up their ideals. They have come to stop the *zaehnie shaoor* [mental consciousness]," she said. In her view, the NGO phenomenon is part of the United States' planning to gain control over the entire world. "NGOs don't bring revolutionary people forward," she added.

Because the *maulavis* are among the groups that NGOs always accuse of defaming them, during the fieldwork I tried to solicit the views of some *maulavis* in the areas I covered. All of the *maulavis* interviewed viewed NGOs as a continuation of Christian missionary work. Unlike the other individuals I interviewed, the *maulavis* seemed to have no consciousness of the international development system. They all blamed NGOs for promoting Western values for monetary gain and viewed them as part of a Christian missionary agenda. Interestingly, however, it was in the rural areas and small towns that the clergy had an additional, very strong critique of NGOs. In these communities, the term *NGO* has become synonymous with a woman who has lost complete respect for her own value system. In these areas, NGOs are the big concern of the clergy's Friday sermons. A staff member of the biggest women's rights NGO in Pakistan noted that it is common for ordinary people in rural areas of Khyber Pakh tunkhwa to say, "An NGO visited today; it was wearing high heels and a short skirt." Although he sat in an organization that funds NGOs and was reasonably progressive, this official shared the public's concern about the culturally insensitive and supposedly completely westernized ideas of the two key nationwide women's rights NGOs.

However, the most damaging evidence of the negative perception of the term *NGO* in Pakistani society came not from the Marxist-oriented activists or the uninformed *maulavis* but from the surveyed NGOs who admitted this problem, as well as from the staff of donor agencies. Almost half of the senior staff members of donor agencies interviewed admitted that many NGOs were set up to attract donor aid for personal gain rather than out of a real commitment to a cause. Furthermore, none of the NGOs included in the survey denied that the term *NGO* is very negatively perceived by the public. Only three of the twenty NGOs interviewed set aside these perceptions as baseless. The majority argued that the negative perceptions of NGOs are based on solid grounds. Seventeen respondents from the NGOs surveyed maintained that NGOs were formed for personal gain rather than to serve a public interest. They claimed, however, that their own organization was different.

The executive director of an education-focused NGO in Karachi that had recently received a large USAID project had this to say about NGO culture:

"NGOs are not grassroots organizations. People in NGOs are visible in speeding cars." He was of the view that what reaches the grassroots through NGO projects is a very small portion of the actual amount available. "For most NGOs the vision is not clear; they keep changing their *kibla* [direction of prayer]. They keep wearing new clothes according to the weather. If donors disappear, they will disappear too," he added. A senior official of an NGO that has become prominent in the Tharparkar Desert maintained, "Criticism of NGOs is by and large valid. Most of the NGOs are involved in some kind of corruption." In his view, NGOs have become family inheritances that the father hands over to the daughter. This reference to "daughter" was also a critique of the dominance of upper-class, foreign-educated women in the NGO sector. "The NGOs are more involved in fashionable jargon. The offices of NGOs in Islamabad are better than the office of the Somalian Embassy," he added. Thus, in his view, big NGOs are more financially resourceful than the governments of poor countries.

One of the top officials of a well-established child rights NGO in Islamabad admitted, "Sometimes it comes as an embarrassment to say one is from an NGO. NGOs are more like business today; they are not voluntary." As she saw it, NGOs get the money first then have to find a way to spend it; VOs, on the other hand, know first what they want to do and then go out to gather funds for it. "The NGO movement will collapse when international donors withdraw," she said. The director of a small NGO in Bahawalpur that in the last four years had acquired quite a few donor-funded projects shared his reservation about disclosing publicly his identity as head of an NGO when he said, "When sitting in a train I will never say that I am the president of an NGO. The people will say you are a *Daku* [bandit], you embezzle money."

The executive director of a Lahore-based NGO that had recently received a multimillion-dollar project from USAID said that he avoids introducing himself as an NGO representative when he goes to the beneficiary groups because of the negative image the term evokes. "I try to explain our work to the community members without using the term *NGO*. But when I explain that we do projects with development money, the people say with that disappointed tone, 'Oh! So it is an NGO.'"

The perceptions of the general public, of specialized groups (including representatives of international donor agencies), and of NGOs, although they are not to be seen as objective data, do support the survey results—that NGOs struggle to win members because of their negative and self-serving image; that the ordinary public makes a clear distinction between VOs and NGOs; and that anyone familiar with the term *NGO* immediately associates it with international donor aid.

## Measuring Motivation

The organizational survey also reveals stark differences between the motivation of leaders of NGOs and the motivation of leaders of VOs (see Table 5.4).

### Material Sacrifice

In the VOs, none of the leaders were paid for their work; they all worked voluntarily. In the NGOs, 100 percent of the leaders were paid for their work, and 95 percent admitted that their salary was higher than the salary of an equivalent position on the government pay scale. Hence, whereas for the leaders of NGOs their work at the organization was their source of income, for the leaders of VOs their work at the organization was completely voluntary, and often in addition to their professional duties elsewhere. Most VO leaders had also made major financial contributions to setting up the organization. Whereas the absence of any monetary benefits in the form of salaries makes it possible to argue that the initiators of the VOs were primarily motivated by ideological incentives, in the case of NGOs it is difficult to establish this claim given that there were clear material incentives for undertaking the work that at times were even more rewarding than what the initiator could receive in the marketplace.

**Table 5.4** Measuring Motivation

| Motivation | NGOs | VOs |
|---|---|---|
| Leader's Salary | 100% drew a salary; for 95% it was more than the salary of an equivalent position on the government scale | 100 percent worked voluntarily; they also invested their own resources in the organization |
| Organization's Origin | 6 were the continuation of donor projects 2 were the continuation of donor consultancies 6 including 2 of the largest women's rights NGOs, resulted from exposure to Western education 5 were responses to local needs | 3 were initiated as a response to a particular incident 17 were initiated as a moral compulsion to address a common problem |
| Beneficiary Population | Project was designed first, beneficiary population was chosen later | Existence of a beneficiary population led to the birth of the organization |
| Material Comfort | 100% were located in a posh area 100% had modern buildings 100% were located away from the project site Majority had four-wheel-drive vehicles | None were located in a posh area 25% had no office building 65% had offices at a project site None maintained four-wheel-drive vehicles |

## Origin of the Organization

An organization's origin is also indicative of the motives of its leaders. The survey shows that an NGO's origins indicate material incentives for the initiators and a VO's origins are embedded mainly in ideological incentives. Continuation of an already existing donor project and the desire to implement a development idea were the two main reasons that leaders gave for starting their NGOs. Six of the twenty NGOs surveyed were established at the closure of a foreign development project when the foreign donor in charge of the project helped the local staff set up local NGOs so that the local manpower trained during the course of the project and the physical infrastructure that was developed would not go to waste. Those who had joined these aid projects as a means to earn a living became leaders of these local NGOs. These individuals had been paid when they joined and they were paid in the new setup. Two of the other NGOs surveyed had come about when their leaders, who had worked for a donor's consultancy project, realized the potential to expand the work by forming an NGO.

In addition to this, the other key explanation for the origin of some of the NGOs interviewed was the initiator's exposure to Western liberal ideas. Two influential women's rights NGOs were set up by initiators who had studied in Western universities. On their return to Pakistan, these initiators had felt the need to challenge the existing gender roles in their society. The same was true for leaders of four other large NGOs in the survey. They had also been exposed to development ideas through foreign education. Nonetheless, with the exception of one NGO, in all these cases, from the very beginning setting up an NGO also ensured the initiators a good income. Five of these from the very start drew on international development aid whereas the one that was set up prior to the availability of development aid moved to receive it as soon as it became available. The existence of clear monetary incentives to undertake this work does not completely rule out the possibility of commitment to ideals on the part of these NGO initiators; it does, however, make it difficult to prove their commitment. It is, thus, difficult to test whether it was the possibility of getting funding for that particular project or a reaction to a local need that made these initiators start the NGO, especially given that they were all well-versed with development discourse and knew which issues were on top of the donors' funding agendas. The initiators of five other NGOs surveyed claimed to have started the NGO in response to a local need. Interestingly, four of these NGOs had started their work with local donations but later moved to receive funding from international donors.

In the case of VOs, on the other hand, there were two main explanations for their origin: one, they were the response of an individual or a group to a particular incident that moved them; or two, they resulted from the realization by a group of individuals who were influential in a given context that a public problem needed to be addressed. Three of the VOs in the survey had originated when the initiators were moved by a particular incident. For example, Anjuman-Faizul-Islam, one of the oldest VOs in Pakistan, was set up in response to a famine in Bengal that left many children orphaned. The other seventeen VOs originated because either one individual or a group of friends or acquaintances felt morally compelled to do something in response to a common need. For example, the APWA, which until the 1970s was very influential but has now been sidelined by the development agencies and the NGOs because it consists largely of women who are housewives rather than professionals, was set up by the wife of the first prime minister of Pakistan in response to the perceived need to mobilize women to contribute to the development of the newly born country. The APWA aimed to engage these women in professional roles while encouraging them to maintain their primary roles as wives and mothers.

The initiators of these organizations had no links to international development aid. These organizations started because the founders decided to use their own resources and seek the help of people around them to address the issues they thought were important. Therefore, whereas, in the case of the NGOs, the survey indicates a strong link between their initiation and the availability of international development aid, in the case of VOs, the reason for their initiation seems to be an urge to respond to a need that matches the initiators' value system. With the exception of one, all of the NGOs surveyed started with the initiators being compensated at the market rate for their work, whereas in the case of the VOs, all of the initiators started by putting in their own resources voluntarily. Arguably they might have sought some social rewards, such as prestige or social status, but there was no evidence of them drawing any economic benefits.

### Commitment to Beneficiaries

If commitment to certain ideals can be measured in terms of how consistently the leaders work with the organization's beneficiaries, the VOs surveyed fared better than the NGOs. For all of the VOs it was the existence of a clearly defined beneficiary population that motivated the leaders; on the other hand, for the NGOs, no specific beneficiary population acted as a motive. For the NGOs, organizational aims were determined by the development projects they had received from their donors, and actual beneficiaries were then sought to match the requirements of the project. Even organizations that worked in a particular region, such as the Thar Desert, focused on different locations, and thus on different beneficiaries within that region, on the basis of the requirements of specific donor projects. As a consequence, the majority of NGOs surveyed had a continuously changing target population.

### Material Comfort

The survey also shows that the initiators of NGOs enjoy much more material comfort in their work than the initiators of VOs. The difference between the two types of organizations was most marked in terms of what was spent out of the organization's resources on making the work environment comfortable for the leaders. All but one of the NGOs surveyed had their offices in the more expensive areas of town in modern buildings with the latest facilities, such as air conditioning and computers. Furthermore, their project sites were usually some distance from these offices. All of the NGOs had many vehicles; many had four-wheel-drive vehicles parked outside their offices.

The VOs, on the other hand, had quite humble offices. Five of them had no office building of their own and were run out of the house or office of the leader. For example, CARE, a VO working on education, does not have an independent office space; its team operates out of a small portion of the commercial office of the initiator. Also, strikingly, thirteen of the VOs had offices at the project site. In contrast to the NGOs' offices, these offices generally consisted of three to four rooms and were very basic. Only two of the VOs maintained offices away from their project site. However, even these were located in small flats in commercial areas of Karachi rather than in the affluent localities that housed the NGOs. The bigger NGOs in the main cities in particular had very lavish offices and expensive vehicles.

## Measuring Performance

The indicators developed to reflect organizational performance also revealed marked differences between the VOs and the NGOs (see Table 5.5).

### Empowerment Versus Dependence

In policy debates on NGOs, VOs and NGOs are often assumed to work with different philosophies: NGOs are expected to undertake development projects that will lead to empowerment and self-reliance within communities; VOs, on the other hand, are assumed to be more concerned with addressing the immediate needs of communities, which often leads to dependence. The survey shows that in using the language of participation NGOs are clearly ahead of VOs. The two types of organizations differ markedly in their use of develop-

**Table 5.5** Measuring Performance

| Performance | NGOs | VOs |
|---|---|---|
| Empowerment vs. Dependence | All claimed their work was different than that of VOs; all defined development as making people stand on their own feet. All were well versed in development discourse. | None of the VOs believed in handouts; even the smallest believed in making people stand on their own feet. None spoke development discourse; all relied on religious or moral diction or Marxist vocabulary. |
| Advocacy vs. Service Delivery | Advocacy-based NGOs focused on workshops and seminars. Social mobilization was interpreted as self-help. | Advocacy-based VOs were very political and much more radical than NGOs. Mobilization was political and often driven by Marxist thinking. |
| | Service-delivery NGOs were neutral toward the state; they focused on moving toward the market. | Service-delivery VOs were neutral toward the state and focused on social responsibility among the well-off. |
| Agenda Setting vs. Agenda Following | Smaller NGOs were more vulnerable to donor pressure but bigger NGOs were not fully independent. | 85% refused aid on ideological grounds; 15% did not pursue due to complicated paperwork. |
| | | 20% had started to accept donor aid but registered problems. |
| Sustainability vs. Fluctuations | All showed dramatic fluctuations in annual budgets in response to aid flows. | Annual budgets were stable, recording only gradual increases or decreases. |
| | Activities kept changing in response to aid flows. | The focus of activities was stable. |
| Elite Domination vs. Grassroots Representation | Leaders came from middle- and upper-income groups. | Leaders came from middle- and upper-income groups. |

ment lingo. NGOs' leaders continually used words like *gender equity, empowerment, beneficiaries,* and *sustainability*. Theirs is a language perfectly in tune with the vocabulary of the international development agencies. The actual understanding of these development concepts was limited to a handful of the bigger NGOs, but the use of the jargon itself was widespread, across the NGO spectrum. Among VOs, however, the language used was very different. Among the service delivery VOs, the language was drawn mainly from religious obligation and a sense of moral and social responsibility; the advocacy-based VOs drew from either religious or Marxist vocabulary. Thus, a VO and an NGO undertaking the same activity, such as running a school, used very different language to explain their main objective. The respondents from NGOs talked about education being a millennium development goal, about the benefits of non-formal education models, and about their knowledge of other international experiences, such as BRAC. The respondents from the VOs undertaking the same activity, however, talked about personal experiences that had convinced them of the need to provide education facilities to poor children, about their sense of social responsibility that motivated them to do this work, and about learning from their own local experiences.

So, even though the two types of organizations used different languages, there was no evidence that the two languages necessarily dealt with different types of activities. None of the respondents from VOs, for example, used the word *empowerment,* but each of them talked about helping their beneficiaries to "stand on their own feet." Each of them aimed at making the poor self-sufficient rather than making them dependent on charity. Even those VOs that had started on a very small scale just to provide immediate relief had eventually expanded their work to address the causes of poverty and deprivation. Service and Development was a very good example of this process. A VO started by two women with very humble ambitions to provide food rations to a few poor families, it soon expanded to providing education scholarships and imparting vocational training, because the initiators realized that distributing food rations alone would not enable the poor families they served to get out of poverty. It is therefore difficult to argue that NGOs work toward empowerment of their beneficiaries but VOs do not. Representatives of an NGO in Bahawalpur that had grown from being a small self-help organization to being largely donor dependent expressed the same view: "Eventually the work we do is exactly the same as we did before receipt of aid money. We ran a school then and we run a school now, but the language is very different."

### Advocacy Versus Service Delivery

Advocacy work that aims to make the state accountable is viewed as a major contribution of NGOs; the VOs, on the other hand, are often viewed as service-delivery focused. The survey shows, however, that advocacy is an equally important activity for NGOs and VOs. Among the NGOs, only four claimed to be primarily advocacy based, and even these had some service-delivery projects. The rest were mainly service-delivery organizations but also engaged in some advocacy work. Among the VOs, the same held true. Five of them were primarily advocacy oriented whereas the rest primarily undertook service delivery, with a small advocacy component.

Furthermore, the survey shows that VOs are more political than NGOs in their advocacy claims. The dominant work model among both advocacy and service-delivery NGOs was to set up self-help village organizations. To the NGOs surveyed, *community mobilization* was a nonpolitical term: the emphasis of this mobilization activity was on making communities pool their resources in order to provide a common good and then to establish good contacts with the government line departments. The advocacy-based VOs, on the other hand, equated *community mobilization* with *political mobilization*. For these organizations, public rallies and demonstrations demanding equitable distribution of economic growth within society through land reforms, water distribution, and reduction in defense spending were key concerns. These VOs were often more confrontational in their tactics than NGOs; whereas NGOs mainly engaged in publishing brochures, disseminating information about rights among the affected communities, and hosting conferences and workshops in hotels, VOs relied heavily on protests, walks, hunger strikes, sit-ins in front of the parliament, and demonstrations that at times led to imprisonment. Thus the two types of organizations differed in terms of the nature of the issues they took up for advocacy and also in the methods they used.

### Agenda Setting Versus Agenda Following

Whether an NGO is an agenda setter or an agenda follower for the donor is one of the critical measures of its performance. The survey findings are not surprising: because NGOs depend on donor agencies rather than on a large constituency of local supporters, they have much less control over setting their agenda than VOs do. More interesting, the survey reveals a stark difference among the NGOs too. An overwhelming majority of the VOs surveyed did not want international development aid for this very reason; they argued that foreign aid comes with its own agenda and leads to an attitude of dependency. In the words of the leader of one advocacy-based VO, "An organization like ours is based on a constituency. We have to be responsive to them. By the same token, the NGOs have to be responsive to their donors. These donors are their constituency."

The NGOs, on the other hand, had a very different approach to international donors. Their main justification for relying on international development aid rather than on local fund raising was, they argued, that more money is available through the former. The bigger NGOs generally had no complaints about donors. They were confident in their ability to resist donor pressure to promote an agenda they did not support. They also had no fear of donor money running out. In fact, they argued that they did not have to go to the donors to seek funds; rather, the donors themselves came to them with project proposals. The smaller NGOs, especially those in remote areas, on the other hand, had many complaints about international donors and about the donors' relationships with NGOs in the big cities. Some blamed the bigger NGOs for cultivating special links with donors, others blamed the donors, and some blamed both. They argued that the bigger NGOs invested in networking with donors and thus got all the big projects. "What do these Islamabad-based NGOs know about the problems in Southern Punjab?" complained the head of a medium-sized NGO in Multan who was very critical of donors' tendency to give the big projects for rural Punjab to these NGOs.

The smaller NGOs were also very open in admitting that their agendas were completely dictated by the donors. "If you go against the donor he will completely sideline you," said the initiator of one of the smaller NGOs in Bahawalpur. In his experience, each and every line of the contract was dictated by the head office of the international donor and the NGO was simply asked to implement the project. "The NGO system is over, it is all contractorship now," he added. The NGO leaders did distinguish between bilateral and multilateral donors and international NGOs in terms of the freedom they gave to the local NGOs to plan their own work, but the survey findings show no signs that different donors have different impacts on an NGO's ability to mobilize members and on the motivation of its leaders.

The survey thus indicates a difference between how international donors interact with the well-established, bigger NGOs and how they interact with the relatively newer and smaller NGOs and CBOs, especially those located in remote areas. There is a good technical explanation for this. The staff members in bigger NGOs are normally more educated and well versed in development discourse and concepts, and because they have been around for a long time they are more tactful in negotiations with donors. Donors' experience with the bigger organizations makes them trust these organizations more than the smaller and newer NGOs, over whom they logically feel the need to have greater control. However, analysis of the overall work trends of the NGOs surveyed shows that although the bigger NGOs might be in a position to ward off direct pressure from the donors over specific projects, their overall work preferences are heavily shaped by the international donors.

The survey shows that all of the NGOs, including the bigger ones, had adapted their activities to their donors' preferences. In the 1980s, donors' funding preferences in Pakistan revolved around women's rights; in the early 1990s they revolved around microcredit; beginning in the mid-1990s donors focused on community empowerment and mobilization; and at the time of my fieldwork their focus was on governance and devolution. The annual reports and brochures of the NGOs show that all of them have followed the same trends. This does seem to indicate that the overall agenda of NGOs is eventually controlled by the donors, or that the liberty that the bigger NGOs enjoy is limited to rejecting or accepting a particular project and not the overall area of intervention. Many local staff members of the donor agencies admitted their influence. In the words of a local official at the UK Department for International Development, "These NGOs all act as contractors; there is no disputing that." Similarly, one of the senior staff members of the Trust for Voluntary Organizations (TVO), a donor agency, admitted, "Beggars cannot be choosers. The donors are like shop owners; they are selling certain ideas. If you are willing to work with those ideas, they will give you money; otherwise you move on to the next shop." He added, "There is no NGO here who will say no to a donor, except a very few big ones. I have seen a lot of NGOs who stay alive by working on child labor one year and moving on to another sector the next year."

The international donors' influence over the agendas of the NGOs can also be studied by observing the NGOs' involvement in the governance debate occurring in Pakistan at the time of the fieldwork. One issue that repeatedly came up in discussions with various groups was the complete absence of critique from the NGOs about General Musharraf's military government. Given that donors link NGOs with the promotion of democracy in developing countries, one would have expected the NGOs in Pakistan to resist military rule. The NGOs, however, were completely silent on the issue. Although *governance* and *public participation* were central to the work of all the NGOs surveyed, none of them, not even the most established advocacy NGOs, were participating in the democracy-versus-military debate taking place in Pakistan. A senior director of one of the largest advocacy NGOs, which at the time was also running many donor-funded projects on governance and decentralization, admitted, "Our failure to take an active part and strong position on LFO [Legal Framework Order, a collection of constitutional amendments that legitimized General Musharraf's rule] has been a weakness. It is an issue that the NGOs did not take any position on it." He added, "There was no intellectual dilemma involved in opposing LFO. All I can think of is that the project workload creates lethargy toward pursuing some of these issues." This comment indicates that even for bigger NGOs, reliance on donor money leads to promoting project guidelines rather than what is actually thought to be important.

Due to General Musharraf's support of the "war on terror" since September 11, 2001, all major donors were very supportive of his regime at the time of the fieldwork, which translated into large aid flows to Pakistan. At that time, *governance*—or more specifically, *devolution*—was the buzzword in international donor and government circles. Almost all donor aid to NGOs was coming through the devolution plan. To criticize General Musharraf's government or have it removed threatened the millions of aid dollars coming to NGOs through the devolution plan. For example, the USAID, which at the time of the fieldwork was disbursing some of the biggest projects to NGOs, had returned to Pakistan, after having withdrawn in the late 1980s, as a sign of support to General Musharraf's policies. The complete silence of NGOs about General Musharraf's regime and the absence of any support from NGOs for the opposition parties was thus not a surprise. It did, however, quite strongly demonstrate the donors' ability to influence the agenda of the NGOs, regardless of the NGOs' scale. The influx of aid to Pakistan in the post-2001 period also highlights the financial vulnerability of NGOs that are reliant on development aid, because aid flows to Pakistan are very vulnerable to the country's geopolitical positioning.

### Sustainability Versus Fluctuations

The ability of NGOs to sustain their activities beyond the donor funding cycle is a key concern in the NGO literature. Annual budgets, which indicate the scale of activity of an organization, are useful indicators of the stability of an organization. The survey shows that the annual budgets of NGOs fluctuate dramatically. At the time of the fieldwork, on the whole, NGO budgets were larger than those of VOs. This seemed linked to the massive expansion of aid flows to Pakistan after September 11. The budgets of some NGOs multiplied more than a hundred times over a period of two years. The availability of large projects from new donors, such as USAID, dramatically enhanced the budgets of three major NGOs whose members I interviewed. One NGO had received Rs. 29,250,000 (£292,500; US$488,475), a considerable amount for an organization whose previous budget had been a little over a million rupees (£10,000; US$16,700). Another organization's budget expanded from Rs. 11 million to Rs. 30 million over one year, and then to Rs. 40 million the following year. As acknowledged by the head of one of the NGOs that had recently received such a project, this growth raises questions about the capacity of organizations to absorb and disburse such money efficiently. For the VOs, on the other hand, the financial expansion was more gradual, but at the same time more stable. No VO recorded such dramatic expansion or reduction in its budget.

The survey also noticed clear differences in the continuity of work between the NGOs and the VOs. The NGOs were very clear that they would carry on a project only as long as there was development aid to support it. In the words of one of the NGO representatives, "We will do the work while we are being paid for it. We can't do it once the funding runs out." For the VOs, on the other hand, there was no concept of the work coming to an end; there was no talk of running a project. This is visible in the approach taken by CARE, a VO in Lahore that has taken over responsibility for improving the quality of education in ten municipal government schools near Lahore. The chief executive of CARE argued, "When taking over schools from the state, we ensured that we get them for at least ten years, because entering into three-year contracts is the approach of the international donors, not ours. We believe in staying involved till the target is achieved."

### Elite Domination Versus Grassroots Representation

The survey records no difference between the economic and social backgrounds of the initiators in the two types of organizations. The leaders of both the NGOs and the VOs came mainly from the upper- and middle-income groups. The majority of them were well educated, with most of the leaders of the NGOs having foreign degrees in development-related subjects. Thus the assumption that giving aid to NGOs will enable members from low-income groups to initiate their own NGOs does not hold true. In the words of the head of a small NGO in Bahawalpur, "NGO work is for educated people; it is not for the common man. A common man cannot write proposals, use e-mail, and the fax machine."

## Conclusion

The survey results thus show that initiators who rely on international development aid fail to mobilize joiners. They also show that those who receive international development aid are motivated by material motives, or that material motives clearly exist in addition to ideological motives, whereas those who rely on the support of local joiners are primarily motivated by ideals, with no proof of material incentives playing a significant role. Finally, the survey results also support the claim that the performance of the VOs is better than that of the NGOs on all of the indicators selected for this study.

Chapter 3 argued that joiners join initiators on the basis of shared ideals, and that they select an initiator by making rational judgments about the motivation and performance of the initiator. The findings discussed in this chapter support this argument. They show that the initiators who are able to mobilize joiners are those who demonstrate clear signs of commitment to their stated ideals and visible signs of high performance, whereas those who fail to show these signs fail to mobilize joiners. The analysis in this chapter thus supports the analysis developed in Chapter 3 and reaffirms the existence of a correlation between the initiator's performance and motivation and the ability to mobilize joiners (see Figure 5.1).

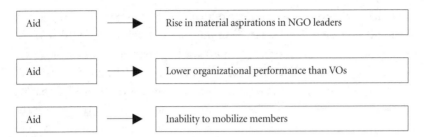

**Figure 5.1**  Strong Correlations

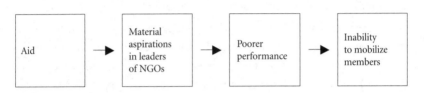

**Figure 5.2**  Plausible Causality Chain

At the same time, this chapter's analysis points to another strong correlation: between the availability of development aid and the increase of material motivation and the worsening of performance on the part of NGO initiators. Analysis of the public's perceptions of NGOs indicates the likelihood of a causal relationship among the three elements whereby international development aid causes material motivation, which, in turn, causes poorer performance, and these factors, in turn, restrict an NGO's ability to mobilize its members (see Figure 5.2).

This conclusion raises two questions. First, why should international development aid lead to material motivation? After all, the international donor also claims commitment to certain ideals—often to universally expressed human rights. Second, why should material motivation on the part of the initiator lead to poor performance compared to the performance of an initiator motivated by ideals?

It is these two questions that are the focus of attention in the next chapter. However, before addressing these questions, the chapter reexamines the existence of the correlations just proposed by analyzing three cases in which initiators initially drew on indigenous funds but then moved to receiving international development aid, to see if there are indications of a causal relationship between international development aid and the rise of material motivation and the worsening of performance on the part of the initiators.

# 6   Why Aid Breaks Down Cooperation

> *It may be objected, that many who are capable of the higher pleasures occasionally, under the influence of temptation, postpone them to the lower.*
>
> John Stuart Mill, "Utilitarianism," [1861] 1982, 258

> *As we know that a man often succumbs to temptation, however, much he may resist it . . . ; fasting, therefore, has a limited use, for a fasting man continues to be swayed by passion.*
>
> Mahatma Gandhi, *All Men Are Brothers*, 1958, 113–114

THE PRECEDING CHAPTER ARGUED that initiators who rely on international development aid tend to be motivated by the pursuit of material interests. Furthermore, the analysis so far has illustrated that these initiators perform poorly compared to initiators driven by the pursuit of ideals. Chapter 5 concluded with two questions: (1) Why should international development aid lead to material motivation? After all, international donors claim to be committed to certain ideals, such as those expressed in the United Nations' Universal Declaration of Human Rights. (2) Why does material motivation on the part of initiators lead to poor performance compared to the performance of initiators motivated by ideals?

This chapter tests the proposed links between international development aid and material motivation and between material motivation and performance by analyzing three cases in which the initiators moved from using indigenous support to using international development aid. The advantage of such a before-and-after comparison over the survey discussed in the previous chapter is that variation in performance can be measured more precisely within one case than when measured across forty cases working in different social sectors and disparate geographical settings. More important, such a before-and-after comparison also makes it possible to record change, as opposed to difference in the initiator's motivation and performance, upon the arrival of international development aid. This chapter thus analyzes three cases to explore further whether there are links between the availability of international development aid and the rise of material motivation in initiators, and between initiators' pursuit of material interest and decreased performance.

The first case studies six CBOs in Sindh that are on record as having shown dramatic shifts in performance after gaining access to donor aid.[1] The information for this study came from individuals in the development sector who funded these organizations and witnessed over time the shift in their behavior after the arrival of development aid, and from documentary evidence, such as project files. The second case documents the experience of Anjuman Mazareen-i-Punjab, the tenant farmers movement studied in Chapter 4, with donor aid. The third case records the shift in performance of three of the VOs covered in Chapter 5—two in Punjab and one in Sindh—upon receipt of international development aid.

## Case 1:
## Oxfam Pakistan and Community-Based Organizations in Sindh

Sindh, the second largest province of Pakistan in terms of population, has a rich tradition of voluntarism and hosts a large number of VOs. However, it was in this very province that I heard the maximum number of complaints about deterioration in the performance of traditional VOs after accepting international development aid. I was able to study these concerns in some depth by focusing on six VOs that in the 1980s moved to receive aid from Oxfam under its civil society-strengthening program. These organizations were often mentioned during my field trips as having experienced dramatic declines in performance after they began receiving international development aid. In-depth interviews and discussions with the former Oxfam official who had been responsible for disbursing funds to these organizations,[2] and with other development professionals

1. Bhatti Welfare Association, Ghot Sudhar Sanghat, Insan Hamdard Sanghat, Marvi Rural Development Organization, Sanghat Faridabad, and Welfare Association Khairpur.

2. This former Oxfam official, a native of Sindh province who today works as a program manager with the UK office of Save the Children, was in charge of this Oxfam project for almost seven years. He was responsible for selecting CBOs to receive aid and then monitoring their performance afterward. He joined Oxfam in the late 1980s, having been hired on the basis

in Sindh who had observed these organizations over time,[3] helped me to map the changes that these organizations underwent, and provided detailed analysis of the reasons for these changes. The six CBOs were prominent organizations when Oxfam approached them with aid in the late 1980s; today, all of them are in the doldrums and have split into small factions, which have filed court cases against one another. Community members have also filed cases against them.[4]

### Performance

Prior to the availability of international development aid, CBOs in Sindh were generally engaged in three distinct activities—charity and welfare (the provision of money and other necessities to those in need of such assistance), lobbying, and local fundraising—though their primary objective was welfare. They were always the first groups to respond to an emergency, even before the government, because of their knowledge of the areas they served and their contacts in those communities. They were also very quick to mobilize public support. For instance, on the basis of its analysis of the situation of the victims of a flood, Insan Hamdard Sanghat managed to collect Rs. 200,000 (£2,000; US$3,340) in just three days. The organization was meticulous in the keeping of its financial accounts; a proper record was maintained of all donations and how they were used, and this record was mailed to all members.

The organizational structure of these CBOs was very democratic: decisions were based on mutual consultation and accounts were open to all community members. "For example, Ghot Sudhar Sanghat maintained meticulous financial accounts and everything was presented in front of the general body," the

---

of his experience of working on local CBO-strengthening programs in Sindh. Within the development community in Pakistan, he enjoys great respect because of his knowledge of the working of VOs in Sindh.

3. Noor Muhammad Bajeer (Regional Director, Strengthening Participatory Organizations, Sindh), Munir Chandio (journalist, Hyderabad), Zafar Ali Junajo (activist, Hyderabad), Ghafar Malik (head of a VO), Gul Mastoi (Regional Officer, Trust for Voluntary Organizations, Sindh), Naseer Memon (works with World Wildlife Fund, Karachi), Amir Mohammad (SPO, Hyderabad), Wali Mohammad (Sindh Graduates Association, Karachi), Mushtaq Meerani (academic and head of an NGO, Hyderabad), Abdul Raheem Mosvi (prominent social worker, Karachi), Ali Palh (SPO, Hyderabad), D. A. A. Qureshi (works on environmental issues), Nazeer Qureshi (activist, Hyderabad), Shamsuddin Sahib (former representative of Amnesty International Pakistan office, Karachi/Islamabad), Sadeka Salauddin (development consultant, Karachi), Rizwan Yaseer (assistant regional officer, Trust for Voluntary Organizations).

4. One of these CBOs was included in the survey presented in the preceding chapter. While arguing that NGOs have a bad name due to public lack of understanding of their activities, the head of this CBO himself mentioned to me that people from the community have at times filed First Information Reports against them, claiming misuse of funds.

former Oxfam official emphasized. General body members were elected on a regular basis from within the community. CBOs maintained close contact with concerned government officials; the government social welfare officer, for example, would monitor the elections of the officeholders and issue official certificates of appointment to them afterward. One copy of each certificate was kept in the office of the social welfare department, the other was kept in the CBO's office. Things were very transparent then.

"There was no written strategy to their work, but they had it in their minds," explained the former Oxfam official. The people running these organizations had no idea what Oxfam was or what terms like *strategic planning* and *capacity building* meant, yet they were very strategic as well as innovative. They were efficient in distributing their workloads among members, who were all volunteers; a teacher, for example, was asked to conduct a survey, or a grocery shop owner was made responsible for distributing food rations. All of these calculations were in the minds of the people running these organizations. They were also strategic and innovative in their fundraising. For example, the members of some CBOs provided their services to landowners at the time of a harvest, and the money they earned through that work went to the CBO. "In the local context, these are the possible innovations. These are people who did their jobs, supported families, and still did this extra work," noted the former Oxfam official.

The main work strategy for many of the CBOs was to influence government policy. Thus they were similarly strategic in their lobbying. If, for example, there was no school in the area, they first wrote a letter to the district government official. They kept the local feudal lord informed about these demands. If the district official failed to respond, they invited the deputy commissioner and the landlord to a function designed to highlight the problem. If the deputy commissioner failed to respond, they invited a member of the parliament to the event. These organizations kept detailed records of all their correspondence, including copies of all the letters they dispatched and a list of the postal registry numbers. This work was not charity; it was serious lobbying work, and the organizations' members did it entirely on their own.

Finally, these CBOs were also strategic about building alliances with other civil society groups, particularly the media, which were used effectively to highlight the organizations' problems. Most CBOs started with distribution of school uniforms and books, and provided burial services. They would then write about their local problems in the newspapers. "In the 1980s it was very common to see such articles and letters in the Sindhi newspapers. This media cooperation was a major support for CBOs," explains the former Oxfam official.

This was all pre-development-aid work. By 1990–1991, however, development aid had reached the CBOs in Pakistan. Oxfam, the South Asia Partnership–Pakistan, and the NGO Resource Centre had come in with development projects intended to strengthen the capacity of the CBOs. Aid made it possible to provide salaries for some of the members of these organizations. This provision changed the dynamics within these groups. Tensions erupted over the question of which members would be paid and which would continue to work voluntarily. Soon accounting also became a problem. When the money was coming through community contributions, every member had access to the accounts. When a major amount came from Oxfam, however, the members who were in charge of the funds became reluctant to share account details. With this money also came the problem of nepotism. A CBO that received Rs. 100,000 (£1,000, US$1,670) for a microcredit program, for example, could not possibly cater to the needs of all of the two hundred farmers in the area; at most it could give credit to only fifty farmers. Criteria were supposedly developed to select the farmers, but in practice it was the farmers who were close to the members who were in charge of the funds who got priority in receiving them. This favoritism increased tension among the members.

Instructions from donors increasingly replaced CBOs' own strategic planning, and the community lost control over the decision-making process. For example, it became the officials of a donor agency who nominated members to attend workshops or meetings, replacing the older practice in which the members collectively nominated one member to represent the organization at an event. As the former Oxfam official commented, "We as donors bypassed this whole system. We started meddling with their accepted code of conduct. This was very dangerous." Three years later it was only the same three or four people who went to every meeting. The more training these members received, the more comfortable it became for the donors to engage with them rather than with other members. Consequently, the other members had increasingly less access to the management of the organization. All of this change has severely hampered the CBOs' ability to mobilize media support. The Sindhi newspapers that in the 1980s regularly carried letters and articles from CBO members are now highly critical of these same CBOs.

## Motivation

All six of the CBOs studied here emerged in response to a specific need of the community. "In 1989–1990, when I first visited these CBOs, the leaders of these organizations were very surprised that they could actually be paid for this work," explained the former Oxfam official. Until then the main motivation for undertaking the work was *sawab* (spiritual rewards); there was no concept of an "NGO." The donors taught people to write proposals, and along came a major shift in people's actions. Members of the CBO started to compete for the material gains that this work could now bring. Internal rivalries started over salaries, opportunities to participate in workshops, and the disbursement of funds. The latter was especially important because the person who spent the aid money enhanced his status in the community. Mutual suspicion arose. Each member became concerned about how the money was spent. "My relatives [the Oxfam official came from that area] said that you are being unwise, these people would just bungle this money," commented the former Oxfam official. The amount given to these organizations was not large—only Rs. 100,000 (£1,000, US$1,670), but the people in these CBOs had never seen this kind of money. "If my capacity is to manage Rs. 50 (£.5) and you put Rs. 200 (£2) in my pocket, there is bound to be a problem," commented the former Oxfam official.

He also noted, "If you look at Insan Hamdard Sanghat now, they are nowhere. In my experience, the organizations that have taken money have never gone back to their original participatory work. They have now seen Islamabad and Karachi; they have seen three-star hotels. Now their motivation has totally changed. They spend whole days in writing proposals." Those who cannot write in English will give from Rs. 2,000 (£20; US$ 34) to Rs. 3,000 (£30; US$50) to a professional to write a proposal for them.

### Ability to Mobilize Joiners

Development aid also affected the ability of these CBOs to mobilize joiners. Each organization had up to thirty people from diverse backgrounds in their working committee, and the total membership of each CBO varied from fifty to three hundred people. After the arrival of international development aid, these organizations gradually lost all their members. Those who quit often complained about domination of the organization by a small group of people who had gotten close to the donors. "People kept getting isolated. From thirty active members, the size of the team shrank to three or four people who had become *workshopias*," commented the former Oxfam official.[5]

This account indicates that there was indeed a shift in initiators' motivation with the arrival of international development aid. It shows that material ambi-

---

5. This is a derogatory term in vogue in the development sector for people who are always attending workshops. The motive for participation is to stay in good hotels and eat good food.

tions, including the drive for salaries, participation in workshops, and material comforts, replaced voluntary commitment. It also reveals a dramatic dip in performance and in initiators' ability to mobilize joiners as a consequence of this change in motivation. This evidence suggests that the acceptance of development aid leads initiators to replace consultative processes and accountability with secrecy and authoritative practices.

## Case 2:
## ActionAid and Anjuman Mazareen-i-Punjab

More evidence of this change in initiators' motivation and performance with the arrival of international development aid is provided by the story of how international development changed the behavior of the leaders of Anjuman Mazareen-i-Punjab. This organization that was studied at length in Chapter 4 initially engaged with international development aid but quickly retracted this policy. The rising popularity of this movement of tenant farmers attracted many potential donors. ActionAid Pakistan signed a £20,000 (US$33,400) contract with the leadership of Anjuman Mazareen-i-Punjab. The money was to be disbursed over a period of two years and was meant to establish a formal secretariat with administrative staff. However, in late 2003 the tenants returned ActionAid's grant and the leaders who had dealt with this money were forced to quit.

Discussions with community members, with the leaders of Anjuman Mazareen, and with members of the People's Rights Movement (PRM) revealed that the tenants returned the money because it negatively affected the leaders' commitment and performance. They explained what happened, which was very similar to what happened to the CBOs discussed earlier in this chapter. From the start, the receipt of aid was shrouded in secrecy, which was the opposite of the open discourse policy followed by the movement. The leaders had not fully consulted the community prior to taking the money, nor did they inform the tenants of the amount they received. The leaders then manifested a clear shift in motivation, from voluntary commitment to desire for material gain. The ActionAid project provided handsome salaries for the leaders and big budgets for activities. The leaders set up a comfortable office in Lahore, the capital of the province of Punjab, instead of in Okara village, the stronghold of the movement. While criticizing how this move distanced the leadership from the tenants, one of the farmers said, "We don't get the chance to go to the Okara city, how would we go to Lahore? How can any leader representing us work for us from so far away? One can enjoy the credit of the movement while sitting in Lahore; one cannot do the work from there."

With these changes, the cost of running the movement multiplied many times. Discussion with the members and written records showed that the movement, which previously had worked entirely on the contributions of local volunteers, was now costing Rs. 80,000 (£800; US$1,333) per month to run the same activities. Prior to receiving aid, meetings took place in community halls, there were no paid staff members and duties were divided among the volunteers, and the leaders collected donations from the tenants to pay for any mass gatherings, for which detailed accounts were maintained. Aid was spent on renting the office in Lahore, purchasing a car for the leaders, paying the salaries of four to five staff members, and other bills. All of this made running the movement a costly exercise. The real problem, however, was not the enhanced cost itself but what these changes in the leaders' behavior did to the movement.

The provision of salaries for four to five paid staff members generated confrontations. As noted earlier, favoritism was shown in selecting staff members, and volunteers began to feel that some members of the community were now making a profit out of the work that others were doing voluntarily. Also, the leaders became less dynamic, that is, they became increasingly reluctant to resist the authorities. They started to talk of accepting the tenants' change of status, and they became averse to using tactics that could lead to imprisonment or cause hardship. This shift in attitude gradually started to break the morale of the whole movement. Referring to the problems they faced after the arrival of the ActionAid money, one of the current leaders of the movement argued, "This was an attempt to make the movement an NGO." What enabled the movement to regain momentum was the community's realization that the change in their leaders' strategies had much to do with their changed priorities following the receipt of aid. PRM members played a key role in bringing this awareness to the movement's members. One of the female officeholders of the Anjuman Mazareen-i-Okara explained to me how, in her view, accepting outside aid made the leadership completely unaccountable to the community: "If we take money from outside, then we don't have to worry about the tenants' views. However, when we collect money from them, then we have to give them account of every penny. Building trust is very difficult. If people think you are making personal gain out of their money, they won't give. They won't come out behind you. Making people follow you is very hard work."

Another reason the movement withdrew from receiving donor aid was the realization that accepting foreign aid damaged the legitimacy of the movement's claims in the eyes of the farm authorities, who started to accuse the tenants of protesting on behalf of foreign interests. As a tenant commented, "If we take money from outside, then we become vulnerable to critique; the government can then very easily accuse us of representing interests of the foreign powers."

This case documents concerns similar to those registered by the CBOs in Sindh. In both cases, donor aid led to initiators succumbing to material temptations, and pursuit of these material temptations led to reduced performance. Both cases also show that increased secrecy and deliberate distancing from the community members marked the process that led to the changes in the initiators' motivation and performance.

## Case 3:
## Some NGO Experiences

Whereas the first case focused on CBOs and the second focused on a movement, this section analyzes some NGOs that have recorded similar problems after the arrival of international development aid. Although I did not study them in as much detail as the previous two cases, it is still worth noting the similar concerns that arose in NGOs. One example is the experience of the Asthan Latif Welfare Trust. In 1996 this organization was very popular among the donor agencies. UNICEF was one of its key donors and promoted it heavily. *Human Development in South Asia 1997* (Haq 1997), published by a prominent Pakistani think tank, profiles the Asthan Latif Welfare Trust as one of the most successful and inspiring examples of a civil society initiative in South Asia.[6] It is a very powerful story of the dedication of one man to the cause of education. He seemingly invested all of his energies in mobilizing the community to contribute resources to provide education opportunities to girls in the community. For many years the organization had operated on a self-help basis by generating funds from local communities, but after the arrival of UNICEF's funding it lost much of its credibility among the donor community. All of the professionals in the aid industry with whom I discussed this organization expressed serious concern about the Asthan Latif Welfare Trust's use of aid money. They claimed, for example, that the schools it reported it had established did not exist anymore. Most of them argued that the influx of aid money had refocused the initiators' attention on material gains and away from the work itself. Pointing to this change in motivation, an official of the Karachi office of the Trust for Voluntary Organizations said, "The huge influx of aid just changed the mind of the father and the son." This official was of the view, however, that part of the

---

6. I was invited to contribute to this report and was involved in selecting this case as a successful initiative. The decision was based mainly on UNICEF's rave reviews.

problem was administrative. As he saw it, the organization was given a project that was far beyond its capacity to carry out. "We told UNICEF not to give him [Latif] more than ten schools, but they gave him a hundred schools in one go. Today no donor wants to engage with him," he concluded.

Another example among many others is the Maternity and Child Welfare Association. Set up by a group of senior medical doctors with a sense of social responsibility, this organization had Fatima Jinnah, sister of Quaid-i-Azam Muhammad Ali Jinnah, the founder of Pakistan, among its patrons. Since its inception in the 1950s, the organization had survived on members' donations and local public contributions, but in the 1990s it moved to accept development aid. I first visited the organization in 2000, when it was recommended to me by staff of one of the international donor agencies in Islamabad. At that time, the Maternity and Child Welfare Association, I was told, had some interesting projects.

My visits to this organization over the years of my research, however, revealed a very different scenario. Its activity gradually declined and eventually the major international donors started to withdraw from supporting its work. The chairman of the organization attributed its changed status to the influx of international development aid. In her view, donor money attracted more opportunists than committed volunteers to the organization. She maintained that the truly committed people left when they saw competition for personal gain set in with the influx of development aid. Although she had been an active member for decades, she eventually left the organization herself because of the changing organizational culture. She returned to help the organization when it was facing severe problems. "The real volunteers got disheartened. The really genuine worker leaves when he sees money come into play. There was competition about who was getting what, and who was going to which conference. I will call this corruption, but some might differ," she added.

Just like the two previous cases, these examples indicate a change of motivation on the part of those who came to dominate the organization when international development aid became available. Furthermore, they show that when the motivation of the initiators changed to material motivation, the practices of the organization also changed, leading to dramatically reduced performance.

## Cross-Case Similarities

The three cases just discussed support the correlations established in the previous chapter, which argued that international development aid restricts the initiation of cooperation between initiators and joiners. The cases analyzed in this chapter confirm that international development aid often prohibits cooperation, even breaking it down where it existed prior to the arrival of such aid. The three cases also support the second finding of the previous chapter, that the availability of international development aid overwhelmingly leads to the pursuit of material interests on the part of initiators, which in turn reduces the organization's performance. Chapter 5 also showed that international aid attracts materially motivated initiators and that the performance of these initiators is poorer than that of initiators driven by commitment to ideals. The cases discussed in this chapter affirm that development aid changes the motivation of initiators from ideals to material gains, and those initiators then record poorer performance than they did when they were driven by ideals.

Given this analysis, three questions demand attention. First, why does international development aid attract materially driven initiators? Second, why does the pursuit of material interests on the part of initiators lead to poor organizational performance? And third, why does international development aid make an initiator committed to ideals give them up and pursue material interests? The next sections attempt to answer these questions by building on the analysis of initiators' and joiners' motivation and decision-making processes developed in Chapters 3 and 4.

### Why Does Aid Attract Materially Motivated Initiators?

The answer to the question of why development aid attracts initiators motivated by material interests rests in the strong material incentives that international aid agencies provide to initiators. Aid agencies approve of spending money on high salaries, rents for big offices in expensive locations, four-wheel-drive vehicles, and conferences in five-star hotels. This attitude creates strong material incentives for materially motivated individuals to become initiators. The initiator of a locally funded VO has to prove his commitment to the cause by clearly demonstrating his willingness to make material sacrifices for that cause. Such an institutional arrangement provides no incentive for individuals seeking material rewards. International development aid, on the other hand, makes setting up an NGO a very attractive proposition for materially driven individuals; in contrast to the initiators of VOs, the initiators of NGOs do not need to sacrifice anything in order to become known as committed activists or welfare workers within international donors' circles. They do not have to provide any proof of their ideological commitment, they just have to claim it. In the process they can earn a living that is even better than what the market can offer them. In a country with a high unemployment rate and limited job opportunities, the possibility of earning a good salary, supporting a comfortable lifestyle, gaining access to elite circles, and having opportunities for foreign travel, not to mention the benefits of being one's own boss, provides strong incentives for rational individuals driven by material self-interest to engage with development aid providers and form NGOs.

## Material Motivation and Diminished Organizational Performance

To answer the question of why material motivation leads to diminished organizational performance, it is useful to revisit the argument about initiators' motives developed in Chapter 3. The three case studies analyzed in that chapter show that initiators' actions are very self-interested and that both initiators and joiners make rational calculations about how to maximize their self-interest. The difference, however, is that initiators' preference is for nonmaterial psychosocial rewards rather than for material ones. Now, if we extend this analysis, it indicates a clear logic for why material motivation leads to lower organizational performance.

## Materially Motivated Initiators and Higher Costs

Chapter 5 discussed that one reason initiators motivated by material incentives perform poorly compared to those motivated by ideals is that the former incur higher costs for the organization. The reason for these higher costs is that whereas it is rational for an initiator driven by ideals to make material sacrifices—in fact, as seen in Chapter 3, such sacrifice is critical if the initiator is to win the leverage or bargaining power that will make others in the community respond to his call for support—it is not rational for the initiator who is primarily motivated by material incentives to make such sacrifices. Because his primary motive is to enhance his own material gains, it is rational for him to charge the highest price possible for his work—the best that the market can offer or, if possible, even more than that. Similarly, it is rational to charge the donor for every input to a project, even if he receives it for free, because those items can now be charged to the project budget. At the extreme, the purely materially driven initiator may even embezzle the aid funds. Unless he is morally restrained, it is only rational for him to apportion as much of the project money as possible for his own personal gain rather than for the cause itself. During my fieldwork, many cases were brought to my attention in which an NGO was set up in the house of the initiator while he drew a high rent payment from the donor, or that he used his personal car but charged high car-rental rates. Similarly, it is very logical for the initiator whose main motive is salary and material comfort to want to have a lavish work environment and to avoid locating the office in the midst of a remote community, even though such conditions multiply the administrative costs. A good location increases the initiator's access to international donors while reducing interference from the community.

Another reason that an activity costs more under a materially motivated initiator than under an initiator motivated by ideals is the failure of the former to mobilize voluntary contributions. In the three case studies analyzed in Chapter 3, as well as in all the VOs studied in Chapter 5, discounts on purchases and free services from specialists were critical for curtailing the organization's costs. It was argued that material sacrifice on the part of the initiator was critical to mobilizing these complementary inputs. When the initiator is materially driven and shows no signs of self-sacrifice (which would be taken as proof of his commitment), he loses the ability to acquire free or discounted inputs from other individuals and businesses. For all these reasons it is rational that the cost-effectiveness of any activity carried out by materially motivated initiators will be lower than that of initiators motivated by commitment to ideals.

### Materially Motivated Initiators and Inconsistency of Work

Another key concern identified in this book is inconsistency in NGOs' pursuit of organizational objectives. We saw in Chapter 5 that materially driven initiators were less consistent than values-driven initiators in working with a particular group of beneficiaries; projects as well as beneficiaries changed when an organization changed donors, or when the funding priorities of the current donor changed. Initiators motivated by ideals worked consistently with the same group of beneficiaries, severing contact with them only after addressing their needs to the organization's maximum ability. This difference in performance is better understood in light of the analysis presented in Chapter 3. Because a materially motivated initiator sets up an NGO's whole system purely or partly to ensure his own income and to acquire personal material gains, it is inevitable that he will change sectors, projects, and beneficiary populations on the basis of the projects he gets from donors rather than continuing to work with the same group of beneficiaries or on a specific project when the money for that project runs out. Most of the NGO initiators I interviewed were clear that their projects could survive only with the continued influx of donor aid. The bigger donor projects lasted for three to five years, the shorter ones for only one to two years. It is thus easy to explain why initiators who are materially motivated show inconsistency in their work: it is rational for them to change their focus to match the availability of donor funds.

## Materially Motivated Initiators and Donor Agendas

The survey results in Chapter 5 also established that materially motivated initiators end up following their donors' agendas. Even if they are influential enough to ward off pressure to undertake specific projects, the sectors on which they focus change when their donors' preferences change. Again, this happens under the influence of the survival instincts of the materially motivated initiator. The survival of his income as well as his organization depends on the continued influx of donor aid. It is therefore only logical for him to adapt his organization's projects to the preferences of the organization's donors. The fact that most NGOs in Pakistan completely avoided critiquing General Musharraf's military rule despite claiming to work on governance and devolution is no surprise when we see that international donors had increased the flow of aid to Pakistan (and thus to NGOs, its key beneficiaries) as a sign of support to General Musharraf. The removal of General Musharraf would have disrupted that flow. It is therefore rational for NGO initiators to avoid the civil-military debate.

## Materially Motivated Initiators and Mass Mobilization

The same logic helps to explain the failure of NGOs to mobilize vertical joiners (those who are simultaneously direct beneficiaries of as well as participants in the organization's work), especially in the form of a mass movement. The NGO professional is simply not capable of doing the work that is needed to mobilize vertical joiners. NGOs operate within the legal system. They must register with the government or they cannot receive international development aid. Under these conditions it simply is not possible for them to consistently challenge the state, which in many cases is the cause of the suppression.

It is just not rational to think that paid professionals could meet the demands of running a movement. Why would they stand by the community when the police are firing on them? Why would they work after 5:00 P.M. and on weekends to help the community? Why would they leave the comfort of their city life and spend weeks at a time in villages, sleeping in the homes of tenant farmers in order to build a lasting relationship with the community? Why would they sit with the people in the scorching heat when they can collect their salary just sitting in their air-conditioned offices? It is not rational for initiators to do all of this when their primary motives for undertaking the work are a good salary, a comfortable life, and career advancement. It is therefore not surprising that despite numerous attempts by many NGOs to engage with the Anjuman Mazareen-i-Punjab, none of them were able to build a lasting relationship with the community. It is thus understandable that NGOs in Pakistan lack power to bring people into the streets for peaceful rallies and demonstrations. When there is a turnout, it is normally in response to the promise of a good meal.

## Rationality of the Changed Process

The three cases analyzed at the outset of this chapter show that the shift from ideal interest to material interest is normally marked by a process of increasing secrecy and distancing on the part of an organization's initiator. There is a rational explanation even for this shift. It has been argued that it is material sacrifice on the part of the initiator that gives him the power to bargain with joiners. It is rational for an initiator motivated by ideals, who is investing his own resources in the work and not drawing any material gains from it, to attract joiners because he is able to give them proof of his commitment and thus strengthen his moral authority over them. It is rational for a materially motivated initiator who is drawing a handsome salary—often even more than the market can offer—to avoid close interaction with the community and sharing of financial accounts, because revealing the organization's financial situation would only cause others to question his commitment given the material rewards he is drawing from the work. This is a critical issue in a society in which many people are jobless or living with very limited means.

Given that even materially motivated initiators want to claim commitment to certain ideals, it is rational for them to try to cover up the material rewards they draw from their work. During the survey, the heads of all the NGOs, despite drawing generous salaries, never acknowledged that they were well paid. They always tried to claim that a voluntary spirit lay behind their work. As one of them argued, "When you include the extra time we put into this work, then the salary is not much. We are volunteers in many ways." This need to keep up the pretense of a voluntary spirit and commitment to certain ideals makes it rational to avoid disclosing much to others about one's work.

Similarly, because foreign aid is received from the foreign donor in a lump sum, it makes no sense for the initiator to open himself to scrutiny by countless members on whose contribution he no longer relies.[7] It is logical to avoid the pressure to be accountable unless it is critical for survival. As we saw in Chapter 3, joiners, especially volunteers, act as constant monitors of the ini-

---

7. This proposition supports James Coleman's (1990) argument that norms develop in response to actions that have externalities that cannot be settled by the market. He argues that in this situation, action can be carried out only when the actor gives to others the right to control his actions. He argues that in order to develop social capital it is essential to build interdependence.

tiator, and the initiator's failure to meet the joiners' expectations creates tension between them. The initiator accepts this pressure because he realizes that withstanding this scrutiny, however frustrating it might be, is the only way to pursue his commitment to his ideals, because without the joiners' contributions the work could not go on. When international donor aid is available, the compulsion to withstand public scrutiny dissipates. It no longer remains rational for the initiator to expose himself to public scrutiny.

This consequence can be observed in the experience of the Anjuman Mazareen-i-Punjab, which has a custom in which the members of the Anjuman go around to each and every household in the community and collect contributions while also spending time chatting and involving the people in making the organization's plans—a process very different in spirit from the practice of simply inviting members to attend a meeting and giving them no role in planning. When I accompanied some of the female members of the Anjuman on their regular visits to all the households in the village, the importance of this interdependence and constant interaction in keeping the movement alive was strikingly obvious. There were suggestions on how to do things, there were agreements, there were disagreements, and finally there were decisions. Such negotiations and collective consensus are rendered unnecessary when large sums of aid from one donor substitute for the community's contributions; in such cases initiators do not feel obliged to win others over, because they do not need their money, and the community members feel they have no right to question the organization's plans.

The three cases analyzed in Chapter 3 make it clear that for initiators motivated by commitment to ideals it is only rational to keep making material sacrifices because the more such sacrifices they make, the more they enhance their personal satisfaction. The Imam in the madrasa, for example, made material sacrifices, and in return increased his well-being because, according to his beliefs, his sacrifices endeared him to God, which for him was the purpose of his life. The same was true for Abdul Sattar Edhi and Akhtar Sheikh. The ideology of change made sacrifice morally and ideologically more rewarding than material gain. In the eyes of the public, all three men made sacrifices, but in their own eyes they were only increasing their own utility by undertaking these activities. Their actions are thus as self-interested as the actions of materially motivated initiators. They are as keen on rewards as materially motivated initiators are. The only difference is that their self-interest is guided by the ideals they hold, and the rewards they seek are psychosocial and rest on the denial of material rewards.

For NGO professionals, who are mainly products of development aid, the motivation for joining an organization is career growth and material gain. For them it is only rational to explore all opportunities to enhance their material prosperity, even at the cost of the cause itself. It is not rational for an NGO professional who initiated the work of an organization in order to earn a handsome living, to increase his chances of obtaining a government advisory position, or to use the work as a launching pad for entering international development institutions to keep fighting for the cause when a donor changes its preferences or when its political agenda stops the flow of aid for that cause. It is not surprising, then, that NGO projects begin and end on the basis of what development aid is available rather than having anything to do with ensuring that the cause that led to the creation of the NGO has been served.

The analysis presented here shows that extending the argument developed in Chapters 3 and 4 helps to explain why material motivation on the part of the initiator leads to diminished organizational performance. The real question, however, is, Why does the pursuit of material rewards replace commitment to ideals? There are two possible explanations for this.

### Material Desires and Commitment to Ideals

One explanation for why initiators shift from operating out of commitment to ideals to pursuing material ambitions when international development aid becomes available is that their commitment to those ideals was weak. It was argued in Chapter 3 that occasionally an activity motivated by ideals could also be an outcome of strategic choice or long-term ambition. For example, a person with a limited educational background, like Abdul Sattar Edhi or the Imam, has only a modest chance of success in a commercial field. Realizing this, they could consciously opt to maximize their spiritual gains. The availability of development aid, however, provides them with the opportunity to satisfy their material ambitions, and their motivation, which is always self-interested, changes from interest in ideals to material interest. In such cases, unless the individual has started to really value the psychosocial rewards he is drawing from his work, the leap from ideal interest to material interest could be quite swift when strong material incentives are provided.

Another explanation for the shift from operating out of commitment to ideals to pursuing material ambitions is that strong material incentives raise the price that the initiator motivated by ideals is paying for his commitment to the cause. The decision to refuse development aid means that the initiator motivated by ideals is then sacrificing not only his own time and money but also substantial amounts of money from international donors that he could acquire by doing the same work. This additional sacrifice increases temptation and requires stronger resistance on the part of the initiator. The increased price of commitment to ideals can weaken the initiator's commitment. This observation is in line with Jean Ensminger's (1992, 10) argument that ideological commitment is not permanent but rather is vulnerable to change when the price of sacrifice rises. Even if the initiator motivated by ideas refuses international development money, the possibility of having it puts extra pressure on the commitment of initiators motivated by ideals.

These explanations leave one key question unanswered, however. Is it not possible to be materially motivated yet also committed to ideals? Is it not possible, for example, to be a highly paid leader of an NGO who is receiving all the material benefits linked with development aid yet staying as committed to ideals as an initiator who is constantly sacrificing for the cause? Can commitment to ideals and material interest coexist? Why should drawing a salary or setting up a physically comfortable office come at the cost of commitment to ideals? Is it not possible to be a highly paid NGO professional yet stay committed to the cause?

This book argues that in most cases it is not. In-depth study of the three other-regarding organizations presented in Chapter 3 revealed that although joiners viewed the initiators of these groups as altruistic and self-sacrificing, the initiators themselves were driven by very self-interested motivations, that is, promoting their organization's particular cause enhanced their self-satisfaction. For the initiator driven by religious ideology, the psychological reward is winning God's goodwill; for the initiator driven by secular intellectual thought, the psychological reward is the soothing of the initiator's ego, the moral satisfaction of having done a good deed, or the prospect of being recorded in history as a martyr. The social rewards, on the other hand, are wide public respect and recognition for the work. The nature of these rewards is such that anyone seeking them has to sacrifice materially, because the reward is contingent on that sacrifice. Winning God's goodwill, for example, requires material sacrifice because that is the route God has outlined. (Chapter 3 covered in detail the emphasis that Islam places on the sacrifice of wealth as the means to this end.) Similarly, for the activist working out of commitment to a political ideology, inner satisfaction is contingent on material sacrifice and doing something above and beyond what ordinary mortals do.

For Akhtar Sheikh, sacrificing his own money and time for his organization's cause was a means of showing others that he is different from the ordinary. It was a silent way of saying that he is superior because he is above material desires. This was the psychological reward he was seeking by undertaking the organization's work. It was critical to his commitment. As Faisal Edhi said in his interview, "If you collect money for yourself you can become a man but not a personality." Winning broad respect and reverence requires convincing people that one is above the material temptations of ordinary individuals and is committed to a higher cause. Material sacrifice is thus the critical foundation of ideal self-interest. Without material sacrifice, the rewards that a rational individual seeks from commitment to certain ideals cannot be attained.

It is here that the real explanation for shifts from ideal self-interest to material self-interest with the onset of international aid is to be found. International development aid promotes the philosophy of paying professionals rather than utilizing volunteers. One of the first things a donor does is provide for the salaries of those who are to work on the donor's project, and these salaries are often higher than what the market offers for similar jobs. The donor also provides money for comfortable offices, computers, and cars. This aid has two effects. First, the initiator can no longer enjoy the psychosocial rewards of undertaking the organization's work, because the foundation of psychosocial rewards is material sacrifice and this high material compensation makes such sacrifice unnecessary and thereby renders those rewards unattainable. Both internal and external factors play a role. Internally, the individual can no longer claim the psychological rewards because he is no longer sacrificing. Externally, the initiator losses the social rewards, because when people see him making a personal profit from the cause to which he claims ideological commitment, they start to doubt him. The wide respect and reverence that were important to all of the initiators and volunteers analyzed in Chapter 3 disappear. Inaccessibility to internal psychological and external social rewards gradually makes it irrational to stay committed to those ideals when there are no gains to be attained from it. Seen in this light, Abdul Sattar Edhi's comment makes sense: "Luxury and commitment to welfare cannot coexist. The merging of the two is impossible without one affecting the other. It is impossible for the committed to live two lives."

Previous studies provide other explanations for why a truly altruistic individual would move to nonaltruistic behavior after receiving strong material incentives. Social psychologists have argued that there are "hidden costs of rewards" and that monetary rewards may reduce intrinsic motivation, that is, the motivation for doing the activity for its own sake (Lepper and Greene 1978). Frey and Oberholzer-Gee (1997) tested this explanation in an economic context and were able to show that the willingness to support socially desirable projects, such as nuclear waste repositories, that impose considerable cost on neighborhoods decreases dramatically with the introduction of monetary incentives. More than three decades ago, Richard M. Titmuss (1970), in his study on blood donors, showed that monetary compensation tends to undermine an individual's sense of civic duty. He illustrated that paying donors affects negatively their willingness to donate blood. From a rational-choice point of view, the reason for this reduction of intrinsically motivated activities is straightforward. If a person derives internal benefits simply by behaving in an altruistic manner or by living up to her civic duty, paying her for this service reduces her option to indulge in altruistic feelings (Frey 1994). Her intrinsic motivation then has a reduced effect on supply of that good. In a different context but with similar emphasis on the utility-maximizing behavior of the individual, anthropologist Ensminger (1992, 10, 168–171) argues that ideology is not resistant to change and is affected by relative price. Therefore, when the price of ideological commitment rises, an individual's ideological commitment can shift. On the other hand, advocates of the institutionalist political economy maintain that one motivation pushes out the other because individuals absorb—that is, internalize—the values of institutions. This view emphasizes institutions and their ability to influence individuals, instead of the utility maximizing behavior of the individual.

None of these approaches emphasize the existence and nature of nonmaterial rewards in explaining the shift in motivation from ideal to material incentives. The argument developed in this book is that the process can be better explained, and with more predictive power, when we see altruistic action as driven by ideal self-interest rather than as an alternative motivation opposed to self-interest. It suggests that the answer to why material incentives push altruistic behavior out of the way lies not in denying that self-interest is the only motive for action, but in accepting that all action is self-interested and as soon as the individual stops gaining utility from an activity, he or she stops undertaking that activity. Such an analysis supports the importance of institutional incentives in shaping human action but places greater emphasis on the process that individuals follow to make conscious choices and on their tendency to maximize their own self-interest in response to changing incentives.

Some of the initiators I spoke with referred to the constant internal struggle with and the strong pull of material temptations. For example, the chairman of Service and Development, who has been making material sacrifices for more than two decades in order to run this organization, said, "We completely avoid the media. We think it corrupts the voluntary spirit. Everyone is human, and once you start getting engaged with material rewards, then there is a tendency to get carried away. It is important not to develop *maen* [the notion of I or me] in oneself. When people praise me a lot I stop them and say that I am a human too; don't praise me so much that I develop an ego." Similarly, in a feedback discussion with PRM members, Akhtar Sheikh said that the "philosopher [one of the PRM members who is considered the thinker in the group] among us has gradually made us realize that eventually this work is not about others; it is about struggle within ourselves."

A few of my respondents admitted that they have given in to material impulses. During administration of the survey discussed in Chapter 5, two initiators who had moved from self-help to donor-funded projects confessed that they could not revert to their old style of work. "I have become used to this comfortable chair now. I can't go back to the old system" was an honest response from the head of a small NGO in Bahawalpur whom I had known for a few years due to my prior professional work. Similarly, the initiator of one of the CBOs involved with the Oxfam case discussed earlier in this chapter said, "When donor money comes in we change. We don't want to go and sit under the sun any more. We prefer to sit in comfortable offices then. Also, innovation goes away."

Support for this argument can also be found in many philosophical traditions and in the experiences of prominent figures. In his reflections on *Brahmachari* (one who desires to practice self-restraint), Gandhi writes about the constant struggle within the individual between material temptations and the pursuit of nobler interests, and the strong pull of material passions and desires: "I have encountered many difficulties in trying to control passion as well as taste, and I cannot claim even now to have brought them under complete subjection" (Gandhi 1958, 29). "We know that a man often succumbs to temptation, however much he may resist it" (8). "Fasting, therefore, has a limited use, for a fasting man continues to be swayed by passion" (113–114).

Even the utilitarian theorists recognize this tension between the "pleasures of the intellect, of the feelings and imagination, and of the moral sentiments" and "those of mere sensation" (Mill [1861] 1982, 258). In his influential paper on utilitarianism, John Stuart Mill acknowledges, "It may be objected, that many who are capable of the higher pleasures occasionally, under the influence of temptation, postpone them to the lower." Similarly, Islamic Sufi thought refers to three centers of the self: the *nafs* (the concupiscent or selfish self), the *qalb* (the heart or intelligent self), and the *ruh* (the spirit or spiritual and intuitional self). It also refers to a similar tension between the *nafs* and the *ruh*, and likewise recognizes the strong pull of the *nafs* (Faridi 1993).

The reason for drawing on these disparate sources is the need to highlight that the tension between ideals and material interest has been recognized by many researchers, yet it has not been given the attention it deserves in policy planning by governments or development agencies.

It is also important to highlight that it is not the intention of this book to say that for the initiator a salary necessarily comes at the expense of psychosocial rewards. The key is that the amount taken in salary should be significantly less than what the initiator could fetch in the marketplace. The more the initiator sacrifices, the more he can draw on the psychosocial rewards. For example, Abdul Sattar Edhi's extremely simple lifestyle, which represents extreme material sacrifice, earns him the broad respect and reverence that few other ideologically motivated initiators can claim because few can match his level of sacrifice. Not all initiators have to sacrifice to this extent to mobilize joiners. However, the bigger the sacrifice, the greater will be the initiator's bargaining power with the public, and the greater will be the psychological rewards he receives.

This analysis identifies individuals, their preferences, and the choices they make as the key reasons for shifts in motivation. It is acknowledged, however, that institutional arrangements are also important in shaping individual action. In this case, very practical factors make it functionally impossible to combine commitment to ideals with professionalism. An initiator relying on development aid cannot keep pushing a cause beyond the timeframe of the project when the funding comes to an end. If an initiator is motivated by commitment to certain ideals, his commitment will require him to pursue an activity until his objectives are attained. If an initiator's primary motive is retaining a salary and other benefits, he will have to keep tailoring his activities to meet the donor's preferences. As one of the former workers of the now-defunct communist party said:

> Most of these leftists who initiated these NGOs in the 1980s did so with good intentions. They thought they would strike roots in the communities through this route. In the beginning they primarily interacted with foreign donors with whom they shared ideological interests. However, as time passed and they developed the organizational infrastructure, their focus shifted from the cause to sustaining the organization. Then they even pursued those donors who propagated very different ideological agendas.

This book thus argues that due to the inherent tension between the reward system for material interest and the reward system for ideal interest, commitment to ideals and material motivation rarely coexist for the same activity. An individual might pursue ideal interest and material interest in different contexts, but rarely together. The initiator who is materially motivated is unlikely to employ for long his commitment to ideals in the activity that is his source of income and material comfort. Overall, the book shows that the human impulse to pursue material interests is stronger then the impulse to pursue ideals and spiritual rewards. More often it is the material desires that push the commitment to ideals out of the way rather than the other way around (North 1990). Individuals who have chosen to pursue psychosocial rewards therefore face constant internal tension to resist material impulses. Ideal motivation is therefore vulnerable to strong material incentives and needs to be nurtured with the right kind of psychosocial incentives. John Stuart Mill argues the same thing in his work on utilitarianism: "Capacity for the nobler feelings is in most natures a very tender plant, easily killed, not only by hostile influences, but by mere want of sustenance; and in the majority of young persons it speedily dies away if the occupations to which their position in life has devoted them, and the society into which it has thrown them, are not favourable to keeping that higher capacity in exercise" (Mill [1861] 1982, 261).

This study thus shows that the promotion of heavy material incentives within the voluntary sector increases self-serving and cheating behavior rather than promoting mutual trust and social capital within civil society. These practical policy issues and the links between the analysis developed here and the existing theoretical debates are discussed in the final chapter of the book.

## Conclusion

The beginning of this chapter argued that donor aid changes ideal motivation to material motivation, and that this change in motivation leads to poorer performance. The chapter went on to explain why international development aid attracts materially motivated initiators, then discussed why material motivation on the part of the initiator leads to diminished performance. The final section of the chapter presented an explanation of why international development aid replaces commitment to ideals with the pursuit of material interests.

The chapter showed that performance deteriorates under the influence of material motivation because it is rational for the materially self-interested initiator to draw maximum material gains from his work even at the cost of the cause itself. It also showed that development aid attracts materially motivated initiators or shifts the allegiance of initiators committed to ideals because it offers very strong material incentives. Most important, it also suggests that there is constant tension between the human need for psychosocial rewards and the desire for material rewards, and strong material incentives can be detrimental to commitment to ideals. The reason for this tension is that the rewards of commitment to ideals rely on the very denial of material desires. Furthermore, change in motivation from ideal to material can be either sudden or gradual, depending on the strength of the person's commitment to ideals.

This chapter's analysis thus raises serious questions about the logic of supplying international development aid with the purpose of strengthening civil society in developing countries when the findings of this book suggest that rather than strengthening voluntary social reformers or activists who are motivated by commitment to ideals, donor aid is giving rise to paid development professionals who have no joiners and exhibit questionable performance. International development aid is also creating incentives that promote material temptations in potential activists and reformers and thus making their internal struggle more difficult. It is also a fact, however, that the serious resource constraints faced by most developing countries limit the ability of self-help collective-action initiatives to bring about large-scale reform. The purpose of this book's analysis has not been to argue that these traditional collective action platforms can solve the development challenges alone, but to show that aid, if given without understanding the complex incentive structures that shape these institutions, can actually hinder rather than enhance their capacity to play the role they can in easing the day-to-day challenges faced by these communities. The final chapter explains how, if at all, aid can set the right incentives—incentives that enhance rather than undermine these institutions of collective action.

# 7 Fixing Incentives
## The Way Forward

*But, since imagination has been taking less lofty flights, and every man's thoughts are centered on himself, . . . one sees that by serving his fellows man serves himself and that doing good is to his private advantage.*

**Alexis de Tocqueville, *Democracy in America*, [1835] 1994, 525**

*If, on the other hand, we accept the proposition that both the knowledge and the computational power of the decision maker are severely limited, then we must distinguish between the real world and the actor's perception of it and reasoning about it. . . . Our theory must include not only the reasoning processes but also the processes that generate the actor's subjective representation of the decision problem, his or her frame.*

**Herbert Simon, "Rationality in Psychology and Economics," 1986, S211**

In *Democracy in America*, Tocqueville attributes Americans' propensity to associate with one another and create dense associational networks to their "enlightened self-interest" or "self-interest properly understood." The duality of self-interest, that is ideal versus material, argued in this volume does not necessarily fit the conception of "enlightened self-interest" that Tocqueville observed in America—a self-interest in which expediency, in contrast to the genuine appeal of ideals, as argued in this book, leads one to engage in other-regarding behavior.[1] What the two concepts have in common, however, is an emphasis

1. A related example in which behavior that appears to be value based is in fact based on self-interest is Pascal's Wager. Blaise Pascal, a seventeenth-century philosopher, suggested that in the absence of certain knowledge about the matter, it is rational to act as though God ex-

on understanding the complex set of incentives that draw individuals to participate in other-regarding action. It is only when we truly understand what individuals gain by engaging in altruistic behavior—as seen in the study of other-regarding groups presented in Chapter 3—that we can understand why the incentives provided by development agencies to mobilize community-based collective action are having the opposite effect. In line with Howard Margolis's (1982) proposition, introduced in Chapter 3, that individuals have two types of utility functions—those that favor group-oriented preferences and those that favor selfish preferences—and that individuals make trade-offs between the two, this volume has shown that collective-action decisions are always subject to complex calculations about whether to maximize one's material utility or ideal utility. In the process it has also shown how, due to the inherent tension between material and ideal rewards, individual preference for participation in a given collective action can prove to be unstable.

This book has thus argued that viewing other-regarding behavior as altruistic—that is, as action initiated primarily as a result of the intention to help others—can lead to wrong conclusions about how to disburse aid in order to support community-based collective action and promote civic association. If other-regarding behavior is seen as a by-product of individuals' search for psychosocial and religious rewards, more reliable predictions can be made to check free-riding in self-regarding groups and generate cooperation in other-regarding groups. Unless aid agencies stop setting reward structures for participants in these groups that directly clash with the psychosocial and spiritual rewards the pursuit of which resulted in the manifestation of the other-regarding behavior in the first place, they will continue to erode community-based collective action. This chapter both analyzes the theoretical and methodological implications of the arguments advanced in this book and explores the specific policy implications resulting from this analysis. A few adjustments in the existing aid disbursement mechanisms can potentially minimize the negative impact of aid on collective action in community-based organizations and civic groups, and dramatically increase the effectiveness of the 30 percent of development aid channeled through them.

---

ists. The idea here is that the negative consequences (hellfire, damnation) of *not believing* in God if God in fact exists are much worse than the negative consequences (regular attendance at church) of *believing* in God if God does not exist. Thus, in the absence of certainty, belief is the safer option.

## Theoretical Concerns

The analysis developed in the preceding chapters informs two critical debates within social theory: how to explain other-regarding collective action, and how to understand the formation of trust within a group of individuals.

### Point 1: Rational Choice Models and Group Behavior

This volume has shown that when collective-action models that draw on variants of rational choice theory are adjusted for the complexity of self-interest and the inherent tension between the attraction of material rewards and the desire for psychosocial rewards, they provide a powerful analytical framework for developing a consistent theory of the rise of both self-regarding and other-regarding groups, without having to change common assumptions about human motivation and decision-making processes in order to explain why those who free-ride in self-regarding groups can voluntarily contribute to other-regarding groups. The cases examined in the book's chapters validate Olson's (1971) prediction that individuals in self-regarding groups are likely to free-ride and would expect others to do the same. They also support Ostrom's (1990) predictions about the kind of institutional arrangements that can overcome free-rider behavior and ensure collectively beneficial outcomes. The book argues that the analytical power of the explanatory variables developed by Ostrom will be enhanced if the role of the initiator's materially sacrificial behavior is also considered a factor in generating cooperative behavior. In addition, it has illustrated the importance of recognizing the incremental and self-transforming nature of institutional change, not just in contexts where institutions that facilitate cooperation are evolving, as Ostrom has argued, but also where existing institutions of this kind are starting to break down.

In the light of this understanding, the question that arises is, Does it serve any purpose to argue that altruistic behavior, rather than being rooted in another motivation, is a version of self-interested action? Why should one argue for a dual notion of self-interest rather than a dual notion of motivation when there is growing recognition of the latter in the recent literature of psychology, economics, and other social sciences? As early as 1970, Titmuss (1970) gave convincing evidence that material incentives can crowd out altruistic behavior: he showed that the number of blood donors dropped when money was offered for blood donations. Using more rigorous evidence, Frey (1994, 1997) advanced a similar position by noting the tensions between intrinsic and extrinsic motivation. This volume has taken this line of reasoning one step further by looking at the precise nature of the rewards associated with the two forms of utility, rather than viewing the tension between them as the result of multiple motivations.

The book has argued that it is important to draw this distinction not just because the empirical evidence suggests as much but, more importantly, because it provides an alternative explanation for the shift in individual preference and changed group behavior discussed in these chapters and thereby leads to different policy recommendations. For example, if it is assumed that some people are driven by altruistic motives to take a particular action, the consequent policy recommendation would be to give NGO professionals more freedom and independence, because failure of cooperation is often attributed to the demands of "upward accountability" to donors. Arguing that "we should acknowledge that there is no need for selfish motivations to dominate behaviour in the public sphere of the state," Chang (2001, 18) maintains that government officials asked to do extensive reporting and kept under strict checks might be less productive because they might feel they are not trusted. He argues that they are likely to be more committed if they perceive they are trusted and if the institution places a premium on noble behavior. Mawdsley, Townsend, and Porter (2005) make a similar recommendation in the context of NGOs.

If we adopt this book's analysis, which acknowledges that the shift from apparently altruistic to selfish behavior occurs in response to internal tension between the attraction of material rewards and the desire for psychosocial rewards, then removing formal accountability mechanisms and giving NGO professionals more independence will not on their own solve the problem. Instead, opportunistic behavior will likely increase, unless the rewards for engaging in NGO activities are adjusted to ensure that the people who get involved in those activities do not do so primarily to get money. Giving NGO professionals greater freedom will therefore not help resolve the problem at hand unless a mechanism is first developed to test whether the leaders of the groups supported by the donors are actually committed to the cause. The explanation of why material incentives crowd out altruistic behavior is therefore based not on denying that self-interest is the only motive for action but on accepting that most action is in fact self-interested—that is, utility maximizing—and on recognizing that as soon as an individual stops gaining utility from an action, he or she stops pursuing that activity. As the cases analyzed in this book show, when initiators can no longer draw psychosocial or spiritual rewards from their other-regarding activities, they stop contributing to them.

The main contribution of this volume, then, is that it identifies the importance of disaggregating the utility calculus and of understanding the inherent tension between the pursuit of material and psychosocial rewards. Becker's (1993) Nobel Prize-winning work in support of the argument that an important step in extending the traditional theory of individual rational choice is to analyze social issues beyond those usually considered by economists—by incorporating into the theory a much richer class of attitudes, preferences, and calculations—is now fully accepted in economics. Although he maintains that all action is self-interested, Becker does not assume that individuals are motivated solely by selfish or material gains; instead he argues that his approach is a method of analysis, not an assumption about particular motivations—that behavior is in fact driven by a much richer set of values and preferences. He does not, however, take into account the need to understand the various reward structures that mark the different sources of utility, and any possible tensions between them. The result, as Goldthorpe (1998, 178) argues, is that "in the face of action that evidently does not conform to the criteria of rationality that are imposed, one response is simply that of postulating hitherto unrecognized features of the situation—unobservable 'psychic' income or costs seem a favourite option . . . which, once taken into account, render the action rational after all. Thus, rather than the theory stimulating further research of any kind, it is in effect 'closed.'"

Although the research presented in this book supports Becker's (1993) argument that even other-regarding behavior is primarily driven by a desire to maximize one's own utility, it also shows that the tension between the rewards associated with material sources of utility and those associated with ideal sources of utility has to be studied in detail if such an all-encompassing concept of self-interest or utility is to be meaningful. As the previous chapter illustrates, the inherent tension between the rewards attached to ideal self-interest and those attached to material self-interest is central to explaining why extrinsic (material) incentives often crowd out intrinsically (ideal) motivated behavior. Because informal institutions are often sustained by members' hopes for psychosocial rewards, the improved understanding of the interface between material and psychosocial rewards presented here has the potential to refine existing institutional analysis of informal institutions. As North (1990, 86) has noted, "we are still at something of a loss to define, in very precise terms, the interplay between changes in relative prices, the ideas and ideologies that form people's perceptions, and the roles that the two play in inducing changes in institutions."

Here it is again important to note that debates on the different kinds of rewards are ongoing in psychology and economics circles; that is, this book is not alone in advancing the position that psychosocial and material rewards constitute separate sources of utility. However, the ideas offered here have not yet made their way into the mainstream economics and development studies literature. Works on psychology and economics do recognize the significance of nonmonetary rewards,[2] and these rewards have been given a variety of labels, including *intrinsic benefits, expressive benefits,* and *participatory benefits.* Psychological rewards are normally interpreted as feelings of efficacy, empowerment, or righteousness, or just the "feel good" feeling. Social rewards, on the other hand, include, among other things, the desire to gain friends, maintain one's social standing, or gain respectability (Chong 1991). These rewards have normally been divided into *external social payment* and *internal self-payment* (Goode 1978). Nonetheless, even though the concept of non-monetary rewards helps explain why rational individuals will support cooperative behavior that apparently entails no material rewards, it is unpopular with many rational choice theorists, for two reasons. First, it seems that nonmonetary rewards can be invoked to explain any outcome whatsoever; and second, nonmonetary rewards are difficult to model. Olson (1971) mentions the existence of social or psychological incentives and acknowledges that the reason he avoids them in his explanation of collective action is that, compared to nonmonetary rewards, material rewards are more easily identifiable and more accurately measured. He argues that "it is not possible to get empirical proof of the motivation behind any person's action; it is not possible definitely to say whether a given individual acted for moral reasons or for other reasons in some particular case. A reliance on moral explanation could thus make the theory untestable" (61). Those who study collective action problems have, however, continued to highlight the significance of these rewards in shaping social action. Emphasizing the importance of nonmonetary benefits in explaining collective action, Chong (1991, 10) asks, "How else can we explain the enthusiasm of participation in public-spirited action?" He argues that what is important is to specify the role and characteristics of nonmonetary rewards more carefully so that not too much collective action is attributed to it.

Similarly, Brennan (1996) highlights the usefulness of the notion of nonmonetary rewards for academic analysis and policy formation while building a model that shows that having a better understanding of the various types of rewards can help an institution attract the right employees. Elaborating on an earlier paper that argued that academics value academic prestige more than they value monetary rewards, he makes the case that in an academic setting individuals with relatively high taste for scholarly activities could be differentially rewarded by a currency—that is, a mixture—of rewards that takes the form of a higher proportion of academic support and a correspondingly lower propor-

---

2. For a good summary of the varied use of this notion, see Chong 1991.

tion of cash, even when agents seeking the different types of rewards cannot be identified (272). This approach, he argues, would prevent nonacademics from presenting fake applications for these positions, because a nonacademic would not see much value in academic rewards. The overuse of the notion of non-monetary rewards for analysis and policy formation and to attract employees or members can be avoided by ensuring that any use of the concept clearly pins down the specific nature of the reward applied to a given activity and how it contributes to the production of a specific good.

### Point 2: Theorizing Trust

At the heart of the collective-action dilemma lies the difficulty of trusting others—that is, everyone expects others to shirk responsibility and leave them with a "sucker's payoff." The study of collective action situations thus indirectly provides insights into what helps build trust. The analysis developed in this book so far provides three interesting insights into the formation of trust. First, it supports Putnam's (1993, 169) view that "Social networks allow trust to become transitive and spread: I trust you, because I trust her and she assures me that she trusts you." That is, trust is an accumulative process. This transitive nature of trust was clearly visible while I was studying the decision-making processes that joiners followed to select an initiator. They often trusted an unknown initiator because a common acquaintance whom they themselves trusted, trusted that initiator. Such trust was not blind, however; people only trusted the word of those of their acquaintances who they knew were well-placed within the networks on which they needed information.

Second, this book also supports Coleman's (1990) argument that the stronger a person's internal compulsion is, the greater is his or her tendency to trust. Although the joiners of self-regarding groups were as suspicious of the motives of the groups' initiators as joiners of other-regarding groups, they were slightly more willing to trust their initiators, because their own immediate concerns were at stake and they therefore had a greater practical need to trust the initiators. However, as noted earlier, building trust was a gradual process. Even the joiners of self-regarding groups increased their contributions to the collective task only gradually, once they saw proof that the initiators did what they said they did.

Overall, the findings of this book support, from among the various theoretical approaches on trust, Bacharach and Gambetta's (2001) work, which uses signaling theory—an extension of rational choice theory—to analyze trust problems. Bacharach and Gambetta have articulated a new theoretical framework for recasting trust games as signaling games. They argue that, except in limited cases, trust-warranting properties are unobservable, but they may be, and often are, known through mediating signs. Whether someone is trustworthy or not is assessed by evaluating observable features of that person that are known to correlate with the unobservable, trust-warranting properties. Gambetta and Hamill (2005, 7) test this theory in an empirical setting and state at the outset, "We suppose, realistically, that the vast majority of basic trust games include some observation by trusters of features of their trustees."

The empirical data in this book have ended up putting forward a similar argument. Chapter 3 shows that the inability of joiners to monitor directly the motivation of the initiator leads to the problem of how to trust him. This trust dilemma is overcome only through developing an indirect monitoring mechanism that consists of evaluating observable features of individual behavior that are correlated with the unobservable trust-warranting features. Thus the reason that visible signs of material self-sacrifice on the part of the initiator play such a critical role in shaping the joiner's decision is that they act as signals of the initiator's commitment to the cause. Material sacrifice on the part of the initiator is the joiner's most cost-efficient monitoring mechanism.

Gambetta and Hamill (2005, 11) write:

> In many real-world cases, however, we are not so lucky and find that most signals at our disposal are not perfectly separating. There are many signs that to some degree are more costly for a mimic (because of, say, penalties for their abuse) but are still emitted by a small number of mimics. . . . When the signal is only partly contaminated, it remains credible enough for a minority of mimics to gain from using it and for the majority of honest signalers to keep using it.

They argue further that the best situation from a truster's perspective is when a genuine trustee can afford to emit these signs, and a nongenuine customer cannot.

Gambetta and Hamill's analysis applies very well to the overall argument developed in this book. It has been shown that international development aid provides strong material incentives to initiators that eventually lead to a breakdown of cooperation between initiators and joiners. If we look at this argument in the light of the analysis presented here, it can be argued that donor aid makes mimicking very easy for initiators and consequently makes it very difficult for joiners to separate honest initiators from those who are mimicking them. Under the rules of donor aid, the initiator can make personal material gains from the cause yet still claim commitment to the cause itself. This option contaminates the signal that joiners had developed to test the motivation of the initiator. This book's findings thus support the reasoning that trust decisions are based on observation of visible signs that are meant to correlate with a characteristic that is not directly observable, and using signaling games to analyze trust problems therefore appears to be a powerful analytical framework.

## Policy Adjustments

What adjustments do donors need to make to their policies for funding civil society groups to ensure that their incentive structures promote rather than erode cooperative behavior among community-based collective-action initiatives? Incentives are the rewards and punishments that individuals perceive to be related to their own and others' actions (Gibson et al. 2005). This book has proposed that the tendency of existing aid disbursement mechanisms to promote the pursuit of material gains among leaders of self-regarding and other-regarding groups is central to the breakdown of cooperation within those groups. The critical question, then, is what can the development agencies do about it? If the search for psychosocial or religious rewards can promote collective action, are donors expected to promote such incentives? And if yes, then how?

Academics are likely to be wary of advising donors to indulge in introducing psychosocial or religious incentives in order to stimulate a desirable policy outcome; the persistence of Talibans, who were initially mobilized by religious incentives but followed a totally unexpected trajectory, confirms this. However, refraining from introducing psychosocial incentives does not mean that donors should not try to ensure that, in contexts where they are proposing to help people overcome their collective problems, such incentives are not crowded out by their interventions.

If the development agencies become more open to studying psychosocial incentives rather than just handing out the material rewards that apparently motivate the actors with whom they are trying to engage, they will be much better positioned to ensure that their support complements the existing cooperative arrangements rather than stifling cooperative behavior. As noted in the cases presented in this book, attempts to replace these psychosocial rewards with material incentives in the hope of professionalizing and formalizing a relatively informal institutional arrangement for coordinating cooperative behavior is often not practically feasible or is a much more costly option. Some very clear policy messages emerge when the role of psychosocial rewards in sustaining community-based collective action and civic association is recognized.

*Adjustment 1:*

*Moving Away from Providing High Salaries to Initiators*

As this book has illustrated, the apparently simple measure of providing high salaries to initiators, supported by the assumption that individuals need to be motivated through high salaries in order to generate civic associations and promote social capital and cooperation within the organization, is central to the explanation of why aid given to generate collective action can end up upsetting the existing institutional arrangements that are regulating cooperative behavior between a group's initiators and joiners. The initiator's willingness to make material sacrifices in order to attain a collective good, along with showing signs of efficacy in meeting the group's stated objectives, is central to mobilizing potential joiners to cooperate with the initiator. High salaries erode cooperative behaviour for two reasons: first, they increase the transaction costs for both potential and current members by making it more costly for the members to gather information and monitor the motivation and commitment of the initiator. Second, in the long term, direct monetary incentives generate tension within the leader over whether to make this work his profession and thus the source of his material achievements, or to continue to invest in this activity as a means to secure psychosocial and religious rewards.

As explained in the previous chapter, if the leader of either of the two forms of groups studied in this book is paid a high salary that is comparable to or more than the market standard, he can no longer gain the psychosocial or religious rewards that could be gained by undertaking the work for nothing. In the long term, this compensation reduces commitment to the cause and introduces a free-rider problem: because the leader can no longer attain psychosocial rewards for his activity, as a rational actor his interest is best served by maximizing his pursuit of material rewards for the activity at the least cost. It is important to remember here that the issue of the leader's salary is distinct from that of the staff's salaries. Members expect staff to have joined the effort as a means of earning income rather than as an expression of commitment to ideas, which they expect from the initiator; therefore, as long as they are not higher than what such people could get in the market, and as long as the staff are not, for example, all relatives of the initiator, salaries for the staff are rarely found to be a concern for the members.

Here it is also important to note that this suggestion does not create a dilemma for the donor whose own staff are paid high salaries; paying the leaders of NGOs less than their foreign or local staff can arguably be seen as discriminatory. The reason is simple: the members of a community-based group are concerned about incentives given to other members of their own group, whether leaders or joiners, and not about the salaries of the staff of foreign donors, especially the expatriate staff, who are seen as external to the local context. Discrimination in the salaries of local and expatriate staff might be an ethical issue for donors, but the salaries of donor agency staff never seemed to affect leaders' and group members' decisions to cooperate.

## Adjustment 2:
### Funding the Activity and Direct Inputs

Rather than offering cash incentives in the form of salaries, agencies that give international development aid can greatly facilitate cooperation by providing the material resources required to meet a community's group objectives. These resources can take the form of funding to support specific activities. Yet here too the style of funding has to change. If activities are funded in lavish ways—for example, paying for conferences in five-star hotels, which is often the norm among the bigger donor-funded NGOs in the developing world—doubts arise among members about the leader's motivation. The key is to remember that anything that is seen as materially benefiting a group's initiator and staff at a level that surpasses their market worth triggers serious concerns among members about the commitment of the leader. The leader is then suspected of undertaking the work for her own benefit rather than for the benefit of the collective or of poor and marginalized groups. Even better than funding such activities would be investing aid in providing the actual material required for the group's activities, or technical support in planning and carrying out certain activities.

## Adjustment 3:
### Monitoring Performance by Designing Better
### Membership Measurement Tools

At present, emphasis is on relying primarily on financial reports and audits to measure the effectiveness of NGOs; however, donors also need to develop innovative tools for measuring the actual membership of these groups and their collective satisfaction resulting from the utilization of the aid made available by the donor. The presence of active members is the most critical feature of the civil society and social capital debate. For Tocqueville ([1835] 1994), it was the members' propensity to associate with one another that determined whether they constituted a vibrant civil society; for Putnam (1993) it is again a dense associational network that forms the foundation of social capital. It is therefore striking that this important indicator for measuring the strength of a civic associational culture has been utterly ignored in measures designed by donors to measure the effectiveness of funds channeled through NGOs, civil society, and community-based initiatives.

## Adjustment 4:
### Willingness to Dialogue as Equals and
### Work with Different Conceptions of Development

If donors adjust the mechanism for disbursing aid to NGOs on the three counts just suggested, one likely outcome will be that the groups left working with donors will demand to enter the dialogue with them as equals. When the leaders of these groups cannot expect to get their salaries from international donors or to attain other material gains through such engagement, they will not have any incentive to follow the donor's plans unless those plans are a natural fit with the group's own objectives. This independence, as illustrated in the case studies of locally funded groups analyzed in Chapters 3 and 4, is critical to these groups' legitimacy and long-term survival and innovation. In order for donors to support these locally embedded groups, their policies will have to be flexible, and they will have to listen to the groups' perspectives and approaches to development. This approach is bound to lead to a more challenging set of engagements for the donors, but such genuine engagement, rather than the sort cultivated by turning activists into paid workers, is the only way to ensure that truly participatory models can evolve. Such an approach should, in principle, fit well with donors' growing recognition of the multiple dimensions of poverty (Alkire 2002) and with Sen's (2001) emphasis on working to increase people's capabilities rather than their functionings. It also forces donors to engage with locally embedded civil society groups in the south, whether religious or secular. These groups might voice a different vision of the world than the one spelled out by the development agencies, but their strong membership base highlights the need to at least assess the appeal of their counterdiscourse and not immediately rule it out as irrelevant. The agendas of some of these locally embedded groups that profess to advocate for and help the poor might indeed be questionable, but not the agendas of all of them.

## Adjustment 5:
### Adjusting Incentives Over Time

The institutional economics literature recognizes that institutions do change, and at times very rapidly. Furthermore, when incentives change, new players enter the field and, at times, old players exit. The relevance of Ostrom's (1990) convincing account of the often incremental and self-transforming nature of in-stitutional change for the study of self-regarding and other-regarding groups has been noted in this volume. Small successes in the beginning of the project can make people contribute more at a later stage. Similarly, the emergence of trust dilemmas from small issues, such as a leader's unwillingness to consult members on the use of donor aid, can result over time in large trust deficits in that the joiners develop such doubts about the leader's motives that cooperation breaks down. In all the organizations studied for this book, the joiners were constantly adapting to the changing behavior of the initiator. It is important that, instead of designing projects with fixed incentive structures, officials in donor agencies learn to view the organization they are supporting as an organic body in which the rules of the game are constantly being renegotiated between the initiators and the joiners. The incentives provided to a group in the first year of project support might not be the same as those needed in the second year, when the activity has taken off, or in the third year, when the activity ideally should be consolidated.

.   .   .

Although this study has highlighted some fundamental problems with the in-centives currently provided by donors to NGOs, it does not suggest the sort of dire conclusions that have led some researchers to argue for the cessation of international development aid altogether. Instead this book proposes that it is possible to identify concrete ways to minimize the negative impact of such aid on community-based organizations of collective action. A general point emerging from this analysis is that although it is important to acknowledge the influence of culture in shaping individual preferences and collective outcomes, it is also important not to interpret cultural practices as purely ideological preferences, because institutions that seem very culturally specific often serve a rational purpose in their societal context. It is much more fruitful, for the purposes of development policy, to approach norms, values, and culture from an institutional economics perspective (North 1990) that, in line with rational choice sociology (Coleman 1990), seeks to identify why individuals cooper-ate with one another to establish norms rather than taking them as given and unchanging.

## Testing the Framework:
## An Experiment with Tsangaya Schools in Kano

In Kano, a northern Nigerian state whose population is 98 percent Muslim, the large-scale provision of Islamic education (there are 25,000 community-run Islamic schools and only 5,600 state-run secular schools) is a result of collective action practices sustained over centuries. The community members actively support the *malams* (religious scholars) to ensure the survival of these religious schools; some contribute because their own children are educated in these schools, others support them for the benefit of the community. In recent years, many donor agencies have been trying to engage with these Islamic schools to explore means to integrate secular subjects into the curriculum because, given the slow growth in the number of state schools, this could be the most cost-effective mechanism to meet the targets of the Education for All movement. The challenge, however, is how to ensure the support of the *malams* and parents in rural areas, who have long distrusted secular education due to its association with colonial rule and Christian missionaries. The problem is particularly severe in the case of the Tsangaya schools, which are boarding schools for boys that historically have focused purely on Quranic education.

It is therefore worth looking at some of the features of a recent intervention undertaken as part of an education sector support program funded by the United Kingdom's Department for International Development (DFID) to introduce modern education into Tsangaya schools. This intervention has had initial successes. *Malams* from 140 Tsangaya schools under three local government authorities have started to release their children to acquire secular education in addition to continuing their Quranic education. This move has benefited close to nine hundred children who otherwise would not have received such education. Although the long-term effectiveness of this program will be assessed only over time, the initial success of this model in mobilizing the cooperation of the *malams* and the community helps to illustrate the importance of the five policy adjustments just discussed.

### Adjustment 1

As in all development projects, the first issue in designing the program was to determine what incentives should be provided to the *malams* to encourage them to take part in the program. Direct cash transfers to them in return for a promise to release the children for certain hours of each day for secular education was one clear option. But such cash incentives, especially if large, would have created a dilemma. The Tsangaya system, due to the boarding arrangement, is characterized by dense informal institutional norms by which parents expect the *malams* to behave in a certain way in return for the parents' granting them extensive control over their children's daily life choices. Cash payments would have provoked suspicion regarding the *malams'* motives for convincing the parents to let their children attend secular education classes. Interviews with community members and parents indicated that payment of a small token fee to the *malams* would be considered fair because of the hard work the *malams* were perceived to do. However, any large cash incentive received by the *malams* would have reduced their credibility among the community members, because then they would not be sure whether the *malams* were convincing the parents to let their children attend secular classes because the *malams* found this to be a religiously legitimate choice or because they were now being paid to encourage the children to gain a secular education.

Enlisting the support of the *malams* was critical for implementation of the program, so when direct financial incentives were found to be problematic, the question became how else to motivate the *malams*. The mobilization team identified two other inputs that could substitute for direct cash incentives: adding technical education to the secular education content, because all of the *malams* genuinely valued their pupils' gaining technical skills; and the provision of lunch to the children once a week, which took some of the pressure of feeding them off the *malams*. Furthermore, the mobilization team consisted of people from the local community and prominent traditional elders who were respected in the areas where the schools were located and had been convinced by the program mobilization team of the importance of this initiative. The reliance on individuals trusted by the community and the willingness to provide inputs that were genuinely valued by the *malams*, rather than trying to buy their cooperation through paying them large salaries, helped the team avoid the creation of parental distrust and at the same time helped to ensure that the *malams* were genuinely involved rather than just paying lip service to the program in anticipation of a handsome reward.

### Adjustment 2

Overcoming the problem of what incentives to provide was not the only challenge; it became clear that it was equally important to ensure that the support provided for carrying out specific activities did not allow perverse incentives to creep in. This need became clear in determining how to provide a meal in each of the schools once a week. To reduce the logistical cost of providing this meal, it was most feasible for the food to be bought and cooked near the schools. Thus, paying the *malams* cash for ensuring provision of the weekly meal was logistically the most cost-effective solution. However, here again the provision of cash to *malams* had inherent problems. In the program model, central schools were created where children from a cluster of five participating

Tsangaya schools came every day for secular education, and the once-a-week meal was to be provided at these central schools. Therefore, only one *malam* was needed to see that the food was prepared for all of the children at each central school, and the money for the meal would be given to this *malam*. However, the *malam* who received the cash was seen by the other *malams* to be benefiting personally, because he could potentially save some money by cooking less food or using cheaper food items, or at the minimum he could save some of the food for his own consumption and for his family. There were signs that failure to resolve this dilemma could lead to some *malams* withdrawing their cooperation. It was therefore decided that preparation of the meals would rotate among the *malams* of the five Tsangaya schools, with a different one cooking each week. In addition, community members and teachers had to be mobilized to monitor that the feeding was being properly carried out.

### Adjustment 3

The designing of tools to assess whether the program was actually engaging with *malams* who had networks of Tsangaya schools and roots within the community was also important in running the program. There was a chance that when they saw the support provided by the program to the *malams* of these schools, other people might claim to have a Tsangaya school without necessarily having one. Because the program team relied on foreign consultants and local staff in the agency's main office, they had limited capacity to assess the legitimacy of a *malam*'s claim about how many children he catered to. This concern was a central challenge that the program's designers could not have overcome without relying heavily on the local association of Quranic *malams*—a network with which all of the *malams* were associated and whose membership mattered to their social recognition—and on the office of the Special Advisor for Tsangaya Education, a government body with the mandate to support the Tsangaya schools. It is only because the staff and senior leadership of these two locally embedded bodies were involved that reliable tools were identified to ensure that *malams* with a genuine following in the community were engaged in the program. To win the cooperation of these two religious bodies, however, adjustment 4 was critical.

### Adjustment 4

At the very outset of designing the program, the main dilemma for DFID was how to engage with Islamic education given that the secular outlook of donor agencies allows little space for acknowledging the value of religious education.

The question therefore was whether the program should just introduce secular education in these schools or actually try to reduce the time spent on teaching religious education, because memorizing the Quran for hours every day, which is what the children in the Tsangaya schools do, does not lead to the growth in analytical skills that is central to the conception of meaningful secular education. Initial research conducted through group discussions in the community established that religious education was highly valued, and it was equally clear that the community wanted its children to have access to secular education—a result that countered the assumption that the *malams* and parents in rural areas are inherently against secular education—but if they had to choose between the two they would definitely choose religious education. Whereas securing a religious education was viewed as a serious religious obligation and as promoting the moral behavior needed to become a good member of society, secular education was thought to be economically advantageous. In the view of most parents, and even the *malams*, both were important.

In such a context, the only way to work effectively with this community was to acknowledge the importance to them of religious education and to respect their pursuit of it rather than attempting to reduce its role. Showing genuine acceptance of this value was central to winning the trust of the two religious bodies mentioned earlier so that the program could be implemented. It was clear that the local actors were very capable of judging the intentions of the donors. It is also important to note that the emphasis on religious education was not entirely motivated by spiritual reasons; its appeal was also shaped by very calculated this-worldly benefits, as was plain in a comment often repeated by parents, that "at least in religious schools they learn to respect the parents, the elders, and the family values. Children in secular schools neither learn good education nor are they able to secure jobs at the end of their schooling because of the poor quality. However, after being in secular schools, they think it is below them to do the traditional jobs that their parents do; the result is that they actually become rude and go around on bikes with their friends, wasting their time."

### Adjustment 5

Finally, from the very start it was clear that it was important to see the program as a constantly evolving process in which the relationships between the program team and the *malams*, as well as among the *malams*, the children, and the community, would change as the program developed. If the children learning in the secular schools started to challenge the *malams*, the cooperation that the *malams* were showing could easily break down. If, however, the *malams* found that the children were gaining a secular and technical education yet retaining respect for their religious values, the cooperation would likely strengthen. At the same time, the *malams'* familiarity with the program team could build trust, which could help greatly to sustain the program in the long run. Relationships would therefore change over time as interaction took place between the different members of the program. The program team had to be conscious of all this and constantly observe the changing relationships and adjust the incentives accordingly if the program was to be successful. As Ostrom (1990) has illustrated, institutions often arise as a result of an incremental self-transforming process, and donors have to learn to adjust their interventions constantly to match these gradual changes.

## Some Methodological Concerns

Rational choice theory has long been criticized for being a product of armchair theorizing, in which theorists armed with assumptions about rationality identify optimal outcomes in different theoretical puzzles (Green and Shapiro 1994). The hypotheses generated by such accounts fail to consider how context and history affect people's preferences and their means–ends calculations. As a result, an increasing clamor of voices demands the empirical testing of rational choice hypotheses and their underlying assumptions in different contexts. Even when empirical studies have been conducted, they have been critiqued for being more eager to vindicate one universalist model or another than to explain actual outcomes (Green and Shapiro 1994). These critics argue that striving to explain observed empirical realities is preferable to fashioning theories according to the dictates of neatness. This book proposes that including the voices of those whose actions are being studied is critical to discovering the rationality of informal institutions.

The studies of rational choice theory remain heavily tilted in favor of quantitative approaches, including mathematical modeling and economic modeling, especially those based on game theory. Admittedly these modeling exercises have remarkable explanatory power: mathematical modeling allows for the systematic checking of logical consistency and the tracking of chains of cause and consequence, and economic modeling helps researchers explore the rationale behind stylized facts once they are identified. But these studies, especially those based on economic modeling, draw on data from standardized questionnaires and surveys that confine the possible responses to a question within the frame of reference of the researcher. This approach leads to a process of generating "post-hoc theory" (Green and Shapiro 1994), in which correlations derived through quantitative research instruments are interpreted in terms of the importance the researcher attributes to those values, rather than in terms of the value they have for the subjects under study.

Although economists' concerns about the subjective nature of interview data are valid, as are their concerns about the generalizability of findings from studies relying on few interviews, it is equally true that large-scale surveys designed without understanding the local value that people attribute to various factors will always run the risk of omitting variables that are critical to shaping choices in a specific context. If institutions result from conscious action on the part of rational individuals, then a real appreciation of the role of these institutions requires giving some weight to the individual's own reasoning about the existence and working of the given institution. Such an exercise requires in-depth engagement with the actual subjects of the study, and reliance on in-depth interviews and observations. This process does not imply doing away with quantitative research techniques; in fact, for certain questions, such as those concerned with the processes that shape the interplay between ideal and material utility, the modeling of biological and cultural evolution holds more promise than qualitative studies. However, it does entail recognizing that quantitative techniques are more appropriate for addressing certain questions than for addressing others, and that sometimes they are better developed after the local logic underlying certain actions has been identified through qualitative research.

# Glossary

Non-English words used only once are translated within the body of the text and are not included in the glossary.

**Alim**  Islamic scholar

**Anjuman Mazareen-i-Punjab**  Organization of Tenants of Punjab

**Dars-i-Nizami**  Islamic curriculum developed in India in the eighteenth century and followed to date in South Asian madrasas

**Haqooq-ul-Abad**  Rights of fellow humans

**Hifz**  Memorization of the Holy Quran

**Jamiat ul Uloom al-Shariah**  Name of a madrasa

**Jazba**  Zeal

**Khankah**  Place of sufi worship

**Langar**  Public kitchen

**Malam**  Religious scholar

**Maulavi**  Title of a religious leader or preacher

**Masjid**  Mosque

**Nazra**  Reading of the Holy Quran

**Pirs**  Local term for a sufi

**Sadaka**  Voluntary religious giving

**Tsangaya**  Traditional Quranic boarding school in northern Nigeria

**Waqf**  Endowed property

**Zakat**  Compulsory religious giving in Islam

# Bibliography

Aga Khan Development Network. 2000. *Enhancing Indigenous Philanthropy for Social Investment: A Report of the Initiative on Indigenous Philanthropy.* Pakistan: Aga Khan Development Network.

Alavi, H. 1966. "The Army and Bureaucracy in Pakistan." *International Socialists Journal* 3(14): 140–181.

Ali, T. 1970. *Pakistan: Military Rule or People's Power?* London: Trinity Press.

———. 1983. *Can Pakistan Survive? The Death of a State.* Harmondsworth, UK: Penguin Books.

Alkire, S. 2002. *Valuing Freedom: Sen's Capability Approach and Poverty Reduction.* Oxford, UK: Oxford University Press.

Alkire, S., and S. Deneulin. 2002. "Individual Motivation, Its Nature, Determinants, and Consequences for Within-Group Behaviour." In J. Heyer, F. Stewart, and S. Throps (eds.), *Group Behaviour and Development: Is the Market Destroying Cooperation?* Oxford, UK: Oxford University Press.

Alt, J. E., and K. A. Shepsle (eds.). 1990. *Perspectives on Positive Political Economy.* Cambridge, UK: Cambridge University Press.

Anheier, H. K., and J. Kendall. 2000. *Trust and Voluntary Organizations: Three Theoretical Approaches.* LSE Civil Society Working Paper 5. London: London School of Economics.

Anheier, H. K., and L. M. Salamon. 1998. *The Nonprofit Sector in the Developing World: A Comparative Analysis.* Manchester, UK: Manchester University Press.

———. 1999. "Volunteering in Cross-National Perspective: Initial Comparisons." *Law and Contemporary Problems* 62: 43–66.

Ansari, K. H. 1990. *The Emergence of Socialist Thought Among North Indian Muslims, 1917–1947.* Lahore, Pakistan: Book Traders.

Ansari, S.F.D. 1992. *Sufi, Saints and State Power: The Pirs of Sindh, 1834–1947.* Cambridge, UK: Cambridge University Press.

Arellano-Lopez, S., and J. Petras. 1994. "NGOs and Poverty Alleviation in Bolivia." *Development and Change* 25 (3): 555–568.

Arrow, K. 2000. "Observations on Social Capital." In P. Dasgupta and I. Serageldin (eds.), *Social Capital: A Multifaceted Perspective.* Washington, DC: World Bank.

Asian Development Bank. 1999. *Cooperation Between Asian Development Bank and Nongovernmental Organizations.* Manila: Asian Development Bank.

———. 2003. *ADB-Government-NGO Cooperation: A Framework For Action, 2003–2005.* Manila: Asian Development Bank.

Bacharach, M., and D. Gambetta. 2001. "Trust in Signs." In K. S. Cook (ed.), *Trust in Society.* New York: Russell Sage Foundation.

Bahadur, K. 1977. *The Jama'at-i-Islami of Pakistan: Political Thought and Political Action.* New Delhi: Chetana Publications.

Ballhatchet, K., and J. Harrison (eds.). 1980. *The City in South Asia: Pre-Modern and Modern.* London: Curzon Press.

Banerjee, A. V. 2007. *Making Aid Work.* Cambridge, MA: MIT Press.

Bano, M. 2008a. "Contested Claims: Public Perceptions and the Decision to Join NGOs in Pakistan." *Journal of South Asian Development* 3 (1): 87–108.

———. 2008b. "Dangerous Correlations: Aid's Impact on NGOs' Performance and Ability to Mobilize Members in Pakistan." *World Development* 36 (11): 2297–2313.

Barrow, O., and M. Jennings. 2001. "The Charitable Impulse: Introduction." In O. Barrow and M. Jennings (eds.), *The Charitable Impulse: NGOs and Development in East and North-East Africa.* Oxford, UK: James Currey.

Bates, R. H. 1990. "Macropolitical Economy in the Field of Development." In J. E. Alt and K. A. Shepsle (eds.), *Perspectives on Positive Political Economy.* Cambridge, UK: Cambridge University Press.

Bayly, C. A. 1971. "Local Control in Indian Towns: The Case of Allahabad, 1880–1920." *Modern Asian Studies* 5: 289–311.

———. 1973. "Patrons and Politics in Northern India." *Modern Asian Studies* 7: 349–388.

———. 1983. *Rulers, Townsmen, and Bazaars: Northern Indian Society in the Age of British Expansion, 1770–1870.* Cambridge, UK: Cambridge University Press.

Bebbington, A., S. Hickey, and D. C. Mitlin. (eds.). 2008. *Can NGOs Make a Difference?: The Challenge of Development Alternatives.* London: Zed.

Bebbington, A. J., M. Woolcock, S. Guggenheim, and E. E. Olson (eds.). 2006. *The Search for Empowerment: Social Capital as Idea and Practice at the World Bank.* Sterling, VA: Kumarian Press.

Becker, G. S. 1993. "Nobel Lecture: The Economic Way of Looking at Behaviour." *Journal of Political Economy* 101 (3): 385–409.

Becker, H. S. 1964. "Problems in the Publication of Field Studies." In A. Vidich, J. Bensman, and M. Stein (eds.), *Reflections on Community Studies.* New York: Harper.

Bennett, J. 1997. *NGOs and Government: A Review of Current Practice for Southern and Eastern NGOs*. Oxford, UK: INTRAC.

Bentham, J. (1789) 1962. "An Introduction to the Principles of Morals and Legislation." In M. Warnock (ed.), *Utilitarianism: On Liberty, Essay on Bentham, John Stuart Mill*. Glasgow, Scotland: William Collins.

Bentley, A. 1949. *The Process of Government*. Evanston, IL: Principia Press.

Berman, S. 1997. "Civil Society and Political Institutionalization." *American Behavioral Scientist* 40 (5): 562.

Bhutto, Z. A. 1969. *The Myth of Independence*. London: Oxford University Press.

Biekart, K. 1999. *The Politics of Civil Society Building: European Aid Agencies and Democratic Transition in Central America*. Utrecht, Netherlands: International Books.

Boudon, R., and F. Bourricaud. 1989. *A Critical Dictionary of Sociology*. London: Routledge.

Boulding, K. E. 1962. "Notes on a Theory of Philanthropy." In F. G. Dickinson (ed.), *Philanthropy and Public Policy*. New York: National Bureau of Economic Research.

Bowles, S. 2004. *Microeconomics: Behavior, Institutions and Evolution*. Princeton, NJ: Princeton University Press.

Braithwaite. C. 1938. *The Voluntary Citizen: An Enquiry into the Place of Philanthropy in the Community*. London: Methuen.

Bratton, M. 1989. "The Politics of Government-NGO Relations in Africa." *World Development* 17 (4): 569–587.

———. 1990. "Non-Governmental Organizations in Africa: Can They Influence Government Policy?" *Development and Change* 21: 87–118.

Brautigam, D. 2000. *Aid Dependence and Governance*. Stockholm, Sweden: Almqvist & Wiksell International.

Brennan, G. 1996. "Selection and the Currency of Rewards." In R. E. Goodin (ed.), *The Theory of Institutional Design*. Cambridge, UK: Cambridge University Press.

Brown, E. 1999. "The Scope of Volunteer Activity and Public Service." *Law and Contemporary Problems* 62: 17–42.

Brown, L. D., and D. Ashman. 1996. "Participation, Social Capital and Intersectoral Problem Solving: African and Asian Cases." *World Development* 24 (9): 1467–1479.

Brown, L. D., and M. H. Moore. 2001. *Accountability, Strategy, and International Non-Governmental Organizations*. Hauser Centre for Non-profit Organizations Working Paper no. 7. Cambridge, MA: Kennedy School of Government, Harvard University.

Brusset, E., W. Pramana, A. Davies, Y. Deshmukh, and S. Pedersen. 2006. *Links Between Relief, Rehabilitation and Development in the Tsunami Response: Indonesia Case Study*. London: Tsunami Evaluation Coalition.

Burnell, P. J. 1991. *Charity, Politics, and the Third World*. London: Harvester Wheatsheaf.

Campbell, R. 1985. "Background for the Uninitiated." In R. Campbell and L. Sowden (eds.), *Paradoxes of Rationality and Cooperation*. Vancouver: University of British Columbia Press.

Carroll. T. F. 1992. *Intermediary NGOs: The Supporting Link in Grassroots Development.* Sterling, VA: Kumarian Press.

Carson, E. D. 1999. "On Defining and Measuring Volunteering in the United States and Abroad." *Law and Contemporary Problems* 62: 67–72.

Chambers, R. 1997. *Whose Reality Counts? Putting the First Last.* London: Intermediate Technology Publications.

Chandhok, N. 1995. *State and Civil Society: Exploration of Political Theory.* New Delhi, India: Sage.

Chang, H.-J. 2001. *Breaking the Mould: An Institutionalist Political Economy Alternative to the Neoliberal Theory of the Market and the State.* Social Policy and Development Programme Paper no. 6. Geneva, Switzerland: UNRISD.

Chaudhry, H. R. 1990. "The Shrine and the Lunger of Golra Sharif." In S. A. Akbar (ed.), *Pakistan: The Social Sciences Perspective.* Karachi, Pakistan: Oxford University Press.

Chong, D. 1991. *Collective Action and the Civil Rights Movement.* Chicago: University of Chicago Press.

———. 1996. "Rational Choice Theory's Mysterious Rivals." In J. Friedman (ed.), *The Rational Choice Controversy: Economic Models of Politics Reconsidered.* New Haven, CT: Yale University Press.

Churchill, E. D., Jr. 1974. "Muslim Societies of the Punjab, 1860–1890." *The Punjab Past and Present* 8: 69–91.

Clark, J. 1991. *Democratising Development: The Role of Voluntary Organizations.* London: Earthscan.

Cohen, J., and W. Easterly (eds.). 2009. *What Works in Development? Thinking Big and Thinking Small.* Washington, DC: Brookings Institution Press.

Cohen, S. P. 1998. *The Pakistan Army.* Karachi, Pakistan: Oxford University Press.

Colclough, C., and J. Manor. 1991. *State or Markets? Neo-Liberalism and the Development Policy Debate.* Oxford, UK: Clarendon Press.

Coleman, J. 1988. "Social Capital in the Creation of Human Capital." *American Journal of Sociology* 94 (Supplement: Organizations and Institutions: Sociological and Economic Approaches to the Analysis of Social Structures): 95–120.

———. 1990. *Foundations of Social Theory.* Cambridge, MA: Harvard University Press.

Colin, R. 2002. *Real World Research: A Resource for Social Scientists and Practitioners.* Oxford, UK: Blackwell.

Collier, C. 2000. "NGOs, the Poor and Local Government." In D. Eade (ed.), *Development, NGOs, and Civil Society.* Oxford, UK: Oxfam.

Cooke, B., and U. Kothari (eds.). 2001. *Participation: The New Tyranny?* London: Zed Books.

Dasgupta, P. 2000. "Economic Progress and the Idea of Social Capital." In P. Dasgupta and I. Serageldin (eds.), *Social Capital: A Multifaceted Perspective.* Washington, DC: World Bank.

Deci, E. L., and R. M. Ryan. 1985. *Intrinsic Motivation and Self-Determination in Human Behavior*. New York: Plenum Press.

Denzin, N. K. 1978. *The Research Act in Sociology: A Theoretical Introduction to Sociological Methods*. New York: McGraw-Hill.

Donnan, H., and P. Werbner (eds.). 1991. *Economy and Culture in Pakistan: Migrants and Cities in a Muslim Society*. Basingstoke, UK: Macmillan.

Dorman, S. R. 2001. "Inclusion and Exclusion: NGOs and Politics in Zimbabwe." Unpublished DPhil thesis, University of Oxford.

Durrani, T. 2001. *Abdul Sattar Edhi: An Autobigraphy—A Mirror to the Blind*. Karachi, Pakistan: Sattar Edhi Foundation.

Eade, D. (ed.). 2000. *Development, NGOs, and Civil Society*. Oxford, UK: Oxfam.

Eade, D., and E. Ligteringen. 2001. *Debating Development*. Oxford, UK: Oxfam.

Eagleton, T. 1991. *Ideology: An Introduction*. London: Verso.

Easterly, W. 2006. *The White Man's Burden: Why the West's Efforts to Aid the Rest Have Done So Much Ill and So Little Good*. New York: Penguin Press.

Ebrahim, A. 2003. *NGOs and Organizational Change: Discourse, Reporting, and Learning*. Cambridge, UK: Cambridge University Press.

Edward, M., and D. Hulme (eds.). 1995. *Non-Governmental Organisations—Performance and Accountability: Beyond the Magic Bullet*. London: Earthscan.

——. 1996. *Making a Difference: NGOs and Development in a Changing World*. London: Earthscan.

Edward, M. 2004. *Civil Society*. Cambridge, UK: Polity.

Elster, J. 1985. "Rationality, Morality, and Collective Action." *Ethics* 96: 136–155.

Elster, J. (ed.). 1986. *Rational Choice*. Oxford, UK: Blackwell.

Ensminger, J. 1992. *Making a Market: The Institutional Transformation of an African Society*. Cambridge, UK: Cambridge University Press.

Escobar, A. 1995. *Encountering Development: The Making and Unmaking of the Third World*. Princeton, NJ: Princeton University Press.

Esman, M. J., and N. T. Uphoff. 1984. *Local Organizations: Intermediaries in Rural Development*. Ithaca, NY: Cornell University Press.

Evans, P. 1995. *Embedded Autonomy: States and Industrial Transformation*. Princeton, NJ: Princeton University Press.

Ewert, C. J. 2010. "The Erosion of Gotong Royong in Post-Tsunami Aceh: An Exploratory Case Study of the Impact of the Cash-for-Work Programme on Social Institutions of Mutual Cooperation." Unpublished MPhil thesis, Oxford University.

Ewing, K. 1983. "The Politics of Sufism: Redefining the Saints of Pakistan." *Journal of Asian Studies* 42: 251–268.

Faridi, Sahidullah. 1993. *Inner Aspects of Faith*. Kuala Lumpur, Malaysia: A. S. Noordeen.

Faris, E., F. Laune, and A. Todd. 1930. *Intelligent Philanthropy*. Chicago: University of Chicago Press.

Farrington, J., and A. Bebbington. 1993. *Reluctant Partners: Non-Governmental Organizations, the State and Sustainable Agricultural Development.* New York: Routledge.

Fine, B. 1999. "The Development State Is Dead—Long Live Social Capital? *Development and Change* 30: 1–19.

Fowler, A. 1988. "NGOs in Africa: Achieving Comparative Advantage in Relief and Micro-Development." Institute of Development Studies Discussion Paper no. 249. Sussex, UK: IDS.

———. 2000. "Civil Society, NGDOs, and Social Development: Changing the Rules for the Game." United Nations Research Institute for Social Development Occasional Paper no. 1. Geneva: UNRISD.

———. 2002. *The Virtuous Spiral: A Guide to Sustainability for Non-Governmental Organisations in International Development.* London: Earthscan.

Fowler, A., and R. James. 1994. "The Role of Southern NGOs in Development Co-operation." INTRAC Occasional Paper no. 2. Oxford, UK: INTRAC.

Freitag, S. B. 1989. *Collective Action and Community: Public Arenas and the Emergence of Communalism in North India.* Berkeley: University of California Press.

Frey, B. S. 1994. "How Intrinsic Motivation Is Crowded Out and In." *Rationality and Society* 6 (3): 334–352.

———. 1997. *Not Just for Money: An Economic Theory of Personal Motivation.* Aldershot, UK: Edward Elgar.

Frey, B. S., and F. Oberholzer-Gee. 1997. "The Cost of Price Incentives: An Empirical Analysis of Motivation Crowding Out. *American Economic Review* 87 (4): 746–755.

Friedman, J. (ed.). 1996. *The Rational Choice Controversy: Economic Models of Politics Reconsidered.* New Haven, CT: Yale University Press.

Fukuyama, F. 1995. *Trust.* New York: Free Press.

———. 2001. "Social Capital, Civil Society and Development." *Third World Quarterly* 22 (1): 7–20.

———. 2002. "Social Capital and Development: The Coming Agenda." *SAIS Review* 22 (1): 23–37.

Gambetta, D. 1988. *Trust: Making and Breaking Cooperative Relations.* Oxford, UK: Blackwell.

———. 2009. *Codes of the Underworld: How Criminals Communicate.* Princeton, NJ: Princeton University Press.

Gambetta, D., and Hamill, H. 2005. *Streetwise: How Taxi Drivers Establish Customers' Trustworthiness.* New York: Russell Sage.

Gamm, G., and R. D. Putnam. 1999. "The Growth of Voluntary Associations in America, 1840–1940." *Journal of Interdisciplinary History* 29 (4): 511–557.

Gandhi, M. 1958. *All Men Are Brothers: Life and Thoughts of Mahatma Gandhi as Told in His Own Words.* Geneva, Switzerland: UNESCO.

Gankovsky, Y. V., and L. R. Gordon-Polonskaya. 1964. *A History of Pakistan 1947–1958.* Lahore: People's Publishing.

Gardner, K., and D. Lewis. 1996. *Anthropology, Development and the Post-Modern Challenge.* London: Pluto Press.

Geertz, C. 1964. "Ideology as a Cultural System." In E. D. Apter (ed.), *Ideology and Discontent.* London: Macmillan.

Gibson, C., K. Andersson, E. Ostrom, and S. Shivakumar. 2005. *The Samaritan's Dilemma: The Political Economy of Development Aid.* Oxford, UK: Oxford University Press.

Giddens, A. 1989. *Sociology.* London: T. J. Press.

Gilmartin, D. 1988. *Empire and Islam: Punjab and the Making of Pakistan.* London: I. B. Tauris.

Glaeser, E. L., D. Laibson, J. A. Scheinkman, and C. L. Soutter. 2000. "Measuring Trust." *Quarterly Journal of Economics* 115 (3): 811.

Glaser, B. G., and A. L. Strauss. 1967. *The Discovery of Grounded Theory: Strategies for Qualitative Research.* New York: Aldine de Gruyter.

Goldthorpe, J. H. 1998. "Rational Action Theory for Sociology." *British Journal of Sociology* 49 (2): 167–192.

Goode, W. J. 1978. *The Celebration of Heroes: Prestige as a Social Control System.* Berkeley: University of California Press.

Goodin, R. E. (ed.). 1996. *The Theory of Institutional Design.* Cambridge, UK: Cambridge University Press.

Grand, J. L. 1997. "Knights, Knaves or Pawns? Human Behaviour and Social Policy." *Journal of Social Policy* 26 (2): 149–169.

Granovetter, M. 1973. "The Strength of Weak Ties." *American Journal of Sociology* 78 (6): 1360–1380.

———. 1985. "Economic Action and Social Structure: The Problem of Embeddedness." *American Journal of Sociology* 91 (3): 481–510.

Green, D. P., and I. Shapiro. 1994. *Pathologies of Rational Choice Theory: A Critique of Applications in Political Science.* New Haven, CT: Yale University Press.

Grootaert, C., and T. V. Bastelaer. 2002. *Understanding and Measuring Social Capital: A Multidisciplinary Tool for Practitioners.* Washington, DC: World Bank.

Hall, J. P. 1995. "In Search of Civil Society." In J. P. Hall (ed.), *Civil Society: Theory, History and Comparison.* Cambridge, UK: Policy Press.

Hammersley, M., and P. Atkinson. 1996. *Ethnography: Principles in Practice.* New York: Routledge.

Hansmann, H. 1980. "The Role of Non-Profit Enterprise." *Yale Law Journal* 89 (5): 835–901.

Haq, M. 1997. *Human Development in South Asia 1997.* Karachi, Pakistan: Oxford University Press.

Hardin, G. 1968. "The Tragedy of the Commons." *Science* 162: 1243–1248.

Hardin, R. 1982. *Collective Action.* Baltimore, MD: Johns Hopkins University Press.

Harper, C. 1996. "Strengthening Civil Society in Transitional South East Asia." In

A. Clayton (ed.), *NGOs, Civil Society and State: Building Democracy in Transitional Societies*. Oxford, UK: INTRAC.

Harriss, J. 2002. *Depoliticising Development: The World Bank and Social Capital*. Glasgow, Scotland: Anthem Press.

Harriss, J., and P. de Renzio. 1997. "'Missing Link' or Analytically Missing? The Concept of Social Capital: An Introductory Bibliographic Essay." *Journal of International Development* 9 (7): 919–937.

Haynes, D. E. 1987. "From Tribute to Philanthropy: The Politics of Gift Giving in a Western Indian City." *Journal of Asian Studies* 46: 339–359.

———. 1992. *Rhetoric and Ritual in Colonial India: The Shaping of a Public Culture in Surat City, 1852–1928*. Delhi, India: Oxford University Press.

Helmke, G., and S. Levitsky. 2004. "Informal Institutions and Comparative Politics: A Research Agenda." *Perspectives on Politics* 2(4): 725–740.

Henderson, S. L. 2002. "Selling Civil Society: Western Aid and the Nongovernmental Organization Sector in Russia." *Comparative Political Studies* 35 (2): 139–167.

Heyer, J., F. Stewart, and S. Throps (eds.). 2002. *Group Behaviour and Development: Is the Market Destroying Cooperation?* Oxford, UK: Oxford University Press.

Hickey, S., and G. Mohan. 2005. "Relocating Participation within a Radical Politics of Development." *Development and Change* 36 (2): 237–262.

Hickey, S., and G. Mohan (eds.). 2004. *Participation: From Tyranny to Transformation? Exploring New Approaches to Participation*. London: Zed Books.

Hirschman, A. O. 1985. "Against Parsimony: Three Easy Ways of Complicating Some Categories of Economic Discourse." *Economics and Philosophy* 1: 7–21.

———. 1986. *Rival Reviews of Market Society and Other Recent Essays*. New York: Penguin.

Hobbes, T. (1651) 2010. *Leviathan: Or the Matter, Forme, and Power of a Common-Wealth Ecclesiasticall and Civill*, ed. I. Shapiro. New Haven, CT: Yale University Press.

Hobsbawm, E., and T. Ranger (eds.). 1996. *The Invention of Tradition*. Cambridge, UK: Cambridge University Press.

Hodgson, G. 2000. "Structures and Institutions: Reflections on Institutionalism, Structuration Theory and Critical Realism." Mimeo. Hertfordshire, UK: Business School, University of Hertfordshire.

Holmén, Hans. 2010. *Snakes in Paradise: NGOs and the Aid Industry in Africa*. Sterling, VA: Kumarian Press.

Howell, J., and J. Pearce. 2000. "Civil Society: Technical Instrument or Social Force for Change?" In D. Lewis and T. Wallace (eds.), *New Roles and Relevance—Development NGOs and the Challenge of Change*. Sterling, VA: Kumarian Press.

Howes, M. 1997. "NGOs and the Institutional Development of Membership Organisations: A Kenyan Case." *Journal of Development Studies* 33 (6): 820–847.

Hudock, A. C. 1999. *NGOs and Civil Society: Democracy by Proxy?* Cambridge, UK: Polity Press.

Human Rights Watch. 2004. *Soiled Hands: The Pakistan Army's Repression of the Punjab Farmers' Movement.* New York: HRW. Available online at http://www.hrw.org/reports /2004/07/20/soiled-hands-pakistan-army-s-repression-punjab-farmers-movement.

Huntington, S. P. 1991. *The Third Wave: Democratization in the Late Twentieth Century.* Norman: University of Oklahoma Press.

———. 1997. "Civil Society, Social Capital, and Development: Dissection of a Complex Discourse." *Studies in Comparative International Development* 32 (1): 3–30.

Hussain, A. 1979. *Elite Politics in an Ideological State: The Case of Pakistan.* Folkestone, UK: Dawson.

Ilchman, W. F., S. A. Katz, and E. L. Queen II. 1998. *Philanthropy in the World's Traditions.* Bloomington: Indiana University Press.

International Crisis Group. 2004. *Devolution in Pakistan: Reform or Regression?* Islamabad, Pakistan: ICG.

INTRAC. 1998. *Direct Funding from a Southern Perspective: Strengthening Civil Society?* Oxford, UK: INTRAC.

Isham, J., Y. Kelly, and S. Ramaswamy. 2002. *Social Capital and Economic Development: Well-Being in Developing Countries.* Cheltenham, UK: Elgar.

Jalal, A. 1990. *The State of Martial Rule: The Origins of Pakistan's Political Economy of Defence.* Cambridge, UK: Cambridge University Press.

———. 1995. *Democracy and Authoritarianism in South Asia: A Comparative Historical Perspective.* Cambridge, UK: Cambridge University Press.

Jenkins, J. C., and Halcli, A. 1999. "Grassrooting the System? The Development and Impact of Social Movement Philanthropy, 1953–1990." In E. C. Lagemann (ed.), *Philanthropic Foundations: New Scholarship, New Possibilities.* Bloomington: Indiana University Press.

Jenkins, R. 2001. "Mistaking 'Governance' for 'Politics': Foreign Aid, Democracy, and the Construction of Civil Society." In S. Kaviraj and S. Khilnani (eds.), *Civil Society: History and Possibilities.* Cambridge, UK: Cambridge University Press

Jones, G. S. 1971. *Outcast London: A Study in the Relationship Between Classes in Victorian Society.* London: Oxford University Press.

Jordan, L., and P. Van Tuijl. (eds.). 2006. *NGO Accountability: Politics, Principles and Innovations.* London: Earthscan.

Kamal, S. 2000. *The NGO-Donor Axis: Suggestions Towards Developing Codes of Conduct for NGOs and Donors in Pakistan.* Pakistan: United Nations Development Programme.

Katherine, E. 1983. "The Politics of Sufism: Redefining the Saints of Pakistan." *Journal of Asian Studies* 42 (2): 251–268.

Kaviraj, S., and Khilnani, S. (eds.) 2001. *Civil Society: History and Possibilities.* Cambridge, UK: Cambridge University Press.

Kendall, J. 2000. *The Mainstreaming of the Third Sector into Public Policy in England in the Late 1990s: Whys and Wherefores.* Civil Society Working Paper no. 2. London: London School of Economics.

Kendall, J., and S. Almond. 1998. *The UK Voluntary (Third) Sector in Comparative Perspective: Exceptional Growth and Transformation.* Mimeo. London: London School of Economics.

————. 2000. *Paid Employment in the Self-Defined Voluntary Sector in 1990s: An Initial Description of Patterns and Trends.* Civil Society Working Paper no. 7. London: London School of Economics.

Khan, A.W.K. 1995. "Life and Thoughts of Badshah Khan." In Nehru Memorial Museum and Library (ed.), *Khan Abdul Ghaffar Khan: A Centennial Tribute.* New Delhi, India: Har-Anan.

Khan, K. A. 1995. "Some Significant Aspects of Badshah Khan's Life." In Nehru Memorial Museum and Library (ed.), *Khan Abdul Ghaffar Khan: A Centennial Tribute.* New Delhi, India: Har-Anan.

Khan, M. A. 1996. *Pakistan, the First Twelve Years: The Pakistan Times Editorials of Mazhar Ali Khan.* Karachi, Pakistan: Oxford University Press.

————. 1998. *Pakistan, the Barren Years: The Viewpoint Editorials and Columns of Mazhar Ali Khan, 1975–1992.* Karachi, Pakistan: Oxford University Press.

King, G., R. Keohane, and S. Verba. 1994. *Designing Social Inquiry.* Princeton, NJ: Princeton University Press.

Kozlowski, G. Z. 1998. "Religious Authority, Reform, and Philanthropy in the Contemporary Muslim World." In W. F. Ilchman, S. A. Katz, and E. L. Queen II (eds.), *Philanthropy in the World's Traditions.* Bloomington: Indiana University Press.

Krebs, D. 1982. "Psychological Approaches to Altruism: An Evaluation." *Ethics* 92: 447–458.

Kreps, D. M. 1997. "The Interaction Between Norms and Economic Incentives: Intrinsic Motivation and Extrinsic Incentives." *American Economic Association Papers and Proceedings* 87 (2): 359–364.

Kuhnert, S. 2001. "An Evolutionary Theory of Collective Action: Schumpeterian Entrepreneurship for the Common Good." *Constitutional Political Economy* 12: 13–29.

Kuratov, S., and A. Solyanik. 1995. "The Glimmer and Glare of Cooperation." *Ecostan News* (August): 3–7.

Lane, R. 1991. *The Market Experience.* Cambridge, UK: Cambridge University Press.

Leadership for Environment and Development. 2002. *Investing in Ourselves: Giving and Fund Raising in Pakistan.* Manila: Asian Development Bank.

Lehmann, D. 1990. *Democracy and Development in Latin America: Economics, Politics and Religion in the Post-War Period.* Cambridge, UK: Polity Press.

Lelyveld. D. 1978. *Aligarh's First Generation.* Princeton, NJ: Princeton University Press.

Lepper, M. R., and Greene, D. (eds.). 1978. *The Hidden Costs of Reward: New Perspectives on the Psychology of Human Motivation.* New York: Erlbaum.

Lewis, D. 2003. "Theorizing the Organization and Management of Non-Governmental

Development Organizations: Towards a Composite Approach." *Public Management Review* 5 (3): 325–344.

———. 2004. "On the Difficulty of Studying 'Civil Society': Reflections on NGO, State, and Democracy in Bangladesh." *Indian Sociology* 38 (3): 299–322.

Lewis, D. (ed.). 1999. *International Perspectives on Voluntary Action: Reshaping the Third Sector.* London: Earthscan.

Liebeskind, C. 1998. *Piety on Its Knees: Three Sufi Traditions in South Asia in Modern Times.* New Delhi, India: Oxford University Press.

Lindbeck, A. 1997. "Incentives and Social Norms in Household Behaviour." *American Economic Association Papers and Proceedings* 87 (2): 370–377.

Locke, J. 1952. *Two Treatises of Civil Government.* London: J. M. Dent.

Malena, C. 1997. *NGO Involvement in World Bank-Financed Social Funds: Lessons Learned.* Environment Department Paper no. 052. Washington, DC: World Bank.

Malik, I. H. 1997. *State and Civil Society in Pakistan: Politics of Authority, Ideology, and Ethnicity.* Basingstoke, UK: Macmillan.

Malik, J. 1996. *Colonialization of Islam: Dissolution of Traditional Institutions in Pakistan.* Lahore, Pakistan: Vanguard.

Mann, E. A. 1989. "Religion, Money and Status: Competition for Resources at the Shrine of Shah Jamal, Aligarh." In C. W. Troll (ed.), *Muslim Shrines in India: Their Character, History and Significance.* New Delhi, India: Oxford University Press.

Margolis, H. 1982. *Selfishness, Altruism, and Rationality; A Theory of Social Choice.* Cambridge, UK: Cambridge University Press.

Marts, A. C. 1953. *Philanthropy's Role in Civilization: Its Contribution to Human Freedom.* New York: Harper.

Marzouk, M. 1995. "The Associative Phenomenon in the Arab World: Engines of Democratisation or Witness to Crisis? In M. Edward and D. Hulme (eds.), *Non-Governmental Organisations—Performance and Accountability: Beyond the Magic Bullet.* London: Earthscan.

Mauss, M. 1954. *The Gift, Forms and Foundation of Exchange in Archaic Societies.* London: Routledge.

Mawdsley, E., J. Townsend, G. Porter, and P. Oakley. 2002. *Knowledge, Power, and Development Agendas.* Oxford, UK: WorldView.

Mawdsley, E., J. Townsend, and G. Porter. 2005. "Trust, Accountability and Face-to-Face Interaction in North-South NGO relations." *Development in Practice* 15 (1): 77–82.

May, T. 2001. *Social Research: Issues, Methods, and Process.* Buckingham, UK: Open University Press.

Metcalf, B. D. 1978. "The Madrasa at Deoband: A Model for Religious Education in India." *Modern Asian Studies* 12: 111–134.

———. 1982. *Islamic Revival in British India: Deoband, 1860–1900.* Princeton, NJ: Princeton University Press.

Meyer, M., and L. Zucker. 1989. *Permanently Failing Organizations.* Thousand Oaks, CA: Sage.

Miles, M. B., and A. M. Huberman. 1994. *Qualitative Data Analysis.* Thousand Oaks, CA: Sage.

Mill, J. S. (1861) 1982. "Utilitarianism: An Introduction to the Principles of Morals and Legislation." In M. Warnock (ed.), *Utilitarianism, On Liberty, Essay on Bentham, John Stuart Mill.* Glasgow, Scotland: William Collins.

Moser, C. A. 1993. *Survey Methods in Social Investigation.* Aldershot, UK: Dartmouth.

Moyo, D. 2008. *Dead Aid: Why Aid Is Not Working and How There Is Another Way for Africa.* London: Allen Lane.

Nabulsi, K. 2005. "The State Building Project: What Went Wrong?" In M. Keating, A. Le More, and R. Lowe (eds.), *Aid, Diplomacy and Facts on the Ground: The Case of Palestine.* London: Chatham House.

Narayan, D., and M. F. Cassidy. 2001. "A Dimensional Approach to Measuring Social Capital and Validation of a Social Capital Inventory." *Current Sociology* 49 (2): 59–102.

Narayan-Parker, D. 2000. *Voices of the Poor: Crying Out for Change.* New York: Oxford University Press for the World Bank.

Nasr, S.V.R. 1994. *The Vanguard of the Islamic Revolution: The Jama'at-i Islami of Pakistan.* Berkeley: University of California Press.

Newton, K. 1997. "Social Capital and Democracy." *American Behavioural Scientist* 40 (5): 575.

NGO Resource Centre. 1999. *The State of the Citizen Sector in Pakistan.* Karachi, Pakistan: NGORC.

———. 2003a. *Directory of Donor Organizations in Pakistan.* Karachi, Pakistan: NGORC.

———. 2003b. *Directory of NGOs.* Karachi, Pakistan: NGORC.

Nizami, F. A. 1983. "Madrasahs, Scholars, Saints: Muslim Response to the British Presence in Delhi and Upper Doab 1803–1857." Unpublished D.Phil dissertation, University of Oxford.

Nizami, K. A. 1998. *The Life and Times of Shaikh Farid-ud-din Ganj-i-Shakar.* Delhi, India: Idarah-I Adabiyat-I Delhi.

Noman, O. 1990. *Pakistan: A Political and Economic History Since 1947.* London: Kegan Paul International.

North, D. C. 1990. *Institutions, Institutional Change and Economic Performance.* Cambridge, UK: Cambridge University Press.

Norton, M. 1996. *The Non-Profit Sector in India.* London: Charities Aid Foundation.

Olson, M. 1971. *The Logic of Collective Action: Public Goods and the Theory of Groups.* Cambridge, MA: Harvard University Press.

Organisation for Economic Co-operation and Development (OECD). 1994. *Development Assistance Committee Report 1993.* Paris: OECD.

———. 2007. *Informal Institutions: How Social Norms Help or Hinder Development.* Paris: OEDC.

Ostrom, E. 1990. *Governing the Commons: The Evolution of Institutions for Collective Action*. Cambridge, UK: Cambridge University Press.

———. 2003. "How Types of Goods and Property Rights Jointly Affect Collective Action." *Journal of Theoretical Politics* 15 (3): 239.

———. 2005. *Doing Institutional Analysis: Digging Deeper Than Markets and Hierarchies*. In C. Menard and M. M. Shirley (eds.), *Handbook of New Institutional Economics*. Dordrecht, Netherlands: Springer.

———. 2007. "Collective Action and Local Development Processes." *Sociologica* 3: 1–32.

Owen, D. 1964. *English Philanthropy 1660–1960*. Cambridge MA: Harvard University Press.

Pakistan Centre for Philanthropy (PCP). 2002. *Creating an Enabling Legal Framework for NPOs in Pakistan*. Islamabad, Pakistan: Aga Khan Foundation.

Pandy, G. (ed.). 1993. *Hindus and Others: The Question of Identity in India Today*. New Delhi, India: Viking.

Pasha, A. G., H. A. Pasha, and M. A. Iqbal. 2002. *Nonprofit Sector in Pakistan: Government Policy and Future Issues*. State Policy and Development Centre Working Paper no. 2. Karachi, Pakistan: SPDC.

Pasha, A. G., J. Haroon, and M. A. Iqbal. 2002. *Dimensions of the Nonprofit Sector in Pakistan*. State Policy and Development Centre Working Paper no. 1. Karachi, Pakistan: SPDC.

Patton, M. Q. 1990. *Qualitative Evaluation and Research Methods*. Thousand Oaks, CA: Sage.

Paul, E. F., F. D. Miller, J. J. Jeffery, and J. Ahrens. 1987. *Beneficence, Philanthropy, and the Public Good*. Oxford: Blackwell.

Pearce, J. 1993. "NGOs and Social Change: Agents and Facilitators?" *Development in Practice* 3 (3): 222–227.

———. 1997. "Between Co-option and Irrelevance: Latin American NGOs in the 1990s." In M. Edwards and D. Hulme (eds.), *NGOs, States and Donors: Too Close for Comfort?* London: Macmillan.

———. 2000. "Development, NGOs and Civil Society: The Debate and Its Future." In D. Eade (ed.), *Development, NGOs, and Civil Society*. Oxford, UK: Oxfam.

Popkin, S. 1979. *The Rational Peasant: The Political Economy of Rural Society in Vietnam*. Berkeley: University of California Press.

Punch, K. F. 1998. *Introduction to Social Research: Quantitative and Qualitative Approaches*. London: Sage Publications.

Punch, M. 1994. "Politics and Ethics in Qualitative Research." In N. K. Denzin and Y. S. Lincoln (eds.), *Handbook of Qualitative Research*. Thousand Oaks, CA: Sage.

Puschiasis, O. 2009. La fertilié: Une ressource "chuchotée": Analyse de la valorisation de la ressource territoriale fertilité par les familes de la zone Intersalar, Bolivie. MA thesis, University of Montpellier.

Putnam, R. 1995. "Bowling Alone: American's Declining Social Capital." *Journal of Democracy* 6 (1): 65–78.

Putnam, R., with R. Leonardi and R. Y. Nanetti. 1993. *Making Democracy Work: Civic Traditions in Modern Italy.* Princeton, NJ: Princeton University Press.

Putnam, R., and G. Gamm. 1999. "The Growth of Voluntary Associations in America, 1840–1940." *Journal of Interdisciplinary History* 29 (4): 511–557.

Rademacher, A., and D. Tamang. 1993. *Democracy, Development and NGOs.* Kathmandu: SEARCH.

Raheja, G. G. 1988. *The Poison in the Gift: Rituals, Presentation, and the Dominant Caste in a Northern Indian Village.* Chicago: University of Chicago Press.

Rahman, A. 2005. History of Urdu Poetry. http://www.urdustan.com

Randel, J., and T. German. 1997. *The Reality of Aid: An Independent Review of International Aid.* London: Earthscan.

Rao, V., and M. Walton (eds.). 2004. *Culture and Public Action.* Stanford, CA: Stanford University Press.

Riddell, R., and M. Robinson. 1995. *Non-governmental Organisations and Rural Poverty Alleviation.* Oxford, UK: Clarendon Press.

Riddell, R. 2005. *Does Foreign Aid Really Work?* Oxford, UK: Oxford University Press.

Robinson, F. 2002. *Islam and Muslim History in South Asia.* New Delhi, India: Oxford University Press.

———. 2001. *The Ulama of Farangi Mahall and Islamic Culture in South Asia.* London: Hurst.

Robinson, M. 1996. "NGOs and Poverty Alleviation: Implications for Scaling Up." In M. Edwards and D. Hulme (eds.), *Making a Difference: NGOs and Development in a Changing World.* London: Earthscan.

Runciman, W. G. (ed.). 1978. *Max Weber: Selections in Translation.* Translated by E. Matthews. Cambridge, UK: Cambridge University Press.

Saeed, A. 1986. *Anjuman-Islamia-Amritsar: 1873–1947.* Lahore, Pakistan: Adara-Thakekat-e-Pakistan.

Salamon, L. M. 1994. "The Rise of the Nonprofit Sector." *Foreign Affairs* (July/August): 109–122.

Salamon, L. M., and H. K. Anheier. 1992. "In Search of the Non-Profit Sector I: The Question of Definition." *VOLUNTAS* 3 (2): 125–153.

———. 1998. "Social Origins of Civil Society." *VOLUNTAS* 9 (3): 213–248.

Salamon, L. M., S. W. Sokolowski, and H. K. Anheier. 2000. *Social Origins of the Civil Society: An Overview.* Working Paper of The Johns Hopkins Comparative Non-Profit Sector Project. Baltimore, MD: Center for Civil Society Studies.

Salamon, L. M., and S. W. Sokolowski. 2001. *Volunteering in Cross-National Perspective: Evidence from 24 Countries.* Working Paper of The Johns Hopkins Comparative Non-profit Sector Project. Baltimore, MD: Center for Civil Society Studies.

Sartori, G. 1969. "Politics, Ideology and Belief Systems." *American Political Science Review* 63: 398–411.

Saxby, J. (1996). "Who Owns the Private Aid Agencies?" In S. David, K. Biekart, and J. Saxby (eds.), *Compassion and Calculation: The Business of Private Foreign Aid.* London: Pluto Press with Transnational Institute.

Schneewind, J. B. (ed.). 1996. *Giving: Western Ideas of Philanthropy.* Indianapolis: Indiana University Press.

Schofield. N. 1996. "Rational Choice and Political Economy." In J. Friedman (ed.), *The Rational Choice Controversy: Economic Models of Politics Reconsidered.* New Haven, CT: Yale University Press.

———. 1985. "Anarchy, Altruism, and Cooperation: A Review." *Social Choice and Welfare* 2: 207–219.

Scitovsky, T. 1976. *The Joyless Economy.* New York: Oxford University Press.

———. 1977. "Protest and Profanation: Agrarian Revolt and the Little Tradition." *Theory and Society* 4: 1–2.

Scott, J. C. 1976. *The Moral Economy of the Peasant: Rebellion and Subsistence in Southeast Asia.* New Haven, CT: Yale University Press.

Seal, A. 1968. *The Emergence of Indian Nationalism: Competition and Collaboration in the Later Nineteenth Century.* Cambridge, UK: Cambridge University Press.

Sen, A. 1977. "Rational Fools: A Critique of the Behavioral Foundations of Economic Theory." *Philosophy and Public Affairs* 6 (4): 317–344.

———. 2001. *Development as Freedom.* Oxford, UK: Oxford University Press.

———. 2002. *Rationality and Freedom.* Cambridge, MA: Belknap Press.

Shaikh, F. 1989. *Community and Consensus in Islam: Muslim Representation in Colonial India, 1860–1947.* Cambridge, UK: Cambridge University Press.

Sharma, S. 2001. *Famine, Philanthropy, and the Colonial State: North India in the Early Nineteenth Century.* New Delhi, India: Oxford University Press.

Sherani, A. R. 1991. "Ulema and Pir in the Politics of Pakistan." In H. Donnan and P. Werbner (eds.), *Economy and Culture in Pakistan: Migrants and Cities in a Muslim Society.*

Shivakumar, S. 2005. *The Constitution of Development: Crafting Capabilities of Self-Governance.* New York: Palgrave Macmillan.

Simon, H. 1986. "Rationality in Psychology and Economics." *Journal of Business* 59 (4, Part 2): S209–S224.

Skocpol, T. 2003. *Diminished Democracy: From Membership to Management in American Civic Life.* Norman: University of Oklahoma Press.

Smillie, I. 1995. *The Alms Bazaar—Altruism Under Fire: Non-Profit Organizations and International Development.* London: Intermediate Technology Publications.

Smillie, I., and H. Helmich. 1993. *Non-Governmental Organisations and Governments: Stakeholders for Development.* Paris: OECD.

Smith, A. 1976. *The Theory of Moral Sentiments.* Oxford, UK: University Press.

Smith, B. 1990. *More than Altruism: The Politics of Private Foreign Aid.* Princeton, NJ: Princeton University Press.

Smith, D. E. (ed.). 1966. *South Asian Politics and Religion.* Princeton, NJ: Princeton University Press.

Sober, E., and D. S. Wilson. 1998. *Unto Others: The Evolution and Psychology of Unselfish Behavior.* Cambridge, MA: Harvard University Press.

Sobhan, B. 1997. *Partners or Contractors? The Relationship Between Official Agencies and NGOs—Bangladesh.* INTRAC Occasional Paper no. 14. Oxford, UK: INTRAC.

Sogge, D. 1996. "Settings and Choices." In S. David, K. Biekart, and J. Saxby (eds.), *Compassion and Calculation: The Business of Private Foreign Aid.* London: Pluto Press with Transnational Institute.

Sperling, V. 1999. *Organizing Women in Contemporary Russia: Engendering Transition.* Cambridge, UK: Cambridge University Press.

Stiles, W. K. 2002. *Civil Society by Design: Donors, NGOs, and the Intermestic Development Circle in Bangladesh.* Santa Barbara, CA: Praeger.

Strauss, A., and Corbin, J. 1998. *Basics of Qualitative Research: Techniques and Procedures for Developing Grounded Theory.* New York: Sage Publications.

Talbot, I. 1998. *Pakistan: A Modern History.* London: Hurst.

Tendler, J. 1982. *Turning Private Voluntary Organizations into Development Agencies: Questions for Evaluation.* Programme Evaluation Discussion Paper no. 12. Washington, DC: USAID.

Tendulkar, D. G. 1967. *Abdul Ghaffar Khan: Faith Is a Battle.* Bombay: Gandhi Peace Foundation.

Tester, K. 1992. *Civil Society.* Routledge: London.

Thompson, J. B. 1990. *Ideology and Modern Culture: Critical Social Theory in the Era of Mass Communication.* Cambridge, UK: Polity Press.

Thorburn, C. 2007. *The Acehnese Gampong Three Years on: Assessing Local Capacity and Reconstruction Assistance in Post-Tsunami Aceh.* Available from http://www.indo .ausaid.gov.au/featurestories/acarpreport.pdf

Titmuss, R. M. 1970. *The Gift Relationship: From Human Blood to Social Policy.* London: Allen and Unwin.

Tocqueville, A. de. (1835) 1994. *Democracy in America.* London: David Campbell.

Tonkiss, F., and A. Passey. 1999. "Trust, Confidence and Voluntary Organizations: Between Values and Institutions." *Sociology* 33 (2): 257–274.

———. 1999. "Democracy and Social Capital." In M. E. Warren (ed.), *Democracy and Trust.* Cambridge, UK: Cambridge University Press.

Troll, C. W. (ed.). 2004. *Muslim Shrines in India: Their Character, History and Significance.* Oxford, UK: Oxford University Press.

Truman, D. B. 1958. *The Governmental Process.* New York: Knopf.

Tvedt, T. 1998. *Angels of Mercy or Development Diplomats? NGOs and Foreign Aid.* Oxford, UK: Africa World Press.

United Nations Development Programme (UNDP). 2010. *Human Development Report 2010*. New York: UNDP.

Uphoff, N. 1995. "Why NGOs Are Not a Third Sector: A Sectoral Analysis with Some Thoughts on Accountability, Sustainability and Evaluation." In M. Edwards and D. Hulme (eds.), *Beyond the Magic Bullet: NGO Performance and Accountability in the Post Cold-War World*. London: Earthscan.

Vakil, A. C. 1997. "Confronting the Classification Problem: Toward a Taxonomy of NGOs." *World Development* 25 (12): 2057–2070.

Viswanath, V. 1994. *The Bank's Cooperation with NGOs*. A Background Paper for Asian Development Bank. Manila: ADB.

Wade, R. 1998. *Village Republics: Economics Conditions for Collective Action in South Asia*. Cambridge, UK: Cambridge University Press.

Wallace, T., S. Crowther, and A. Shepherd. 1997. *Standardising Development: Influences on UK NGOs' Policies and Procedures*. Oxford, UK: WorldView.

Wax, R. H. 1971. *Doing Fieldwork: Warnings and Advice*. Chicago: University of Chicago Press.

Weber, M. 1978. *Economy and Society: An Outline of Interpretive Sociology*. Vol. 1. Edited by G. Roth and C. Wittich. Berkeley: University of California Press.

Weisbrod, B. A. 1988. *The Nonprofit Economy*. Cambridge, MA: Harvard University Press.

Williamson, O. 1975. *Markets and Hierarchies—Analysis and Antitrust Implications: A Study in the Economics of Internal Organization*. New York: Free Press.

———. 1985. *The Economic Institutions of Capitalism*. New York: Free Press.

———. 2000. "The New Institutional Economics: Taking Stock, Looking Ahead." *Journal of Economic Literature* 38 (3): 595–613.

Woods, N. 1995. "Economic Ideas and International Relations: Beyond National Neglect." *International Studies Quarterly* 39: 161–180.

World Bank. 1997. *World Development Report 1997: The State in a Changing World*. Washington, DC: Oxford University Press.

———. 2000a. *Consultations with Civil Society Organizations: General Guidelines for World Bank Staff*. Washington, DC: World Bank.

———. 2000b. *Good Practices: Involving Nongovernmental Organizations in Bank-Supported Activities*. World Bank Operational Manual, NGO/Civil Society Unit. Washington, DC: World Bank.

———. 2001. *World Development Report 2000/2001: Attacking Poverty*. Washington, DC: Oxford University Press.

———. 2005. *Issues and Options for Improving Engagement Between the World Bank and Civil Society Organizations*. Washington, DC: World Bank.

Wright, K. 2002. *Generosity Versus Altruism: Philanthropy and Charity in the US and UK*. London School of Economics Civil Society Working Paper no. 17. London: London School of Economics.

Zadak, S. 1996. "Looking Back from 2010." In S. David, K. Biekart, and J. Saxby (eds.), *Compassion and Calculation: The Business of Private Foreign Aid*. London: Pluto Press with Transnational Institute.

Zaidi, A. S. 1999a. *Issues in Pakistan's Economy*. Karachi, Pakistan: Oxford University Press.

———. 1999b. "NGO Failure and the Need to Bring Back the State." *Journal of International Development* 11 (2): 259–271.

Zaman, M. Q. 2002. *The Ulama in Contemporary Islam: Custodians of Change*. Princeton, NJ: Princeton University Press.

Zeno. 1994. "Professor Ahmed Ali and Progressive Writers Movement." *Annual of Urdu Studies* 9 (Special Feature: Ahmed Ali—A Tribute): 39–43.

Ziring, L. 1997. *Pakistan in the Twentieth Century: A Political History*. Karachi, Pakistan: Oxford University Press.

# Index

Abdul Sattar Edhi International Foundation, *see* Edhi Foundation

accountability: failure of cooperation attributed to upward, 170; small lapses trigger a dynamic that leads to complete breakdown of, 20

accounting systems, 25, 79–81

Aceh (Indonesia), 2–3, 15

ActionAid Pakistan, 108, 149–51

advocacy versus service delivery, 136–37

Aga Khan Foundation, 127n

Aga Khan RSP, 52

agenda setting versus agenda following, 137–40

aid: accusations of representing foreign interests due to, 150–51; adjustments in existing disbursement mechanisms, 168–84; commitment to ideals undermined by, 161–65; as critical to Pakistan, 32–33; erodes rather than strengthens cooperation, xi, 1–4, 7–8, 13, 19–20, 25, 174, 175; increased flows to NGOs, 10; material motivation increased by, 141–42, 143, 153; performance worsened by, 142, 153; questioning logic of, 166; reduces initiators' ability to mobilize or retain members, 18, 148–49; removes dependence of initiators on joiners, 20; reward structures that clash with psychosocial and spiritual rewards, 168; testing whether it breaks down cooperation, 119–42; why it attracts the materially motivated initiator, 153–54; why it breaks down cooperation, 24, 143–66. *See also* international donors

Alavi, Hamza, 128

Ali, T., 31, 32–33, 45

Alkire, S., 19

All Pakistan Alliance Baray Katchi Abadi, 98

All Pakistan Power Looms Association, 98

All Pakistan Women's Association (APWA), 125, 133

altruism: high salaries for initiators erodes, 25, 26; in madrasas, 35; material incentives and shift to nonaltruistic behavior, 161–62, 169–70; self-interest in, 65, 162, 169, 170; versus self-interest in other-regarding groups, 18–19; understanding what individuals gain from, 168, 169–73; why initiators initiate, 64, 65

*Ambrose* (newspaper), 44

Andersson, K., 4, 15

Anheier, H. K., 8–9

Anjuman-Faizul-Islam, 47, 133

Anjuman-i-Himayat-i-Islam, 40–41, 47

Anjuman-i-Islamia Amritsar, 47–48

Anjuman Mazareen-i-Punjab: brief history of, 98–101; collective identity increases in, 116–17; conflict with Pakistani military, 98, 100, 104, 107, 111; factors that helped sustain, 113–16; international